The campaign to direct material aid
from the rich countries to the poor –
whether carried on by international
organizations, national governments or
charitable bodies – is seldom out of the
headlines; and this trenchant and
polemical study of aid and its
implications claims that beneath all
the effort to help the underdeveloped
peoples of the world there is a subtle
and destructive ambiguity. To such an
extent is our response mixed –
alternately succouring the poor and
bombing them back to the Stone Age –
that Mr. Hensman sees the confrontation
as essentially one of hostility and rivalry.
Aid, he argues, must not be a balm
to conscience but must be based
on a thorough understanding of the
economic infrastructure of Third
World countries and a way of allowing
these countries to make a great leap
forward for themselves. In many cases
aid is so tethered by strings that it
constitutes a process of anti-
development, retarding ambition, skills
and human resources. Mr. Hensman, the
author of *From Gandhi to Guevara*, has
assembled a vast range of material from
all corners of the Third World and from
some rarely illuminated parts of the
prosperous West. His book makes
alarming reading and poses one vital
question: are we fighting an unacknow-
ledged war with the poor peoples of
the world?

C. R. Hensman is a freelance writer,
broadcaster and lecturer. Born in 1923
in Ceylon, he became a teacher after
he graduated from the University of
Ceylon. From 1954 to 1958 he edited
the quarterly *Community*; then he
became Research Secretary of the
Overseas Council in London. He has also
worked as a producer for the BBC.
C. R. Hensman has travelled extensively
in south and south-east Asia, the Middle
East, and in east and central Africa.

C. R. HENSMAN

Rich Against Poor

THE REALITY OF AID

SCHENKMAN PUBLISHING COMPANY
Cambridge, Massachusetts

First published in 1971
Allen Lane The Penguin Press
London W.1, England

First published in the U.S.A., 1971
Schenkman Publishing Company
Cambridge, Massachusetts

ISBN A7073 294 3

Printed in Great Britain by
Cox & Wyman Ltd, London, Fakenham, Reading
Set in Monotype Garamond

Schenkman books are distributed by
General Learning Press
Morristown, New Jersey

Contents

1 THE WAR AGAINST WORLD POVERTY 1

2 RAPID DEVELOPMENT IS A RECENT
PHENOMENON 42

3 THE DEVELOPMENT PROCESS 63

4 THE PROCESS OF ANTI-DEVELOPMENT 86

5 ANTI-DEVELOPMENT: MALIGNANT
FORMS OF GROWTH 123

6 ANTI-DEVELOPMENT:
INTERNATIONAL PARTNERSHIP 162

7 THE AID RELATIONSHIP:
THE BENEFACTORS, MODELS AND
TEACHERS 189

8 THE AID RELATIONSHIP: THE
RHETORIC AND THE REALITY 233

9 JOINING THE REAL WAR ON POVERTY 270

INDEX 289

CHAPTER I

The War Against World Poverty

MULTIPLYING PEOPLE AND DIMINISHING FOOD SUPPLIES

FOR most working people in the West, the job of keeping themselves and their families alive, healthy and contented seems never-ending. Time, energy and attention are exhausted by the insistent demands of unfinished duties and unsatisfied wants. What is enjoyed of the good life, as it is presented through the shop windows, the magazines and television, is tantalizing. The more satisfying and more glorious existence striven after appears the best possible – the creation of generations of European technology, progress and democracy. But the hold that ordinary people have on it is so precarious that invitations to participate, by the use of their imaginations and moral sense, in the sufferings of remote people in the Caribbean or south-east Asia or southern Africa, and to assist *their* struggles against want and oppression must seem to issue from a universe totally foreign to the 'real' business of living.

In their more thoughtful and sensitive moments people may become aware that in their work and their personal relationships they are unfulfilled, uncreative, frustrated, unhappy – that they cannot respect themselves for docilely devoting themselves to looking after themselves and their families and the source of their income. They adapt themselves, however, to an inglorious and imperfect existence. For they know that without a regular weekly or monthly income they would have nowhere to live and nothing to eat, and would have to beg to be given work and a wage or allowance. The pictures (of shrivelled and mangled bodies) and the words and figures which symbolize the plight and need of the poor and oppressed outside their gates are thrust on them as part of the information and entertainment provided by newspapers and television. But any implication that their own aspirations, loyalties and interests have some bearing on what goes on outside appears as an affront, and even obscene. If each individual has to strive in his isolation to keep himself from destitution and suffering even in an affluent society, sentimental involvement in distant suffering which one cannot relieve appears to be wrong. Their copies of the *Daily Sensation* or the *Times of Crisis* tell them that the world is full of danger and insecurity. Recessions and slumps, tax increases and 'subversion' lie in wait round the corner. In less ordered societies hardly a day passes without an earthquake, flood, famine, riot, assassination, a conspiracy discovered, somewhere in the world. The assurance that their bosses and rulers give them, therefore, of a placid and pleasant existence, however undignified and restricted it is, appears as a piece of good fortune.

The hunger, frustration and misery of others cannot affect them as long as the rich and the poor exist as remote, separate, self-contained societies. But what if the poor are crowding near the gates within which are their sources of income and much else that is precious? How can they feel secure in the face of what they are told is a massive danger to all mankind: famine on an unprecedented scale and a world population beyond the earth's capacity to sustain? Must the fast-breeding poor be their problem? A few years ago they were told that while it had taken all of human history for the world population to reach 3,500,000,000, it would take only the next forty years for that figure to double. The scale of such an impending catastrophe has forced people in the West to pay heed to facts and figures about other peoples. One day they read that the population increase in the world every day is 180,000; shortly afterwards that it is 190,000. One year they learn that the world's population increases by sixty million a year. The following year they are given the figure of seventy million. And, all the time, the world's food production, already known to be seriously below current needs, is reported to be increasing at a much slower rate than its population. Several countries in which much of the

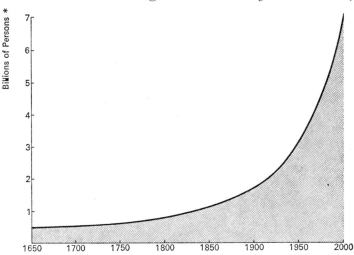

population is already afflicted by extreme hunger will, it is also reported, double their population in less than thirty years, at the present rate of increase.

The sense of material security and privileged existence into which the citizens of Western countries are lulled by the much-advertised abundance of goods and cheap entertainment is, therefore, continually undermined by the fearful, even apocalyptic warnings of the wrath to come, like the following:

The human race has 10 years to solve its food shortage problems or face extinction, Professor George Borgstrom, adviser to the United Nations Food and Agriculture Organization, told a teach-in on population crisis at the University of Toronto. Instead of launching a large-scale programme to find food for the exploding world population the 'have' nations were continuing trade patterns 'that present the absurd spectacle of the hungry feeding the rich and self-satisfied', he said.

Professor Borgstrom added: we would need to 'double the world's present agricultural production just to provide for those now living'.†

* 'Billion' is used in this book in the American sense of 'one thousand million'.

† *Guardian,* 29 October 1968.

The world is on the threshold of the biggest famine in history. If present trends continue, it seems likely that famine will reach serious proportions in India, Pakistan and China in the early 1970s . . . a famine will be of massive proportions affecting hundreds of millions.*

Unless the less developed countries sharply increase their agricultural productivity, and soon, mass famine will take place. Thus more human lives hang in the balance in the race between food and people than have been lost in all the wars in history.†

The next 24 to 28 years are going to be the most critical. . . . If the rate of food production cannot be significantly increased, we must be prepared for the four horsemen of the Apocalypse.‡

The four horsemen in the vision of the writer of the Book of Revelation were, of course, war, pestilence, famine and death. The massive hunger and poverty are seen here as a problem which, if it is not solved quickly, could lead to the end of all civilized life on our planet. Dr Sen, and the organization which he headed, the Food and Agriculture Organization of the United Nations, have been giving a good deal of publicity to the extent of hunger in the world. Some people may have noticed that in August 1965 he circularized Ministers of Agriculture in a number of countries, pointing out the implications of the lack of increase of *per capita* food production in the developing countries:

The stark fact is that it is now no less than seven years since there was any appreciable increase in food production per head of the world's population, seven very lean years for the developing countries. The outlook is alarming.

All this meant, if FAO's conclusions were correct, that by the early 1970s some of the major Third World countries, like China, India, Pakistan, Indonesia and Egypt, would experience

* Dr Raymond Ewell, in December 1962, quoted in W. & P. Paddock, *Famine 1975*.

† US Secretary of Agriculture, Orville L. Freeman, 21 July 1966.

‡ Dr B. R. Sen, Director-General FAO, *The Times*, 18 October 1966.

serious famines. On these grounds the newspapers were justified in publishing alarmist reports and features.

Dr Sen's reference to the 'horsemen of the Apocalypse' drew attention to something more alarming than the danger of food shortages in Europe and North America. The super-fear of what the 'hungry nations' would do has given rise to a horrendous political analysis of the problems facing the nations which have achieved material prosperity and abundance. Reports and articles prophesy that the fast-increasing multitude of backward and hungry Latin Americans, Asians and Africans (the peoples of the tri-continental 'south'), desperately seeking food and living space, would seize what the Europeans (both Eastern and Western), North Americans, Australians and Japanese (the 'north') already possess. 'They want,' as President Lyndon B. Johnson said, 'what we have.' The less amenable the hungry are to control by the powers of the 'developed' world, and the better organized and diligent on their own account, the greater cause for 'northern' anxiety. A few years ago the backward peoples were 2,000,000,000 in number, already forming two thirds of the world's population. By the turn of the century they will have increased to four fifths.

Hungry people are combustible people [argued a distinguished scientist, Professor Harrison Brown]. The growing number of 'combustible people' are, understandably, willing to take almost any action which they believe might mean more food for their families. Add to this the glimpses they get of the abundant life in the rich nations. Add to this the feeling of hopelessness concerning the rate of improvement of their personal situations. They see little change for the better from year to year, and often (particularly with respect to food) they see changes for the worse.

Cuba, the Congo, the Dominican Republic, Ghana, Indonesia, Nigeria and Vietnam are examples of countries which have recently been torn by strife and bloodshed. That list is destined to become much longer, unless something dramatically new is injected into the international picture. We must ask, if we double the number of combustible people and magnify their personal agonies how many explosions will we experience in the next decade? Perhaps ten? Twenty? Thirty?

Rich Against Poor

World Population and Projection for the Year 2000

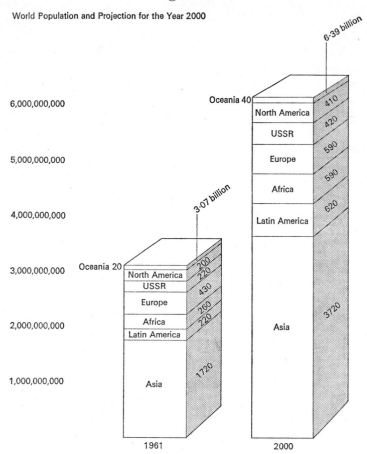

After referring to the earth's population, and the prospects of a population of 7,500 million by the turn of the century, Dr Harrison Brown continued:

It seems clear to me that in the absence of truly substantial help from outside, the poorer nations are headed squarely towards famine, pestilence, revolution and bloodshed on a massive scale, with consequences for the rest of the world which are difficult to foresee.

The article concludes with a proposal that the massive United States role in dealing with the situation should be directed by a new organization, not the Agency for International Development.*

The argument that hunger and poverty breed violence which threatens the affluent countries was also developed by United States Secretary of Defense, Robert McNamara, who later moved to the International Bank for Reconstruction and Development to become its President. A speech of his in Canada to the American Society of Newspaper Editors on 18 May 1966 may be recalled. He pointed out the correlation he saw between growing poverty and growing violence: whereas early in 1958 there were thirty-four outbreaks of violence (twenty-three continued insurgences) in the world, by February 1966 there were seventy-eight (forty of them prolonged insurgences). Only one of the twenty-seven nations in the richest category, according to Mr McNamara, experienced a serious violent upheaval, but eighty-seven per cent of the very poor (in the lowest category) did so.†

U Thant, the Secretary General of the United Nations, speaking to the UN Economic and Social Council's session in Geneva in the summer of 1968,‡ echoed this idea that a failure to assist the poorer nations to bridge the gap separating them from the rich countries was an 'invitation to violence'. U Thant spoke of the 'need to persuade people in the developed countries that their future prosperity and security, and that of their children and grandchildren, is inextricably linked with the well-being of people in the developing countries'.

Here were clear warnings that unless the explosive and revolutionary potentiality of the hungry peoples was de-fused, the 'good fortune' of the ordinary man and woman in the materially affluent societies might not last. Some of them may

* *New York Herald Tribune*, international edition (*NYHTI*), 24 May 1967. The reference to Ghana is difficult to understand. A similar portrayal of the dangers of 'upheaval' and a proposal to replace AID was made in a report on 9 January 1969 to Mr Nixon by an advisory group chaired by Professor James A. Perkins.

† The *New York Times* the next week-end published adjacent maps of the world to show that *Where the Poverty Is Is Where the Insurgency Is.*

‡ *NYHTI*, 9 July 1968.

have taken it that 'the natives were restless'. But humanitarian considerations, too, have persuaded many people in Britain, the United States, the Western European countries and perhaps Japan that the suffering caused by increasing hunger and world poverty must be brought to an end, not merely for reasons of preserving the privileged position of the 'high-income' countries, but for the sake of the men, women and children of the 'low-income' countries. The ordinary newspaper reader or television viewer gets his attention drawn to these world problems partly because a small minority of humane and sensitive persons, among whom are to be found journalists, are anxious enough to want to tell more, and find out more.

The feeling that there is an emergency on a world-wide scale has not been fostered merely by statements and headlines expressing alarm and horror, such as this from a Trenton, New Jersey, local newspaper in March 1967.

HUNGER – The Toll: 40,320 Dead Each Day

Carefully researched facts and statistics have been presented in all manner of publications. In October 1966 a panel of 'experts' appointed by FAO published a well-documented progress report on an 'Indicative World Plan for Agricultural Development', for the two decades ending in 1985. This plan, completed in October 1969, was to be discussed and used at a high-level meeting in Rome. Other agencies, too, publicize facts and statistics. But how all this activity and the anxieties expressed nowadays about the dangers of outbreaks of violence, revolt and revolution, came about we can understand only if we move further back in time than the mid-1960s.

THE WAR-TIME AND POST-WAR DISCOVERY
OF WORLD POVERTY

A convenient starting-point is the political awakening of a number of people in the 'developed' countries of the anti-Fascist alliance who had, during and just after the Second

World War, come to discover the facts about world economic conditions. Previously, most of those from the early-industrializing, imperial metropoles travelling in Latin America, Africa and colonial or semi-colonial Asia had been government officials, businessmen and traders, bankers, planters, officers, missionaries, mercenary troops and affluent tourists. They had on the whole no intimate knowledge of the situation of the industrial working class and the rural poor in their own communities.* The disruption of the old order in conditions of general war, especially in Asia, coincided with the travel to North Africa and Asia of large numbers of North Americans and Europeans who had themselves experienced poverty, or who were politically sensitive about economic exploitation and about the extreme disparity in living standards and political power between the rich on the one hand and the poor on the other. Some of them saw 'the East' with eyes different from those of tourists, colonial administrators, diplomats or missionaries; the economic and political conditions which 'the natives' found intolerable and against which revolts were taking place appeared intolerable to some of them, too. The much-propounded notion that colonial or semi-colonial status had been beneficial – had introduced civilization, peace, prosperity and progress – seemed to be contradicted by conditions which journalists as well as conscripted intellectuals, workers and others on war service saw for themselves.

To people who had to make the terrible sacrifices which brought little personal reward, the notion that they were fighting to create a better world was more than the rhetoric of politicians. But it appeared that to do this something more than the military defeat of the Fascist powers was needed. In the Kuomintang-controlled areas of China, for example, what some writers soberly recorded as *normal* conditions in the midst of the most serious crisis seemed almost beyond description: the heartless and cruel way in which the ruling *élites* treated the

* In the years following the First World War and the Great Slump there had been some working-class militancy. But those who supported this knew little at first hand and cared little about conditions in the colonies.

people was in sharp contrast to the glowing accounts given earlier by those who had favoured Chiang Kai-shek's bid to establish his dictatorship over all of China. The poor impression created by the wanton cruelty, cynicism and selfishness of the landlords, bureaucracy, military officers, ruling families and other forces of law and order supported by the major powers was made much worse by such examples of brutality as the treatment of the peasants in Honan Province during the terrible famine of 1942. The contrast in conditions and values and morale in the revolutionary areas under Mao Tse-tung's government were also reluctantly noted. The dignity, political consciousness, courage and fighting qualities of the peasant revolutionaries seemed ominous for the post-war future.* Here in China was the most important, and almost the poorest, of the colonial and semi-colonial countries, and the discontented poor were offered no alternative to increasing misery and oppression but a revolutionary break with the established order. To some observers, who were moved by what they saw as a struggle for social justice, for freedom from humiliating and impoverishing foreign rule or domination, and for the reconstruction of a modern China by its own people, the movement of revolt was a revelation of a new vitality in Asia, and a sign of hope. Sympathetic foreigners assisted during the war in the creation of a cooperative movement in the interior, and after it helped to publicize the facts about China.

In China the improvement of the political status and the living and working conditions of the peasants and the other working people had increasingly been the aim of the revolution led by Sun Yat-sen, and, after his death in 1925, by his revolutionary heirs. India, the other major colonial country, had not experienced war and invasion in the same way as China had in the twentieth century. Nationalist leaders, such as Mahatma Gandhi and Jawaharlal Nehru, had vigorously denounced what appeared to them as the ruinously exploitative and impoverish-

* Theodore White and Annalee Jacoby, *Thunder Out of China* (New York, 1946); Gunther Stein, *The Challenge of Red China* (London, 1945); Harold R. Isaacs, *No Peace for Asia* (New York, 1947).

ing system which British rule had imposed. In the course of the campaign for national independence the peasant masses were being stirred politically. Among the nationalists there were people who thought and worked in terms of a socialist India. Plans for a post-colonial economic reconstruction of the Indian economy after the overthrow of imperial rule were drawn up not only by Gandhians and native capitalists but also by the Indian Federation of Labour and the other left-wing forces. In other countries, especially in the Japanese empire into which the lately conquered colonies in Asia of the rival European and North American imperial powers had been incorporated, guerrilla movements for national liberation had been active during the anti-Fascist war. In the Philippines popular forces (especially in the island of Luzon) took action against their Japanese rulers and against Filipino collaborators, whom they saw as members of the same class which had served the former US rulers. An agrarian revolution began in the countryside, and the peasants gathered strength. From Korea (where, too, an anti-imperialist resistance continued its activities) to south-west Asia, the spark of popular discontent was threatening to start a major conflagration in which the foundations and structures of the order created during the period of imperial rule could be destroyed totally. In the jungles of Burma and Malaya, in north-eastern Thailand and Indochina, the people spontaneously took to armed resistance to the old order.

All over the region the conditions of poverty in which the great majority of the people lived were made much worse by the devastation of international war and civil war. These conditions were favourable for militant left-wing nationalists who were convinced that the traditional structures of authority and privilege, and the international system of capitalism into which the traditional order had been incorporated, were the cause of social and economic backwardness, of the repression of movements for popular democracy, and of the imprisoning and killing of popular leaders. To the masses who had woken to the fact that they had been the victims of tyranny they

B

offered political analyses and proposed organized action which could issue in attacks on landlords, colonial administrators, *compradors*, the colonial economic relations, and so on. The defeat and departure of the forces defending the far-reaching Japanese empire (as well as German and Italian empires) was to mark for them the beginning of a new, post-colonial and post-traditional way of life.

The conservative middle classes and the Westernized *élites* had themselves to adopt a mildly anti-imperialist stand and accept the need for a redistribution of power and wealth in order to retain their positions. Where they failed to do so, they were swept aside by revolutionary forces. The clamour for change drew world-wide attention to the poverty in the 'low-income' countries. The idea was spreading that poverty and racial humiliation could be wiped out only by the creation of new institutions and structures in place of the framework in which pre-colonial and colonial forms of society continued to exist. In this view it was from a radical upheaval and turmoil that progressive and just societies might be created. In the post-war years the shift in assumptions was to be seen also in the West and in the activities of the UN bodies. Scholars were taking a critical look at colonial policies and practices. Some were even urging support of movements for revolutionary change. In the United Nations the movement in favour of radical decoloniza-tion was so strong that the fundamental right of colonial peoples to take back national economic assets which had been seized from them very nearly came to be recognized interna-tionally. The necessity of land reform was the basis of a study undertaken on instructions from the UN General Assembly. Some of the things being said or written, and the statis-tics published, even by people who were far from being in support of revolutionary change and socialist forms of democracy, helped to expose the oppressive and institutional nature of the poverty and misery in Latin America, Asia and Africa.*

* UN, *Land Reform. Defects in Agrarian Structure as Obstacles to Economic Development* (New York, 1951).

The suffering and misery in the war-devastated areas was as great in Europe as anywhere else in the world. But while the formerly industrialized areas of Europe were able to recover quickly, the economic situation in Asia as a whole (where more than half of the world's poor lived) continued to be intolerable. There were a number of developments which accounted for the persistence of conditions of economic backwardness.

In the years since the end of the Second World War many people in the highly industrialized countries (the imperial powers of the nineteenth and early twentieth centuries) have had cause to worry about the dangers of nuclear annihilation and of war between the two super-powers. They have sought stability and quiet. But the number of those who have been outraged and scandalized by the nature and extent of the chronic hunger and poverty of hundreds of millions of men, women and children also has grown. The surge of genuine sympathy for nations in which starvation or serious malnutrition were normal for the masses, was certainly a factor making for a growing interest in the study of the social and economic conditions which bred poverty and the strategy of ending it.* The facts of hunger and economic backwardness were investigated, and comparisons of the living conditions of people in the 'rich' and the 'poor' countries were made and elaborated. There was analysis and argument. Solutions were prescribed and debated. Never before had the poverty and lack of economic development in the colonial world been so much talked about.

The United Nations Food and Agriculture Organization, which had come into existence towards the end of the war, the regional economic agencies of the United Nations, and economists and statisticians working for other UN organizations, regularly produced statistics and made comparative studies which were useful, and of interest, to journalists and politicians, as much as to scholars. The facts established the

* How important a factor it was, and what part other factors played, is a matter for inquiry. It would be interesting to relate this to the kind of interest which led to the Beveridge Report and the welfare state in Britain.

extent to which the impoverished areas, because of their size
and population, helped to depress economic standards in the
world as a whole. For example, it was shown that the food output per person, taken as an average for the world, was extremely
low. The figures for 1947–8 were the equivalent of 0·42 metric
tons of wheat for the world (excluding the Soviet Union, for
which statistics were not available to the UN). Yet the figure
for the North American and Central American region alone
was 2·57 metric tons. Non-Soviet Asia (with fifty-three per cent
of the world's population) had (according to these statistics) a
food output of only 0·22, and Africa 0·12 metric tons *per capita*.

*Productivity of the agricultural population by continents
and for the world,* pre-war and 1947–8.†*

Continent	Yield per hectare			Yield per person in agriculture		
	pre-war	1947–8	1947–8 as per cent of pre-war	pre-war	1947–8	1947–8 as per cent of pre-war
	metric tons			metric tons		
WORLD AVERAGE	1·24	1·30	105	0·42	0·42	100
North and Central America	1·07	1·50	140	1·80	2·57	143
South America	1·28	1·39	109	0·58	0·48	83
Europe	1·51	1·34	89	1·04	0·88	85
Oceania	1·06	1·20	113	1·94	2·38	123
Asia	1·26	1·20	95	0·24	0·22	92
Africa	0·77	0·73	95	0·12	0·12	100

As far as the knowledge which students of human nutrition
had at the time permitted, FAO worked it out that minimum
nutritional needs, on an average, should be equal to 2,200
calories a day. But according to estimates, whereas twenty-two
per cent of the non-Soviet world population had a *per capita*
consumption of over 2,700 calories, and twelve per cent between
2,200 and 2,700, the remaining sixty-six per cent had diets

* Table 2 in *Land Reform, op. cit.*   † Excluding USSR.

which gave them less than 2,200 calories.* By this count, two thirds of the world's population were getting less than the minimum number of required calories, and were therefore 'under-fed'. These included 1,299 million out of 1,300 million in Asia, and 184 million out of 198 million in Africa.†

Comparisons which began, perhaps, with levels of food consumption, were extended to other aspects of living and economic activity, such as consumption per head of energy for industrial use, mineral consumption, literacy, school accommodation available, and so on. The gap between rich and poor was shown to be fantastically wide. The commercial energy consumption *per capita* in the United States was eighty times and in the United Kingdom forty-five times that in India.‡ United States government figures, published in a report called 'Resources for Freedom' in 1952, indicated that of the non-Soviet world's consumption of 'important metals' (pig-iron, copper, lead, zinc and tin) ninety to ninety-seven per cent of each was consumed in the 'developed' countries, which had only twenty-four per cent of the total population. Disparities on this scale explained the low *per capita* incomes in the 'poor' countries at the end of the 1940s (see table on p. 16).

Per capita income and use of industrial energy were only some of the indices, it became clear, of what came, variously, to be called 'backwardness', 'underdevelopment', 'stagnation' and so on. The people in the 'poor' nations were shown to be dependent for employment, trade and consumption almost exclusively on the cultivation, often inefficient cultivation, of

* The respective percentage figures for the pre-war period were estimated as twenty-four, twenty-seven, and forty-nine.

† The 2,200 calories minimum has, justifiably, been the subject of controversy. It was noticed that in Ceylon, where detailed research into diets was carried out, normally healthy people who regularly ate a variety of good food (and could afford to eat as much as they wanted) were by this 'minimum' classed as 'under-fed'. It would, of course, have been gross exaggeration on the basis of these figures to say that two thirds of the world is hungry.

‡ UN, *Statistical Yearbook 1954*. 'Commercial energy' included all solid fuels, liquid fuels and natural gas, hydro-electric and nuclear power.

Per capita incomes (dollars)*	
Indonesia	25
China	27
Burma	36
India	57
Egypt	100
Brazil	112
United Kingdom	773
Switzerland	849
Canada	870
USA	1,453

one or two crops. The economic relationships (both domestic and international) established in the pre-war period were not, however, to be changed easily; the export of one or two primary commodities to the former metropolitan countries continued; the low incomes and standard of living made savings almost impossible, and locally generated capital for investment in new economic ventures and modernization generally was very scarce. There had been little economic expansion for several generations when populations had been growing, and there was a large proportion of adults of working age who were unemployed or only partly employed.

As study and analysis revealed the features of the *society* which was economically 'underdeveloped', the lines on which remedial action should be taken were sketched out, and a worldwide theoretical discussion on the social and political origins of poverty began. There were among the subject peoples of the colonial and neo-colonial territories which had become 'independent' some who made (as we noted earlier) a profound and comprehensive analysis of their situation and advocated action (to end poverty) which consisted in reversing the directions taken in the past or in other ways radically changing the economic patterns and relationships established in the previous century, and even earlier. Much of the thinking

* The figures for Indonesia, China and Burma are 'post-war'. The others are 1949 figures.

underlying this kind of analysis and action derived from a belief that the interests of the rich and powerful were antagonistic to those of the poor and powerless. In opposition to this view (which tended to blame the systematic exploitation of the land, resources and people of Latin America, Africa and Asia by profit-seeking international capitalists for the poverty and lack of industrialization) other theories were advanced of how countries must develop, and the 'stages' through which economically developing countries must pass. These stressed continuity with the processes established in the colonial period and collaboration between the 'developed' and the 'underdeveloped'.* In fact, the Second World War had hardly ended before the war between those seeking the contradictory lines of development began.

To recall all this as we have done, briefly, is to recognize that the theoretical interest in economic growth on a world-wide basis is very much a post-war phenomenon. The widespread public interest in the plight of the poor peoples of the 'southern' continents, and the professed eagerness to get rid of world-wide

---

* '. . . The sins of imperialism are still today appealed to in many countries of Asia and even Latin America, even though the former imperialists have lost control and, in many cases, have completely withdrawn from these countries' (B. F. Hoselitz, 'Nationalism, Economic Development and Democracy', in Hoselitz (ed.), *Agrarian Societies in Transition. Annals*, May 1956). A different view of 'the spectacular upsurge of interest in the underdeveloped areas' was expressed by Douglas F. Dowd: 'There remains good reason to differ with the basic assumption underlying most proposals for developing these areas – the assumption that such development can at once be beneficial to all concerned and take place within an institutional framework basically the same as that which now exists. What is required to bring about the economic development of the underdeveloped areas is nothing less than a comprehensive social transformation, and a substantial modification of their place in the world economy. Isolated attacks on specific scarcities . . . where they do not represent a naïve approach to the problem, may well lend themselves to a perpetuation of colonial relationship' ('Two Thirds of the World', *Antioch Review*, Fall 1953). See also J. K. Galbraith, 'Conditions for Economic Change in Underdeveloped Countries', *Journal of Farm Economics*, vol. 33, 1951.

hunger and poverty contrast curiously with the indifference to the plight of the poor which had prevailed till then.*

AID FOR THE POOR: VOLUNTARY AND OFFICIAL

The Voluntary Agencies

The manifest inequalities of a world-wide community in which comparisons can easily be made, and in which information and opinion can be communicated quickly and easily, have been a cause of discontent and dissatisfaction. The powers which were divesting themselves in the late 1940s and 1950s of the responsibilities of direct imperial administration had very limited time to make good their declared intention of helping the low-income countries substantially to ameliorate their material and cultural situation, and thus to demonstrate the irrelevance of attempts to seek to create a new society on new, non-Western foundations. Their theories and policies had sought to convince all those who were not prepared to tolerate existing inequalities that if there was the correct know-how about economic development, cultural change, technical change, political development, modernization, the right type of *élites*, development of communications, agricultural development, educational development, and so on, the war on world poverty would be won. The 'developed' countries have since the beginning of independence increasingly taken over responsibility for training technicians, organizing agriculture, conducting scientific research, recruiting and training officers and soldiers, organizing police and security forces, advising government tax departments, teaching in universities and schools, and deciding policy, in various Third World countries.

* The stream of academic literature explaining 'underdevelopment' on conservative lines began in the early 1950s, e.g. B. F. Hoselitz (ed.), *The Progress of Underdeveloped Areas* (Chicago, 1952); Eugene Staley, the author of *The Future of Underdeveloped Countries* (New York, 1954), later played an important role as the author of the Staley Plan for dealing with the Vietnamese.

Hundreds of thousands of their people have been compelled to go to the Third World countries on government service. Many people in the affluent countries like Britain and the United States believe, however, that the governments of the high-income countries have not been successful in relieving the misery, hunger and oppression of the hundreds of millions who constitute the majority of the men, women and children in the 'poor' countries. The failure to get results from 'aid' has increased the impatience and anxiety of the donors.

The gap between the richest nations and the poorest nations is even greater now than it was two decades ago, when the much-publicized attempt to close the gap can be said to have begun. Obviously, the distance between the richest million people in the world and the poorest million in regard to their material possessions and income and status, and power over their destinies, increases fantastically. The very conception of a single humanity which encompasses such nearly total contradictions is a strain on the imagination. Idealistic young people and students, eager to end the humbug and the injustices which they see prevailing in their own societies, have been eager to rescue the poor and oppressed abroad from the human, material and institutional forces which seem to exploit them and oppress them.

The growth of scientific and technological knowledge since the war has been remarkable. So has progress in the organization of agriculture and industry. But the claim of the Western governments that they are helping overseas development is not always convincing. For that is not development which rapidly diminishes the numbers of the poor, and of their houses, fields and towns, even while well-fed men and women thousands of miles away watch on television and listen to gruesome on-the-spot reports. In many homes young men and women are moved by the suffering of people of other lands and races in ways which their parents, full of their own immediate cares and anxieties, cannot easily understand. As famines recur, and warnings of major famine and war increase, more people form or join organizations actively engaged in fighting world hunger and poverty. They help conduct expensive campaigns advertising the situation of the poor abroad. They collect funds. They organize fasts, teach-ins, demonstrations and conferences on hunger and poverty. All this may be seen as a peaceful struggle waged against world poverty, which the peoples of Africa, Asia and Latin America do not seem, to some of the enthusiastic activists at least, to be doing much to overcome. Some voluntary work is therefore also carried on abroad, through short-term organized service. The 'world' of the poor is not as remote and foreign to the young in the West as it is to the middle-aged and old.

In Britain organizations such as Oxfam, Christian Aid, War on Want and Voluntary Service Overseas are widely known. There are a number of others, and new ones are coming into being. Sometimes existing organizations and agencies combine to conduct campaigns or co-ordinate their work. The Churches, too, have drawn attention to the development needs of overseas countries. Similar work is done by groups of people in other European countries and in North America. All these not only continually confront the public with the facts and challenges of world-wide hunger and poverty, but in addition sometimes sponsor or initiate agricultural and other projects which in their view will improve living standards in Asia and Africa, or show people there how things should be done.

Voluntary agencies of any kind are not easy to organize internationally. But there have been some international agencies, such as the Red Cross, CARE and Church World Service, which have taken an important part in stirring people's consciences about the suffering and misery resulting from war devastation, large-scale migrations, famines and floods, and the general shortage of food, housing and other resources in some countries or areas. They have also collected and distributed funds, and recruited volunteers for relief and development work. The international organizations of the Christian Churches have been active in this manner, often in collaboration with the international agencies of the United Nations. The World Council of Churches, for example, has helped in relief work, as well as provided study of 'areas of rapid social change', and responsible action to help them.

Official Aid

As we look back over the last twenty-five years we may notice how vigorously some voluntary agencies have acted as a political 'lobby' on behalf of the poor countries, pressing the governments of the industrialized countries with the highest *per capita* incomes to allocate a small part of the national budget to aid the underdeveloped (or, as they came to be called, 'developing') countries. They have helped to prepare 'public opinion' in these countries for government-sponsored aid programmes. The coming into being of the Ministry of Overseas Development in Britain has been one consequence. The arguments used for voting money for loans, grants, technical assistance and other forms of 'aid' have been varied; chief among them have been those of humanitarianism, social justice and self-interest. Governments have been able to allocate much larger sums of money than voluntary agencies, depending on individual contributions, have been able to distribute or spend. Anyone who was familiar with the relationships between the European peoples and the rest before the war would have been struck by the way in which programmes of 'aid' or 'assistance' from one to the other have come to be accepted by the poor countries as an aspect of international relations in the last two decades.

It is not possible to examine the different governmental aid programmes of the major industrial countries in any detail here. The Organization for Economic Cooperation and Development* has a Development Assistance Committee which co-ordinates and stimulates aid programmes, conducts some research and makes a comparative survey of aid programmes of

---

* Its members are the United Kingdom, West Germany, Eire, France, Austria, Iceland, Sweden, the Netherlands, Belgium, Turkey, Switzerland, Denmark, Italy, Norway, Portugal, Luxemburg, Greece, Canada, the United States and Japan.

member-countries. The main 'donors' of aid are, according to
its surveys of what has been disbursed, France, the United
States, the United Kingdom and West Germany. An interesting
fact is that France's official payments of what its government
considers as 'aid' have been the highest, as a percentage of the
national income. The figures for the early 1960s indicate this.

*Official aid of main donors (net disbursements)**

	Totals ($ million)			As percentage of the national income		
	1962	1963	1964	1962	1963	1964
France	977	843	841	1·76	1·38	1·26
Germany	427	421	499	0·62	0·58	0·58
USA	3,713	3,842	3,534	0·82	0·81	0·70
UK	418	414	490	0·64	0·61	0·67

But the government which is recorded as having provided
most 'aid' is that of the United States.† The sums voted by the
United States in the 1950s and the 1960s are so large, in
comparison with what most poor countries can take from the
proceeds of taxation for investment in development projects,
that we shall be justified in discussing in some detail the United
States as the most important aid donor among the 'high-
income' countries.

During the Second World War the people of the United
States had been taken much further into the world outside than

* From *French Aid* by Teresa Hayter (London, 1966). For further
information on French aid this book is worth consulting. This volume is
one of a series of studies of overseas aid and investment.

† The United States had entered the war as the richest and technologically most advanced industrial power. She emerged after the war after
four years in which enormous amounts of money and effort had been
invested in the development of her technology and economy, with a much
bigger lead over her rivals. The home territory of the United States had
emerged unscathed after the war, though American war casualties were
heavy. Every one of the other major industrial powers suffered badly in
the war, up to then by far the most destructive in world history.

ever before. The notion that their nation was not like other nations, but was unique, with a world-wide mission or destiny, had from time to time been propounded (and acted upon). But in the century and a half following the founding of the republic it was the territories and peoples to their south and west which had been regarded as of special interest for the United States. In practical terms, and compared with the other European peoples and the Japanese, the Americans had not been very closely involved in the Asian and African continents as a whole up to the 1930s.

The technological gap between the societies in which development had been arrested largely at a pre-industrial stage and the United States made its modern technology and 'know-how' more desirable than ever. During the war, and partly because of the value to the United States of the political support and resources of the Latin American countries, a series of conferences had resulted in technical assistance programmes beginning in Latin America. The Institute of Inter-American Affairs was created in March 1942 for this purpose.* The substantial aid given to the Chiang Kai-shek government in China during the war was continued after it. Then came the European Recovery Programme (or Marshall Plan) of 1948, to administer which the Economic Cooperation Administration was created. By passing the Act for International Development in May 1950 Congress also authorized the creation of the Technical Cooperation Administration. When ECA ceased functioning in 1951, the Mutual Security Agency was created to administer aid programmes. This ended in July 1953, but the Foreign Operations Administration then took over, to hand over its economic and technical aid functions at the end of June 1955 to the International Cooperation Administration; later (in 1957) there was the Development Loan Fund. In November 1961 Congress passed the Foreign Assistance Act, and under it the Agency for International Development (AID) was set up, to oversee and administer the different aspects of foreign aid.

* Gordon Connell-Smith, *The Inter-American System* (London and New York, 1966), pp. 123 ff.

On the initiative taken by President Kennedy in March 1961, the Alliance for Progress was set up to provide for inter-American cooperation in developing Latin America. It is also relevant to add that in 1954 Congress had passed the Agricultural Trade Development Act (which became known as PL 480), providing for the sale abroad of US agricultural surpluses. This was amended in 1966, and is also referred to as the 'Food for Peace Act' and the 'Food for Freedom Act'.

The listing of a series of agencies, programmes and laws can cause confusion if all these names are in current use. In fact, for practical purposes the Agency for International Development is the main US agency today for non-military forms of aid, providing development loans and administering technical cooperation; it also provides 'supporting assistance'. The confusion of aims and practice reflected in the frequent changes has been criticized in the United States.* Nevertheless, the United States' Foreign Assistance programme received high praise from a panel appointed by President Johnson: '*It still stands as a pioneering, humanitarian effort without parallel in all of history.*'†

President Johnson also declared that the United States was specially qualified to take responsibility for and give leadership to the development of the backward countries.‡ It makes sense therefore for us to learn more about the role the United

* I. W. Moomaw is reported as writing in 1966 of the aid programme: 'In the years since the beginning of Point Four, ten different directors have been in charge. Each sought to effect his own ideas for change. No other arena of governmental responsibility has been so frequently surveyed and changed. Eight Presidential Committees have scrutinized it. Three administrations have completely overhauled it. . . .' Quoted in *The World Food Problem* (Washington DC, 1967), p. 117.

† *ibid.*, p. 118. Italic in original.

‡ 'We are the richest nation in history. We have much to do that is urgent and pressing at home and abroad, but we must maintain our involvement in the world-wide war on want' (9 October 1968). 'The people of the world . . . are looking to our system to show them the way into the twentieth century. And we must not fail because the alternative is anarchy and through anarchy the enemies of freedom will triumph!' Quoted in *The Aid Story* (Washington DC, n.d.).

States has played in countries whose peoples have sought to eliminate poverty and oppression.

The total aid in loans and grants authorized to be administered by the US Agency for International Development and the agencies which preceded it was $44,824 million from 1948 to the end of the fiscal year 1967. Of this $40,688 million were spent. The details are as follows:

	US fiscal year	Total of net obligations and loan authorizations (loans and grants) ($ million)*
Marshall Plan Period	1948 (April to June)	766
	1949	5,517
	1950	3,614
	1951	2,622
	1952	1,985
Mutual Security Act Period	1953	1,960
	1954	2,228
	1955	1,821
	1956	1,506
	1957	1,627
	1958	1,620
	1959	1,916
	1960	1,866
	1961	2,012
AID Period	1962	2,508
	1963	2,297
	1964	2,136
	1965	2,026
	1966	2,545
	1967	2,249

It must be noted that this amount excludes large sums allocated for military assistance programmes, the 'Food for

* From *US Economic Assistance Programs Administered by the Agency for International Development and Predecessor Agencies. April 3, 1948 – June 30, 1967.*

Freedom' programme and certain other expenditures, information about which is classified. For the last two years of this
period, for example, AID allocations and Food for Freedom
allocations (in millions of dollars) were:

	1966	1967
AID	2,655	2,415
Food for Freedom	1,941	1,177

These figures are sufficient to indicate how considerable the
volume of US official foreign aid is. According to AID, the
funds are used for a variety of purposes: to provide the services
of highly trained or skilled technicians and experts from
universities, engineering and construction companies, business
firms, cooperatives, trade unions and other institutions; to send
iron and steel, industrial machinery, chemicals, motor vehicles,
fertilizers, construction equipment, electrical apparatus, copper
and petroleum products; to provide training for citizens of
developing countries; to encourage private investment in
developing countries by insuring investors against losses from
inconvertibility of currency, expropriation, war, revolution
and insurrection, and against long-term business risks; to make
investment surveys to determine whether overseas investments
are feasible; to encourage US voluntary agencies; to provide
relief in the event of natural disasters; to make grants to
American-sponsored schools and hospitals abroad; to finance
research; and so on. The food programme also has several
uses.

The official aid programmes of the United States are administered by Federal government agencies. But the increasingly elaborate activities connected with 'international
development' have given rise to a number of organizations
which have played a semi-official role; projects and research
programmes relating to US action in the Third World have
involved universities, research councils and foundations. It
is these which have issued the literature on various aspects of
'development'.

When all that the American taxpayer spends on all aspects of official and semi-official study of and action in the Third World is taken into account the total since the Second World War must be several hundreds of billions of dollars.

United Nations and Other International Aid

Part of governmental aid to developing countries is channelled through United Nations bodies and other international agencies. Increasing demands from both the developing countries and from pro-aid enthusiasts in the high-income countries for more vigorous international action to help the poor nations has kept 'development aid' near the top of the list of the UN's concerns. The programmes of national organizations active in relieving hunger and poverty have sometimes been devoted to helping schemes sponsored by the United Nations Organizations.

FAO's work in drawing attention to the need to grow more food has already been mentioned. From its founding at Yellow Springs, Virginia, in 1943 to its attempt to draw up and implement an Indicative World Plan for agricultural development it has helped rich and poor countries to work together. The Freedom From Hunger Campaign was supported throughout the world by the formation of local Freedom From Hunger committees and organizations.

The work of the regional economic commissions of the UN, the International Labour Organization, the Economic and Social Council, FAO, WHO, UNICEF, UNESCO, UNWRRA, and numerous other bodies has added to the volume of work which is believed to assist the developing countries. It was on the initiative of the UN secretariat that the 1960s were designated the Development Decade, with the aim of raising the annual rate of growth of the developing countries from about $3\frac{1}{2}$ per cent to five per cent, and, ultimately, to six per cent – an ambitious and optimistic aim. Other 'targets' to be reached during the Development Decade were a modest increase in the developing countries' share of world trade, and the raising of development assistance from the high-income countries to one per cent of national income. The Development Decade has now drawn to a close, and an estimate of the success and relevance of such campaigns as this is timely.

While attempts were being made to remedy the poor start to the Development Decade, initiatives taken within the Third World led to the calling, under United Nations' auspices, of the Conference on Trade and Development, in 1964. The Conference made it necessary for a new UN body to be created, and subsequently a second conference was called, at New Delhi in 1968.

While all this was going on, technical assistance, development loans and other aid programmes were being devised and carried out under the auspices of such bodies as the Colombo Plan, the International Bank for Reconstruction and Development (the 'World Bank') and the Inter-American Development Bank. The work of OECD's Development Assistance Committee (which stimulates and co-ordinates, but does not give aid) has already been mentioned.

IS 'INTERNATIONAL DEVELOPMENT' THE SOLUTION?

If the reader is tired of all the details, which are by no means complete, of agencies promoting, giving, reviewing, discussing development aid, his reaction is understandable. The organizations, their research and publications, their activities and their expenditure, are themselves a subject for study. The contrast between the pre-war world and the post-war world in regard to the interest in 'development' and 'developing' countries is as marked in the fields of teaching, research and publications as in anything else. Sociologists, political scientists, psychologists, economists, international relations experts, educationists and others now talk of 'development' as an aspect of their respective subjects of specialization.* But it is not as a subject of academic interest that the problems of world-wide hunger and poverty strike most sensitive people. They are more concerned about

* See Nicholas A. Sims, *Opting for Development* (London, 1968) for an account of development studies in Britain.

whether something can be done to avert the consequences of the growing gap between rich and poor, and dissatisfied with existing programmes. They would like to know what can be done to make aid more relevant and effective than it has been.

One of the many official and semi-official responses to the criticisms was the report issued recently by a Commission under the chairmanship of Mr Lester Pearson, former Prime Minister of Canada.* The Commission had been appointed by Mr Robert McNamara, the President of the World Bank. The Commission did not attempt any radical examination of the world situation, but it made an extensive review of the problems arising from and the prospects for 'international co-operation in development' of Asia, Africa and Latin America, and recommended what it called a 'strategy'. It proposed also that Mr McNamara should convene an international conference 'to consider the creation of machinery essential to the efficiency and co-ordination of the international aid system'.†

It is clear that for many other people, too, 'a new and interdependent world community' will be associated with the kind of conservative 'strategy' proposed by this commission. Many of the assumptions taken for granted today were considered highly questionable in the immediate post-war years.‡ More-

---

* *Partners in Development*, Report of the Commission on International Development (London, 1959). It opened with these words:

CRISIS IN AID

'The widening gap between the developed and developing countries has become a central issue of our time.

'The effort to reduce it has inspired the nations left behind by the technological revolution to mobilize their resources for economic growth. It has also produced a transfer of resources on an unprecedented scale from richer to poorer countries. International cooperation for development over the last twenty years has been of a nature and on a scale new in history . . .'

† *ibid.*, p. 22.

‡ See Nasser's and Nehru's views in my *From Gandhi to Guevara: The Polemics of Revolt* (London, 1970), pp. 111 ff., pp. 277 ff. Also Indian Council of World Affairs, *Asian Relations – Proceedings and Documentation of the first Asian Relations Conference* (New Delhi, 1948).

over, the 'crisis' in the development of the formerly colonial
areas occurs after solutions to the hunger and world poverty
have been attempted through 'aid'. Thirty years ago it was
taken for granted by nationalists in Asia that it would be
impossible to achieve modernization within the confines of the
Western-dominated world economy and polity. In recent years a
different idea has gained wide acceptance in some of the capitals
of the former colonies. It is the idea that the industrially
developed 'northern' powers of Europe, North America and
Japan are willing to make sacrifices to guide and lead the more
backward peoples in the ways of economic and political
modernization, and even to lay the foundations of economies
which would eradicate hunger, poverty and ignorance. The
generous 'transfer of resources' from the economically
advanced north to the southern, underdeveloped, areas is
regarded as an earnest of what the high-income countries were
prepared to do to eliminate remaining imperialist practices and
institutions in Latin America, Asia and Africa, and in that way
to strengthen political freedom and national independence. The
need for an increase of aid is acknowledged, as the under developed countries need more technical help, materials, equipment, know-how, leadership, foreign exchange and protection
than has been made available. Those who press for a greater
volume of aid, and criticize the decline in the percentage of their
national income which the high-income countries are prepared
to make available for aid, are in fact arguing that foreign aid to
the 'south' has been absolutely vital for political and economic
development in that area, and must be increased in order to
prevent the disruption of the world order by revolution, or by
the large-scale famines and epidemics which would signal
failure to prevent serious over-population. The cry 'Not
enough aid' is also raised to contradict those who argue that the
developed countries could afford to go their own way, or that
aid is wasted by its recipients, who do not even bother to feel
grateful to the donors. The notion that the peoples of the non-
developed areas are incapable of helping themselves is thus
confirmed by both sides of the argument. The 'More aid'

lobby argue, in effect, that not contempt and condemnation, but more pity and compassion, more generosity towards the less fortunate, should be the order of the day. They also argue that the economic system on which their own affluence and power depends will be undermined and rendered insecure if the situation in the Third World is not taken in hand more firmly.*

Some of those who argue that aid is effective when the desired political and cultural conditions exist in the recipient countries, refer to the 'success stories'. They claim high rates of economic growth in the Chinese province of Taiwan, Mexico, Brazil, South Korea and Iran and cite these as testimony to the effectiveness of aid, and what it might achieve in the long run to further the interests of both donors and recipients. Pakistan's rapid progress and India's success in increasing wheat production are also cited, as was the rapid economic growth in the southern half of Vietnam. It is also argued that the concern shown for over-population and world poverty may point to the remarkable awakening of conscience on behalf of the poor in distant lands, and to the uplifting moral effects of the personal self-denial and practical help of many who collect and give money, organize fasts and teach-ins on behalf of people of different races and nationalities, and sometimes go out to distant lands to render personal service to the less fortunate.

Nevertheless, the kind of 'war on world poverty' which is led and directed in the ways described has come in for very critical attention. I am referring not only to the kind of campaign which concentrates on raising the official aid figure to one per cent of the national income of the developed countries, and on securing more favourable terms of trade for the developing countries than they are now able to get. I am also referring to

* Both President Johnson in his attempt to persuade Congress not to cut down his requests for a high level of technical and military aid, loans, etc. and Barbara Ward argue in this way, but with differing aims. See my *From Gandhi to Guevara, op. cit.*, pp. 250–55, for opposing views by Barbara Ward and Professor Peter Bauer.

those who are hoping that the US and British governments, the World Bank and UN agencies will be able to improve their own aid policies and administration so as to take account of the fact that progress is not moving fast enough to avert catastrophic famine and revolution. The Pearson Commission, for example, in *Partners in Development*, has offered the world what it claims is a piece of rethinking on aid policies. Other bodies have made similar criticisms and suggestions. Is there then any need to go any further than they have into questions about the relevance and effectiveness of the present 'wars' on poverty, hunger, ignorance and underdevelopment?

There are good reasons for thinking that there is. I hope that a few brief observations will explain why the appraisal of the revolt against hunger and oppression, and the response to it over the past twenty-five years, are unsatisfactory. These observations are not made in any systematic way, but rather to indicate that there are good grounds for doubting both the relevance of the conservative prescriptions for eradicating world poverty and the efficacy of Western and Soviet 'aid' for the struggle of the poor against poverty.

Firstly, let us look at the widening income gap between the rich and the poor. It has been given a great deal of publicity. The statistics which show this, and which make projections for the future, are impressive. But we have not had an analysis of the power-structure, institutions and economic processes which make for the widening gap. The *relation* between the colonial system and the original gap, on the one hand, and between the post-war 'gap' and the conservative prescriptions followed for decolonization, on the other, should have been examined, but they were not. The *system* which by its working plainly impoverishes some and *at the same time* enriches others also should have been analysed. Barbara Ward, one of the most distinguished supporters of 'aid', argued in a lecture she gave in May 1968 for 'realism'.

Our starting point [she said], can only be the recognition that in normal times most people do not concern themselves with other peoples' misery, least of all what is happening to other races in other lands. There may be a minority committed to action and perhaps a rather larger group ready for charity. But so long as world development is dependent simply upon generous instincts, we shall not get very far. . . . The central concerns of the rich are their own living standards, their trading positions and the relationships among wealthy nations that border on the North Atlantic Ocean, forming a select rich man's club.

She nevertheless presents what she claims is a realistic argument for 'a properly integrated and expanded strategy for world development'. The thinking is serious, and well-informed.* But what are 'normal times'? Is her argument, which implies that the end of 'the deepening poverty of the developing continents' will stabilize and strengthen the international capitalist economy, a valid one? Can 'world development' be achieved today (by the same class of people who developed the national economies of Britain, France and the United States in the last two centuries) without considerable and expensive military coercion? In any case, is Barbara Ward concerned about the eradication of poverty? Does she think that the poor will respect 'the central concerns of the rich'? There are many questions for which answers have to be found outside the present 'aid' lobbies.

Secondly, there are good grounds for inquiring if the 'success stories' refer to authentic cases of communities which have made genuine progress in economic and political reconstruction and have in fact become 'developed' countries. One example often cited is China's province of Taiwan, over which since 1949 the Chinese government has been denied jurisdiction by the United States. Taiwan had been seized from China by the Japanese in 1895, and though a colonial possession been fairly well developed economically before it was restored to China on Japan's defeat in 1945. Both socially and economically the extension of the Chiang Kai-shek dictatorship to it was disastrous for the province. It was occupied and administered by Chiang and his forces when the Chinese people drove them out of the mainland in 1949. From that year to 1961 the United

* *Poverty and Politics* (London, 1968), pp. 1, 2, 7.

States allocated, apart from immense amounts of military aid and 'Food for Peace' aid, over $1,300 million ($1,000 *per capita*) in aid (of which only $175 million were loans). In addition, it has been its policy to attract foreign private capitalists to invest heavily in industry in Taiwan. (Foreign 'investments' rose by nearly $100 million in the three-year period, 1964–6.) The utmost care and ingenuity has been devoted by the United States government to making Taiwan an example of the type of development it favours. The island, with a population of under fourteen million, had a *per capita* income in 1967 of over $274. But 'success stories' of this kind (assuming for the moment that the goals of genuine development have been reached) can be multiplied if one selects particular *areas* or provinces in a number of countries. Moreover, Taiwan's progress is overshadowed by that of some other provinces of China and even by that of China as a whole. For this, and possibly for other reasons, such as twenty years of martial law and the maintenance by the Chiang dictatorship of a military force of 600,000, this example of what the US has achieved in Taiwan is a spurious one. But, more significantly, the assiduous advertising of Taiwan, dominated by an expensive and unproductive police apparatus of which its citizens live in terror, as a model of what 'international development' can achieve, calls for more discussion of the kind of society the United States, Britain, Japan and other affluent countries would like to 'develop' in the Third World.

South Korea is another showpiece. From 1953, when the Korean peace was achieved, to 1967 the government in Seoul was voted $2,750 million in aid (in addition to specifically military aid), nearly ninety per cent of it as direct grants. (This may be compared with non-food aid to India during the same period of $2,940 million – nearly $2,600 million as loans.) Annual aid allocations have been reduced annually, until the 1967 figure was $112·9 million. But PL 480 'aid' that year alone totalled over $44 million, and military aid was estimated at $320 million. The South Korean government has also been receiving help from Japan. But its economy and regime would hardly commend themselves to the Third World countries as models of development. It is well known that wage rates are nearly the lowest in the world. South Korea's foreign liabilities in 1968 were $1,128 million (according to the *Far Eastern Economic Review*), and the fact that some 100 foreign firms find it profitable and safe to set up business in Korea gives cause for inquiry into the criteria by which the success of 'international development' is assessed.

There has also been lavish praise for the economic growth of Mexico under capitalism. The Mexican Revolution, and the radical reforms under President Cardenas in the 1930s, had achieved a level of economic equality and justice which made Mexico at one time one of the most advanced countries in Latin America. The statistics of Mexico's rate of economic growth (six per cent or more a year) in recent years have been impressive. Yet Mexico is one of the Third World countries in which the distress of the working people has actually been increasing while the rich have been getting richer. Whoever praises Mexico for the wealth it offers, it is not the majority of Mexicans, who live in slums of town and countryside. Far from poverty being eliminated, it has increased. There is a new-rich *élite*, but the income gap between the mass of wage-earners and the *élite* has been widening. It is also an odd commitment to development which leads Mexico's rulers to imprison or massacre those seeking redress of grievances, instead of treating people with respect.* The stable and progressive

---

* The nature of Mexican 'development' is viewed critically even by some of its admirers. *The Times* said: 'Mexico has made small headway in reducing her overwhelming economic dependence on the Americans. . . . American corporations hold a substantial position in Mexico's industry, as leaders in the automotive and several other sectors of manufacturing. . . . In television, films, radio, publishing and advertising, the American influence is all pervasive. . . . A kind of Coca-Cola culture has reached into the fabric of Mexican society . . .' ('Sovereignty Not for Sale' by S. T. Wise). 'Millions of Mexican peasants are still waiting for a piece of land; land hunger is recognized by the Government as a social problem. . . . Excessive

economy of Pakistan, another major aid-recipient, has been another success story. Success in East Pakistan, according to a leading expert on the developing countries, Lucian Pye, was 'possibly the most dramatic'. Yet the real income of the labouring masses actually fell while the GNP doubled in the 1960s. This model of Western-type development was presented in an unflattering light when severe economic distress throughout that populous country caused a mass uprising early in 1969, and the overthrow of the Ayub Khan government. What in fact was 'most dramatic' in East Pakistan was the way in which the poor decided to 'tell it as it is'. One heard at that time, how, during the period of 'aid', only twenty families had been 'developing'. The very real possibility that Pakistan's foreign debt will be enormous (over 100 billion rupees by 1985) is also cause for further thought.

Thirdly, a hard look at the seemingly generous flow of donations in *their* direction makes one cautious about the extent to which the developing countries are recipients of undeserved and unearned benefactions. Recently there was a discussion in *The Times* about how much Britain officially contributes in overseas aid. The official figure of £221 million was cut down by correspondents, who pointed out that in order to measure the amount which was in practice 'given away' in 1968 account would have to be taken of loan repayments and interest payments received, the profit margins on goods which had to be bought in Britain, and the additional business which consequently accrued to British interests. What would be left would amount to very little indeed. Beyond all this, the British economy, like the American economy, is boosted by the considerably large amounts which move in the direction of

---

disparities between wealth and poverty have rather grown than been curbed of recent years. The peasant communities remain remote from the cities and powerless (more than half the population in all rural areas at the last census was unable to read and write); but the shanty town problem with its inhuman living conditions and heavy under-employment represents a growing serious threat . . .' (Richard Wigg, 'A Country of Two Nations', *The Times*, 28 July 1969).

the developed countries – as profits, gains owing to favourable terms of trade, and so on.*

There is also the growing bill which the people in the poor countries must pay in order to service and repay the aid requested and accepted by their leaders. The following table tells a small part of the story.

Asia's aid indebtedness in 1967 (in $ million)†

	External public debt outstanding on 1 January 1967			Total grants and loans received in 1966 debt service thereon		
	total	as a product of exports	in $ per head	total	total	as per cent of grants and loans
India	7,318	4·6	15	1,462	319	22
Pakistan	2,533	4·2	24	517	84	16
South Korea	552	2·2	19	317	12	·4
Philippines	429	0·5	13	98	74	76
Thailand	352	0·5	11	160	30	19
Malaysia	350	0·3	36	50	19	38
Taiwan (*sic*)	321	0·6	25	77	23	30
Ceylon	169	0·5	15	49	10	21
Singapore	51	—	27	15	1	9

The indebtedness of the Latin America peoples is as great as that of Asian 'aid'-recipients. The political and economic implications of entering into the debtor–creditor relationship were plain in earlier times. The examples of nineteenth-century Egypt and China are not very reassuring.

* 'Aid', a British House of Commons Estimates Committee recommended, should be 'increasingly concentrated on those countries which offer the greatest potential markets'.

† Taken from *Far Eastern Economic Review, 1969 Year Book* (Hong Kong, 1969), p. 81. The major country in the region, China, had no external debt at all, except for current credits in trade. As most of the aid to Taiwan, South Korea and the Philippines was in grants, the amount owed on loans is only a small fraction of what was received from foreign backers of the regimes there.

Fourthly, the idealistic enthusiasm for the ending of poverty and hunger in the 'poor' world often shows a 'concern' which is so restricted and selective as to be inexplicable in terms of the plight and the needs of the poor themselves. It must be considered strange and irrational for a war on world poverty to be conceived, as the literature tells us, as a form of security for the rich minority and the privileged *élites*. One has cause to wonder, after talking and listening to the enthusiasts for this kind of aid who are anxious about and disapproving of the peasants and workers, whether the sensitiveness and compassion, the seeking after justice and equity, is more in the rhetoric than in the heart, the mind and the act. Even radical proposals for aiding the poor countries seem to show indifference, hostility, even hatred towards large numbers of the poor, and opposition to the hard struggles they are waging against the root causes of chronic hunger and poverty. The joining of the struggle *against* the oppressed and impoverished who have taken in hand the eradication of the conditions which breed poverty is a *motive* for supporting 'aid' programmes. These are strange contradictions.

The Haslemere Declaration, one of the most radical and critical statements of the need to end exploitation and help genuine development, must be commended as a valuable document. Yet the indifference or hostility of its authors to the one third of the poor who are Chinese is plain. There is one hostile and untruthful reference to them. One discerns in this and many other examples a lack of respect for the poor. A relationship between rich and poor which is one of equality, mutual respect, mutual benefit and non-interference is not envisaged by some professedly radical do-gooders who want to assist the poor countries to 'develop'. We need therefore to know more about the value of the 'aid' they give in regard to the insubordinate or the revolutionary poor who are being harassed, starved, tortured and killed. A large proportion of military and civilian 'aid' voted for the benefit of the 'developing' countries is expended in their lands, or 'consumed' by them. The large sums taken from tax-payers in the donor countries for helping recipient countries are not spent in undermining the poverty-creating order and opposing the people who are causing the hunger and poverty, but in rather different ways. The contradictions call for more careful scrutiny. If aid is not to serve peoples who are eliminating tyranny and exploitation, and by hard work making their nations self-reliant, independent of foreign control and secure against invasion and conquest, what is it for?*

Fifthly, the role played by the high-income countries in political, economic and cultural development has still to be explained. The Pearson Report recommends closer consultation between donors and recipients. What is it that specially qualifies United States or British government personnel or business men or other 'experts' for directing or supervising the modernization and development of the Latin American, Asian and African peoples? What experience or achievement makes them expert in the elimination of poverty and oppression? What, for example, do the American worker, taxpayer and development 'expert' do for the peasants of underpopulated Laos, the world's leading beneficiary of 'aid'? If the Pearson Commission is to be believed when it claims that 'international cooperation for development over the last twenty years has been of a nature and on a scale new in history' why has so much of it been military in character?† The answers to these questions could make the 'donor' status clearer than it has so far been made.

One could go on with this list of points, to include the frustration of the early post-war efforts at decolonization; the early struggle by the governments of the 'donor' countries in the United Nations to prevent a definition of fundamental

* The Haslemere Declaration was issued early in 1968 (London).

† For example, during the Mutual Security Act Period FY 1953–61 of the $39,738 million spent on 'aid' by the US government, $23,182 million was purely military, leaving $16,556 million for 'non-military' aid. Of this, $11,455 million was for surveillance, suppression and pacification of the poor engaged in revolutionary activity, leaving only $5,101 million as purely economic aid. See Richard Barnet, *Intervention and Revolution* (New York, 1968), pp. 19–20, footnote 8.

rights which would entitle the poor peoples to reclaim sovereignty over all the economic resources in their national territory; the failure to create the Special United Nations Fund for Economic Development, and to make a success of the Development Decade and of the Trade and Development Conferences; the massive arms and military expenditures, going into many hundreds of billions of dollars, in the high-income countries, for action against Third World countries; the unsatisfactory definitions of both 'underdeveloped' and 'development' in the overwhelming mass of semi-officially sponsored literature and expertise on 'development' emanating from North America and Europe; and the vagueness about what actually is going on in the Third World countries.

A superficial discussion of these doubts and misgivings is not going to be edifying. If, as there is good reason to suppose, the analysis of the world situation on which the voluntary agencies as well as governments base their activities has not been done properly – if the situation, in other words, has been wrongly described and the action wrongly conceived – it seems best to dig a little deeper into the historical and human realities which are overlaid with the rhetoric of the new missionary movement to rescue the non-European peoples. There can be no doubt that if all those who are trying genuinely to make a contribution (in money, by energetic work, by taking careful thought together with the victims of poverty and exploitation, by developing and making available special skills and equipment) to the eradication of world poverty do so on the correct lines, and following the right strategy, the war on poverty can be won in our time. But then, if the elimination of all that causes poverty is indeed the highest priority, one may have to be prepared to see the whole international order transformed and shaken up. For, presumably, then, those who comprise twenty per cent of the world's population will not be monopolizing eighty per cent of the world's productive resources. To renounce the kind of war which terrorizes and subdues the economically and politically developing poor, and to join the actual, authentic war being waged against all that degrades, impoverishes and starves them, is indeed to aid the struggle for development. Is the rapid development of the poor nations in fact being aided by the rich? We must now take a closer look at that struggle in its actual historical and social context. The anxieties and efforts, declarations of intent and programmes, which now dominate the 'world development' organizations can be seen in proper perspective only after the struggle for development is put in the correct historical and political context.

CHAPTER 2

Rapid Development is a Recent Phenomenon

SOME centuries have passed since the inhabitants of a country like Britain experienced the worst effects of famine – people dying of hunger and some even resorting to cannibalism to keep alive. There are still those who are continually cold and under-nourished, and there is still a wide gap between richest and poorest. But if, over the past few decades, there have been deaths from starvation or extreme poverty they have been individual or accidental rather than the norm. However, pictures and reports describing the long-term physical, moral and social consequences of continuous lack of food, housing and medical care leave little to the imagination of well-fed people. Although few people are thought to experience chronic hunger and desperate poverty in the areas of the world where European peoples live or have settled, it is only the complacent and selfish who are immune to the horror of what they see of themselves in the faces, bodies and minds of the starving. Famines abroad still get publicity. And recently the suffering which is *normal* for whole classes and communities in such places as north-eastern Brazil, the Andean region of Peru or Chad has engaged the attention of thoughtful and curious people, for whom poverty anywhere is a universal scandal. A call to mobilize for the 'war on world poverty' is evoking some response in countries where, relatively speaking, there is an abundance and variety of food, clothing, housing, sanitary facilities, schools, opportunities for work, books, music, cheap travel, labour-saving domestic gadgets and entertainment of all kinds.

Like the 'war to end war', the war on world poverty may be

a delusion; or, like the contemporary crusade of Western governments and big business to destroy 'the enemies of freedom', it may be specious rhetoric. What it actually is, we have to discover by a study of the historical facts and social processes. For, without careful inspection of actual policies, events, relationships and seriously intended action, we have no way of knowing whether peoples and governments are actually going about the business of eliminating poverty. Moral commitment to end poverty must be evident not only in observable actions, but in the institutions and organizations established to end it.

We live in an era in which scientifically, politically and sociologically poverty is an anachronism. What man can find out about the earth, what he can get, use, build and manufacture is almost without limit. All over the world the poor have decided that poverty and exploitation are neither inevitable nor tolerable any longer. New forms of human organization for fighting the causes of poverty and living a humanly meaningful existence have been tested successfully. The persistence of poverty needs then to be explained. People in the centuries before the nineteenth of the Christian era had their conceptions of Utopia. But they could not have talked (as we can) in a matter-of-fact way about poverty as a transitional, historical phenomenon. It must seem strange to those who are impatient to see that every community and person is adequately fed, clothed, housed and equipped for modern life to realize that for nearly the whole of the history of civilized man poverty was not regarded as a social phenomenon or even a particularly unfortunate condition. Even morally sensitive thinkers with the noblest and most ambitious conceptions of what every man, woman and child was destined to achieve, were, with few exceptions, more concerned with escaping the worst features of poverty than with eradicating it. Those to whom the poor yielded their rights and their substance – the rich and the powerful – were admired and honoured. The main cultural tradition has tended to present the poor as less deserving of consideration, respect and service than the rich.

c

It is instructive to recall that Christian churchgoers used, till recently, to include with

> *All things bright and beautiful*
> *All creatures great and small*
> *All things wise and wonderful*

which 'the Lord God' made,

> *The rich man in his castle*
> *The poor man at his gate.*

The poor man whom they proclaimed as part of the lovely creation was not, of course, the frugal hardworking cultivator or artisan but the wretched beggar all covered with sores, Lazarus, for whose suffering Jesus held the unfeeling and luxury-loving Dives responsible. The Christian Church, or rather its bureaucracy, has indeed been very severe with members acting on the belief that poverty is an evil for which bad rulers are responsible.*

Poverty in the pre-industrial period of human civilization was, of course, different from what we mean by the word today. It was not poverty amid abundance, as it is today – poverty in spite of man's capacity to produce incomparably more abundantly than ever before the means necessary for the sustenance and growth of body, intellect and spirit. It was not poverty that the oppressed and poor could vanquish. But today it is part of their poverty that the poor grow daily poorer in the capacity to cope with social forces which have deprived them of the means of life available to all. They are violently driven

---

* The Jesus whose authority they invoked in fact acted and spoke in the tradition of certain 'prophets' who preceded him in south-west Asia, notably the herdsman Amos, who denounced in the strongest terms the rich and their exploitation of the poor. But his teaching has carried little weight against that of the Church's official teaching, which at best enjoined its adherents to relieve the sufferings of poor individuals but not to attack the causes and very existence of poverty. Dives, when he comes to the inevitable judgement of total self-knowledge, burns with the agony of remorse and horror which it is too late to relieve by action. For social and economic conditions in the highly 'modern' Jerusalem of the parable see Joachim Jeremias, *Jerusalem in the Time of Jesus* (London, 1969).

further and further away from an inheritance which has the power to make the earth bear as never before and to enhance their ability to build, create and communicate. In the past, whole communities of people perished from famines, floods or other similar disasters, partly because they were, given the small-scale organization of society and simple technology, isolated. But the desperation and desolation of the poor in the last hundred years is of a new kind. The world of the poor has become the whole of the civilized world. What does this world do to or for them? The twentieth-century meaning of the suffering and desolation of poverty has to be explored. Those who press on us the familiar and discredited assumptions of 'stable development', and would confine discussion of rich and poor to questions about how the benevolence of the rich may be made more 'effective', are side-tracking the search for an understanding of *development* which will show how the poor can turn oppression and misery into a memory.

THE PROBLEMS OF AFFLUENCE

The revolutionary expansion of man's power to produce, communicate and make war has, as we have noted, given a totally new character to the plight of the poor peoples. It has also created the problem of over-affluence. Talk about 'the overweight society', and 'overdevelopment' is as characteristic of our age as talk about 'underdevelopment'. It is important for the struggle against underdevelopment for us to know if it is linked in any organic and significant way with overdevelopment. Is the war on world poverty related to a 'war on world affluence'? Can we speak of 'hindering overdevelopment' as part of the strategy of assisting development? More fundamentally, in what way should the immense knowledge and power to construct, transform and create which are now available to man be possessed and used, in order that it should serve all the world's peoples? Some of the new possibilities of rapid economic growth and technological progress have been realized before the answers to these questions have been worked out. We may even discover that the rich and powerful have taken and kept to themselves the very means necessary for the liberation of mankind from poverty and oppression.

The characteristics and problems of the super-rich society and the new rich may be shown in what is known about national income, wealthy corporations and personal wealth in typically affluent societies. A British scholar recently devised a complex system of 'indicators of affluence' to compare private consumption per head of population in the rich countries. It showed that in 1968 Americans were twice as affluent as Frenchmen or Belgians, and ten times as affluent as the Chinese.* Whether this is precisely correct or not, it draws attention to the super-affluence of the US. Its *per capita* income two decades ago, in 1949, according to UN figures, was $1,453.† It was already ahead of all other countries on this score. America's total national income in 1967 was working out to an income per head of population of $3,280. The source of wealth is mainly manufacturing activity and trade. A news item dealing with business activity by the 'top 500' US corporations in 1968 quoted the comment by *Fortune* magazine: 'Business was terrific from the beginning of the year to the end.' It then went on:

Total sales of all firms jumped some 13 per cent to a massive $405,000m. while profits, even after the surcharge's bite, increased by around the same amount to top $24,000m.

Topping the 1968 growth league, as it has done for years, comes General Motors, whose sales reached an awe-inspiring $22,755m. The next four biggest are also unchanged from last year's tables: Standard Oil (NJ), Ford Motor, General Electric and Chrysler.

In the next five, IBM crept up one place to finish sixth, Mobil

* Dr William Beckerman of Balliol College, Oxford. The study was made for the Development Centre of OECD. *NYHTI*, 24 August 1968.

† UN, *Statistical Yearbook 1953*. In a statement on conservation in 1962 President Kennedy said: 'During the last thirty years this nation has consumed more minerals than all the peoples of the world had previously used.'

Oil dropped one down to seventh, and Texaco, Gulf Oil and United States Steel held their respective rankings.

Looking at the 500 as a whole, *Fortune* reports that their share of total business in the United States grew once again, this time from 62 to 64 per cent. Profits represent 74·4 per cent of all profits made by the nation's businesses.*

We learn then that in that year only 500 firms (a tiny proportion of US enterprises) accounted for sixty-four per cent, nearly two thirds, of $405 billion worth of business activity; and secured 74·4 per cent of total business profits of $24 billion. To get an idea of the total revenue of these 500 firms one must compare it with the gross national product of major industrial countries like Britain and France and highly affluent countries like Sweden and Switzerland.† These firms are able to account for as much business as they have because of the scope of their activities and their size.‡ The capital assets ($35 billion in 1967) of a firm like International Business Machines (IBM) and its annual business are enormous when compared with the economic assets and national product of the 500 million people of India. In addition to these corporations there are the financial houses and banks, whose assets and business are, at the top, of the same magnitude: in 1967

* *NYHTI,* 15 May 1969.

† Britain's national income in 1967 was just under $86 billion. Michael Harrington writes: 'After all, General Motors has the eighteenth largest GNP on the globe (at 20·2 billion in 1967 it ranked ahead of Argentina, Belgium, Switzerland and Czechoslovakia, among others). Ford is the twenty-third richest industrial power, Standard Oil of New Jersey the twenty-fourth, and General Electric, at the thirty-fourth position, has more of an output than Greece' ('The Road to 1972', in *Dissent,* 1969). The American Telephone and Telegraph Company, which is not an industrial corporation, is even bigger and richer than General Motors.

‡ F. Lundberg, in *The Rich and the Super-Rich: A Study in the Power of Wealth Today* (London, 1969), p. 178, cites a study showing that the *net* income of AT & T, after taxes, is approximately equal to the national income of Sweden. Standard Oil (NJ)'s own fleet of tankers exceeded in size that of the Soviet Union (*New York Times*, international edition (*NYTI*), 2 September 1966).

Prudential Life Insurance, $25·1 billion; Metropolitan Life Insurance, $24·6 billion; Bank of America, $21·3 billion; Chase Manhattan Bank, $17·7 billion; First National City Bank, $17·5 billion, and so on.*

Since control over these private firms and banks is exercised, in the interests of maximum profits, by a few individuals and families it is not surprising that the affluent society is one in which the richest families get income, own property and exercise power which in comparison with wealth and power in past eras, and most governmental incomes and power today, is enormous. Ferdinand Lundberg's *The Rich and the Super-Rich: A Study in the Power of Wealth Today* estimates the total holdings of the Du Pont family as $7 billion, of the Rockefeller and Mellon families as around $5 billion each, and of the Ford family as about $2 billion. Although much of the present wealth of these families (and lesser ones like the McCormicks, Pews, Harknesses and so on) was built up over generations, it is important to remember that in historical perspective the wealth is of comparatively recent origin. Individual members of these families, and others who own and profit from industrial and financial activity, have personal wealth which would be staggering in size if one had not already got accustomed to thinking and talking in billions of dollars. But though it would be almost commonplace in the super-affluent society to have two individuals with fortunes of over a billion dollars, and twenty-six others with fortunes ranging from $1 billion to $200 million,†

* For comparison, here are some details about the five largest non-US industrial companies in 1968, with assets, sales and net profit respectively in thousands of dollars: Royal Dutch/Shell (14,303,287 – 9,215,772 – 934,723); Unilever (3,431,760 – 5,533,680 – 206,160); British Petroleum (5,056,320 – 3,260,160 – 242,880); Imperial Chemical Industries (ICI) (4,387,680 – 2,969,520 – 206,160); Volkswagenwerk (1,604,750 – 2,925,000 – 125,000). The top 200 of these, with total sales worth $174,251 million and profits of over $6,847 million, owned assets worth $196,823 million. The assets of the fifty biggest non-US banks totalled $277,071 million. They were easily headed by Barclays Bank, with deposits of $12,844,769,000 and assets of $13,495,707,000 (*Fortune*, 15 August 1969).

† See *Fortune*, 1968, and Lundberg, *op. cit.*

it is a contrast with the wealth of the vast majority of people today, who cannot own even 1,000 dollars-worth of personal property.

There are affluent societies other than the United States: Sweden, for example, which according to Dr Beckerman ranks second. Even Britain is an affluent country. There are super-rich people in other, less industrialized countries whose wealth in land or livestock is fantastic. But since the point at the moment is to illustrate the unprecedented problems of affluence, the United States provides the best examples of the social and moral problems which engage a great deal of attention, and tend to make other kinds of problems appear small in comparison. The tremendous business and industrial turnover which makes the high consumption and huge profits possible indicates an enormous appetite for raw materials, energy resources and, in the case of the consumer, a constant supply of new commodities. The fact that less than seven per cent of the world's population are consuming about sixty-seven per cent of the world's wealth indicates a voracious appetite for new materials and resources. There are also other consequences. It is not only the riches of the wealthy that have to be measured in millions and billions, or only their national income that doubles in two decades. A society in which a few rush frantically into unprecedented affluence may itself be rushing into disaster.

Here is an American bemoaning the loss of a lake:

THE EFFLUENT SOCIETY

Once upon a time there was a lake.

It was a thing of magnificent beauty, left a breathtaking blue by departing glaciers. It was thirty miles wide in some places, nearly sixty in others, and more than 240 miles long. Ten thousand square miles of lake, over 200 feet deep, it lived on a still larger sister to the north, and fed a somewhat smaller sister to the east. . . .

Today, Lake Erie is virtually dead. Detroit, Cleveland, Buffalo, Akron, Toledo and a dozen other cities pour millions of *tons* of *sewage* into the lake every *day*. Some of it is carefully treated; much of it (especially Detroit's) is not.

The Detroit River, which feeds Lake Erie, carries every *day*, in addition to Detroit's largely untreated sewage, 19,000 gallons of oil; 10,000 pounds of iron; 200,000 pounds of various acids; and two million pounds of chemical salts. The fertiliser used on the farms of Ohio and Pennsylvania and New York drains into streams which pour into Lake Erie. Paper mills in the Monroe area of Michigan pour volumes of pollutant waste into the lake. Steelmakers pour in mill scale and oil and grease and pickling solution and rinse water. The engineers of the area dredge the harbor and channels of the area and dump the sludge into the middle of Lake Erie.

Normally, a lake receives from various sources a certain amount of nutrient material, which is consumed by plankton or algae or bottom vegetation or bacteria. The fish eat the plankton and the algae, the bacteria mess around with the nitrogen, a couple of hundred other processes simultaneously take place, and it all works out.

So you dump a bunch of sewage or fertiliser or other biologically rich material into the water, and the algae, for instance, grow faster than the fish can eat them. Algae are life forms just like you and me, but (like you and me) in large numbers they stink. They also use up whatever free oxygen might be in the water, which makes it tough for the other life forms. Beaches become covered with algae in the form of slime, and so does the surface of the lake. The lake, in ecological terms, 'dies'.

Lake Erie has had it. . . .

Sewage aside, an urban unit of a million people produces, every day, another 2,000 tons of solid waste that has to be disposed of. On top of this it throws into the air, every day, 1,000 tons of particles, sulfur dioxide, nitrogen oxides, hydrocarbons and carbon dioxide. In 1963, American mines, every day, discarded 90,400,000 tons of waste rock and tailings. In 1965, every day, 16,000 automobiles were scrapped (joining from 25 to 40 million already on junkpiles).

Every year, America manufactures 48 billion cans, 26 billion bottles and jars, 65 billion metal and plastic caps, virtually all of which become, almost instantly, solid waste (and aluminium cans and Saranwrap don't degenerate easily like easy rusting steel cans and paper) . . .*

The rapid death of a lake created over millennia is only a

* From Gene Marine, 'America the Raped' in *Ramparts*, April 1967. The problem of the disposal of surplus poison gas and of chemical and biological weapons generally became serious in 1969.

symbol of rapid 'development'. These are only some of the statistics of the waste and pollution which accompany the creation of the massive personal and corporate fortunes which have been described earlier. The consequences are by no means only localized. In the past century the amount of carbon dioxide in the air has been increased by ten per cent, and the oceans have been polluted in the frantic business of increasing affluence. Further, there is the rapid increase in the crime rate.* The increase in alcoholism, drug addiction and venereal disease was also steep. The number of people killed on the roads is also high.

What is called affluence – the consequence of the type of rapid economic development which occurred from about the middle of the nineteenth century – is in a real sense an abundance not just of serious problems which machines cannot solve, but of hopeless poverty: the physical insecurity, personal unhappiness, the intensified mortality, the sense of being dwarfed by vast and uncontrollable physical, mechanical and corporate structures, the hatred and contempt of other peoples, the lack of opportunity for contemplation, the loss of community life. Amidst the planned obsolescence, the decaying cities, the deadly machines and chemistry, the surfeit of advertising, the bills to be paid, and the prohibitions and prescriptions, actual men, women and children in the affluent society do not seem very much better off than the ordinary people in societies which have not experienced the same kind of rapid development. The United States only manifests the features of overdevelopment in a more marked way than do Sweden, Switzerland, West Germany and even Britain, which reached an advanced stage of economic development fairly

---

* According to FBI statistics the increase over the previous year's figures for serious crime – murder, rape, felonious assault and robbery – in 1966 was eleven per cent, in 1967 sixteen per cent and in 1968 seventeen per cent. There had been a 122 per cent increase since 1960. 'A murder was committed every 39 minutes; forcible rape every 17 minutes; aggravated assault and robbery every two minutes . . .' (*The Times*, 14 August 1969).

gradually, and with more of its pre-capitalist heritage intact. Japan, whose problems are growing as rapidly as the fortunes of its barons of business and industry, provides another demonstration of the features of overdevelopment.

A discussion of the problems of societies which have enormous wealth at their disposal would have sounded insane more than a hundred years ago. Rapid development is very recent, and its consequences could then have only been prophesied. Today it is commonplace for sociologists, economists, social workers, politicians, architects, town planners, psychologists, doctors, educators and engineers to discuss ways of repairing the fabric of the affluent society after 100 years of frenzied and unrestricted 'development'. The seekers of enormous wealth and power found it possible, by adapting the newly available scientific knowledge and technology to their purpose, to get what they wanted. But their super-rich countries, as well as the world generally, have been impoverished in a far more disastrous and ultimate sense than ever before. To try to understand the whole of man's possibilities and achievements over thousands of years with minds made sick by the 'effluence' of capitalist ideology and practice is inevitably to get the true dimensions of man as discoverer, inventor, creator, worker and administrator out of true proportion. The modern age, with its peculiar problems, needs to be viewed freshly in the light of the rich and varied history of what man has dared to think and do.

PRE-MODERN AND MODERN:
MAN LEAPS INTO THE FUTURE

What is the problem posed by the poor? Is it that they are breeding too fast? Is it that they are not doing anything to improve their own situation? Is it that they are too actively discontented? The stock images and concepts of the mass media, government agencies and politicians in the high-income countries and the Westernized capitals in the Third World add to the confusion about how the poor can 'develop' out of their underdevelopment. There they are in their millions, with their hunger, misery, continual death, without money, land to work, access to factories and mines, moral or political choices, and dirty, diseased, illiterate. They are cut off from the farmlands, the factories and mines, the banks, the schools, the libraries, the scientific laboratories, the radio and television studios, the printing presses, the tax offices, the shops, the armouries, the presidential palaces, the chambers of deputies and sometimes even from the ballot box. What are they doing in that enclosed and deprived existence? Why don't they get out of that ghetto or wilderness, and help themselves? Yet, as we continually hear, when they cross that line they are no longer the poor seeking to end their poverty, but 'Communists'. Obviously, no rational analysis of the development process is possible if we are trapped in this terminology. Too many people act as if they believed that the poor are idle, unproductive people who either beg or want to appropriate what God has given to others or what others have created by their own efforts and self-sacrifice.

The terraced fields, the irrigation channels, the varieties of plants, the herds of cattle, the fabrics, the exquisite carvings and sculptures with their power to delight for hundreds of years, the roads, the factories, the mines, the goods in the shops: all this wealth is so much taken for granted. It seems very naïve to ask where it came from. It seems almost irrelevant to recall that wealth is created largely by the hands and brains of countless millions of obscure men and women, using what others in earlier generations or distant lands have handed over to them as well as the powers of the earth which have been discovered to be usable. When we recall that fact we come to recognize that, while rapid development is a recent possibility, development itself is something that has gone on for hundreds of thousands of years.

In the distant past, too, there were very rich families and persons. In fiction and satire, art and drama, we encounter classes of over-fed people who are exploiters of others. Societies of the past were not so poor that they could afford only frugal, austere living for all. The sumptuous living they could afford for a few is evidenced by what was devised, by cultivator, trader and cook, for finely cultivated palates and elaborate ritual eating; and by miners, weavers, artisans, masons, metal-workers and artists and poets for lovers of rich brocades, jewels, palaces, cities and entertainments. It would be a mistake for anyone to be so blinded by the brilliance of modern tech-nology and the garishness of modern display of wealth as to think that progress in methods of production and technology, in the continuous transformation of what the earth is, and in forms of social organization, had to wait for the modern scientific tradition.*

The story of the arduous work done by men and women to create the material conditions which even in the early empires of 5,000 years ago were taken for granted is a long one. Man's tremendous capacity to produce all manner of goods and services had a beginning and a development long before times recorded by historians. The making of some of the things enjoyed, consumed and even destroyed today was begun many hundreds and even thousands of years ago. It ill becomes today's flabby, timid and moronic slave of the machine to feel superior to heroic 'early man', who solved stupendous prob-lems in the course of his dangerous existence as a food-gatherer, and thus made of himself and the earth something never conceived before. How he got his ideas and solved his problems can tell us a great deal about the fundamentals of the struggle to eradicate poverty. The more abundant fruits and herbs were, the more competition man had from other animals and insects. Such berries, leaves, seeds and roots as he could collect must have lacked taste and variety. And food obtained by catching birds, insects and animals must, to start with, have

---

* The time and skills needed to maintain a high standard of living for some families or ruling classes could be accumulated and organized only if they claimed vast material possessions, including the lives and services of resident men, women and children. The lavish living of King Solomon in the tenth century BC was made possible by an elaborate system of exploitation which the Old Testament describes.

been rare. To live was to struggle. In the long pre-agricultural phase of their development men faced a number of threats, apart from climatic changes, to their continued existence and growth. Countless small communities must have failed to withstand the threats to their continued existence, and just died out. The great migrations, like that from north-east Asia into and through America, were great adventures which radically transformed the earth.

The extensive living space needed by early man made the common thought and action vital for progress very difficult to achieve. If they could survive by consuming such berries and roots, or fish, or animals as had not been appropriated by other living creatures, a small band of men and women required a vast amount of space to move about in. Even very much later, when they used slash-and-burn methods of agriculture to grow part of their food supply, or having domesticated the horse could move quickly and easily, a good deal of living space was needed. A life lived in the open, amidst conditions of great insecurity, must always have been one of severe physical exertion, and beyond the capacity of weak children, sick adults and the old. Every advance which improved these conditions, and added to the store or quality of tools which made digging, hunting, transporting and building easier, was a stupendous achievement. The easier ground of tested knowledge and taught skill could not have been reached without the original discoveries and creations. Knowledge and experience – all that there is of them – were not in the first place derived from some pre-existent manual, or transmitted by 'experts' or brought by angels from another planet. They were acquired by the imaginative daring, collective practice and thinking of men and women even when they struggled for survival in the primitive band of food-gatherers or hunters. They had to cross the lines which bounded their capacities and perceptions. Every step which took them beyond the familiar and customary was a stupendous achievement. It must have required great courage to break with the past, to conceive the hitherto inconceivable, **to imagine and create the hitherto unimaginable. And new** tools, material improvements, new words and concepts, indeed a new earth, continually demanded the recreation of the moral order, too.

All over the world bands of men must have repeated the same discoveries of new human possibilities, both in the earliest times and when the complex civilizations of Egypt, the Indus valley and Iraq were created. The ability to preserve and transmit their powers and knowledge grew with their ingenuity in acquiring or producing more stocks of food than the food-producers and their young currently needed. With more economic use of the energies, work-time and skills necessary to ensure the continued survival of the tribe, there was a surplus which, whether shared equitably or not, enabled men to look beyond their immediate struggle for survival. The distance from which men could reflect on their own lives and activities progressively increased.

It might be supposed that, since it is in the interests of those whose work supported the community to make their tasks less laborious, hazardous and time-consuming, the development of the technology of production would have accelerated. Animals make a claim on the food supply. But machines for lifting, ploughing, transporting and grinding do not. It *could* have happened that economic conditions generally improved, and life became less of a struggle. But instead the struggle became more complex, and new predators and new hazards had to be dealt with as the opportunities for the acquisition of material goods increased. Development possibilities were snatched away by political and ideological devices. Some men made the discovery that by capturing members of other communities, or inducing submission in the bodies and minds of their own fellows, they could consume the energies, the fruits of labour and whatever else was enjoyable in other men and women; and this created the social and ideological context for a new struggle by their victim for survival and progress in the face of exploitation and subjection. For a subject class, tribe or nation must be denied the freedom to develop economically, scientifically and politically. Inequality had to be created and hallowed.

The barriers against the creative leaps had to be maintained by terror and force or by fraud; so that the rulers could make scientific knowledge, technology and political skill advance only their own power and wealth.

The beginnings of settled agriculture (first in south-west Asia and then in the Nile valley) required complex social organization and new skills in caring for what was built and cultivated, draining swamps and marshes, controlling rivers, domesticating animals and protecting the community against attack and pestilence. The advances made in learning about new crops, or in changing from the trapping of animals and fish to breeding them, were enormous. It must be supposed that thousands of years ago questions about what life is for must have been formed in the minds of men as they were required to determine the long-term purposes of their actions; and curiosity about the interrelatedness of things, phenomena and social conditions must have been aroused. We know very little about those thousands of years when all living beyond the most austere and frugal standards had been outside the reach of men. But for thousands of years before recorded history begins life must also have been spiritually as complex and intense as it is in the affluent societies today. It is because men had learnt to make distinctions between the transitory and the lasting, between sense and nonsense, between the just and the unjust, that the great civilizations could have come into existence at all. For man is as material a reality as anything else on the earth. His transformation of himself and the world outside himself – through his intelligence, persistence, imagination, daring, power of reasoning, and, perhaps, love – had revolutionized the material conditions for the creation of the vast systems of thought and social order which have come and gone in history, passing on an accumulation of ideas and techniques, as well as a much-transformed perception of the earth itself. The peoples of east Asia, south-east Asia, south Asia, south-west Asia, Egypt, and some parts of America are still living on capital created a long time ago, by the hard work of millions of men and women.

The revolutionary 'leaps forward' by which humanity

advances became longer and more frequent from the time of the Sumerian civilization in south-west Asia, and particularly since the early centuries of the first millennium BC, during which man leapt into city life. Improved communications and the invention of writing helped ideas to spread, oppose one another and intermingle. Advanced systems of thought and life, with their sensitive appreciation of human responsibility and beauty, took highly particularized forms as local cultural traditions. These were passed on, refined and enriched; but, paradoxically, they became barriers to further progress for those schooled in them. For science could develop only in a universal language. Some civilizations disappeared, without being able to achieve a more universal form of thought and life. But it was in the civilization of the city that the seeds of truly universal development were planted.

The developments in scientific thought, philosophy and social organization which took place in Greece and, later, in the Roman empire, are fairly well known. The remarkable achievements and original contributions to human progress of the Asian and native American peoples is far less frequently told. The qualities and capabilities which have continually pushed man to greater achievements are universally human; they are not a peculiar attribute of some races or class. It is when we look at the whole story that we are in a position to realize how resourceful, inventive and revolutionary man has always been. As the light of discovery and progress grew dim in one place it grew brighter in another. Whether in east Asia, south Asia, west Asia or southern Europe, thought and learning, technological invention and wisdom have flourished throughout the Christian era. Metallurgy and the various branches of mathematics were developed, great engineering schemes devised, new machines invented, universities and research institutes founded and hospitals built.*

* See J. S. Needham, *Science and Civilization in China* (Cambridge, 1954), vol. 1, pp. 150 ff.; *Within the Four Seas* (London, 1969), Chapter 12, 'The House of Wisdom'; and A. C. Crombie (ed.), *Scientific Change* (London, 1963), Chapters 5, 6 and 7.

When Europe entered the period known as the Dark Ages, political, economic, scientific and technological progress in the Asian regions, especially China, continued. The cost of some of this progress was heavy in human terms, and included the vitality and dignity of the common people. During this period what was slowly at first, but later rapidly, taking place in Europe was a social transformation, which was to be of decisive importance for its later economic growth. The transformation began in the Dark Ages with the marriage of European traditions and forms with those of the alien Semitic peoples of south-west Asia, and was completed by the scientific revolution in the time of Galileo and after, by the voyages of discovery, and by the dominance of new classes with revolutionary aims. Their readiness to learn from other, more advanced, peoples and to make use of what they had developed, and their readiness to break with traditional ideas, structures and sanctities was of fundamental importance. During the two centuries from the end of the sixteenth there was evident in Europe a freshness and vigour, a curiosity and artistic and political creativity, which contrasted markedly with what was happening in the more highly organized and previously more advanced non-European civilizations. The changes in ways of thinking and feeling, and in forms of community, were evident in the new forms of production as much as in music, drama, poetry, scientific research and exploration. Man surpassed all his previous achievements, and found a new momentum of change. The eighteenth century, when the non-European civilizations had declined, was the period of the Enlightenment, and belief in the power of human reason; the rapid spread of literacy had also begun. The foundations had been laid for the industrial revolution and the world-wide expansion of the power of the European middle classes.*

* In all periods and societies the great ethical and intellectual advances were the work of people who were in revolt against the values and standards of the minority who held power in the prevailing order. But the massive and elaborate organization of the great empires, with their large populations, commerce and security against foreign attack, their guilds and

The pace of change in the environment and of growth in the capacity to produce and manufacture things has been so rapid since about 1850 that it can be called the greatest economic revolution since the beginning of agriculture. We have got accustomed to it in the West, but there are some communities in the world which cannot yet take for granted the economic and technological developments of our age. What the rate of economic growth has been, what variations there have been in different countries at different times, these are questions which are argued even by economic historians. We must make the best we can of the details, and make a rough estimate of the changes which have taken place in the world as a whole and in some of the economically developed countries in the century between 1850 and 1950. During this period the world population, which is estimated as 1,200 million for 1850, doubled. By 1960 the world's industrial output was thirty or forty times what it was in 1860. Britain and France, the two leading industrial nations at the beginning of that century, had increased their outputs eight and ten times respectively, Germany twenty-seven times and the United States over fifty times. Another interesting

---

associations, their elaborate hierarchies and legal systems, tended to slow down the pace of revolutionary change. Ruling classes or bureaucracies found it necessary (and possible) to stifle creativity and innovation, which would create turmoil and encourage the rejection of much that was built up and stabilized over centuries – much that buttressed their own power, esteem and privileges. Sanctified usage is not easy to break through. Stability is in some conditions indistinguishable from inertia and slow decay. China, for example, which for over a thousand years was in many ways ahead, sometimes far ahead, of Europe in political organization, science and technology, fell far behind, and the lot of her people grew worse than that of their ancestors. The remarkable labour-saving devices which were to hand in China, for example, the creative potentialities of printing from movable type, gunpowder, the mariner's compass, the sternpost rudder and similar achievements which had brought the ancient civilizations to the threshold of a new age could not be realized because the struggle to break out of an increasingly oppressive social order failed again and again. The failure of the Mayan civilization to modernize is also instructive.

fact is that, although the world population only doubled in this period, the industrial output per head increased fifteen to twenty times. But the rise in standards of living is more significant. If we take the *per capita* income figures as an indication of standards of living we can see how wide the disparity is between the poor countries of the Third World and the industrialized countries after a century of rapid development.

But at the start of that century there was no striking disparity. Even including Britain (the pioneer in industrialization and the beneficiary of a great empire) and the United States (which had an abundance of resources), the industrialized countries in 1850 were only about seventy per cent higher in *per capita* income than the pre-industrialized countries. (And there is evidence for believing that some of these countries – China, for example – at that time were worse off than they had been a century or two earlier.) In any case, we cannot assume that there was any *steady* rise in *per capita* income before that. The economist Surendra J. Patel argues that:

At a steady growth of only one-tenth of one per cent per year *per capita* income would rise about 7 times in 2,000 years, 20 times in 3,000 years, 50 times in 4,000 years and nearly 340 times in 6,000 years. This would imply that the average person in Egypt, Sumer or the Indus valley, at the height of its glory, was fifty times poorer than today – or had an annual income of less than $2 in 1960 prices! An absurdly impossible proposition.*

In the world as a whole man's stock of scientific and technological knowledge, and his capacity to produce, has not increased as rapidly as industrial production over the century that Dr Patel is talking about. But the increase has been very rapid. But whereas the long history of development and invention and progress was shared by many peoples and areas in the preceding centuries and millennia, the nineteenth century and the first half of the twentieth are a period when development was deliberately limited to certain areas and races. It was very lopsided development indeed. When we scrutinize

* In *Essays on Economic Transition* (Bombay, 1965), from which the material on industrial growth rates is taken.

the period just before this, that of preparation for the great leap in human science and technology, industry and learning, we notice that the tendencies towards the retardation of some regions and races and the selective advancement of others had already begun.

The European merchants, settlers, administrators and industrialists did develop their possessions in Latin America, Asia and Africa. Colonial or semi-colonial status implied for India, parts of China, Peru, Mexico, Brazil, Ceylon, Vietnam, Indonesia, Egypt and West Africa an unprecedented type of economic development. But colonial development was part of the struggle of the ruling classes in the imperial countries for the progress of *their* power, production and technology. Not only were the imagination, ingenuity, daring, experimentation, intellectual struggle, creative powers, organizational ability and foresight of the non-European peoples *not* a condition of the colonial type of development; it was a necessary condition for it that these should not be brought into play.

'World development' of the colonial type *may* increase the statistical total of what is produced. But whether it is directed by Western governments, the World Bank or the 'experts' of US foundations and agencies, it will increase the lopsidedness of the world economy, and push the obedient peoples further back from the frontiers of progress in knowledge, skill and power. World development cannot take place until all the peoples of the world conduct their own struggle to realize their full potentialities and those of mankind as a whole through the independent, determined and bold utilization of all the powers and resources properly at the disposal of modern man. They must institute and accelerate the process of development which has been held up for so long. What this process is by which the large-scale poverty and hunger of our time may be brought to an end we have now to consider.

CHAPTER 3

The Development Process

'DEVELOPMENT' HIERARCHIES

Lists of countries arranged in order of the size of the national income per head of population are frequently to be seen in books dealing with development. They are meant as an indication of the order of achievement and of excellence of the different countries of the contemporary world. Taking *per capita* income figures for 1966 (as far as these have been worked out by United Nations statisticians) the listing would begin in this manner:

	Country	Estimated national income *per capita* in dollars
1	United States	3,175
2	Sweden	2,500
3	Iceland	2,080
4	Switzerland	2,059
5	Canada	1,990
6	Denmark	1,815
7	Australia	1,759
8	New Zealand	1,730
9	France	1,634
10	Norway	1,544
11	United Kingdom	1,535
12	West Germany	1,528
13	Belgium	1,519
14	Finland	1,484
15	Netherlands	1,352
16	Israel	1,159
17	Austria	1,033
18	Italy	949
19	Ireland	797
20	Japan	791

Twenty countries have been listed so far. Even if it is agreed that very small countries, such as Luxemburg, should not be considered for inclusion, the list may be challenged by those who would argue that East Germany, the Soviet Union, and possibly even Czechoslovakia, should be in the group of 'top nations'. The exact statistical figures for the Soviet Union are not provided in the United Nations' *Statistical Yearbook*, but it would be safe to include the Soviet Union in this group.

What is significant is the absence so far of any country in the Third World. It is as we go on and come to the bottom of the list that we see where the countries of the Third World stand in relation to those of Europe and North America, on the basis of these statistics. Venezuela, on the score of her *per capita* income statistics of $735, is the 'leading' Third World country, and comes rather high on the list. It appears to belong to a different category from countries which usually are classed as 'under-developed', with *per capita* incomes of $200 and less. But the industry which accounts for ninety per cent of exports and twenty per cent of GNP – petroleum, of which Venezuela is the world's biggest exporter – is foreign-owned; it provides employment for only two per cent of the work force in a country where large numbers have no work. Iron-mining is also owned by foreign corporations, which are expanding their operations. Hundreds of thousands of peasants in this vast country have no land, and food has to be imported. Except in the case of raw materials, prices are much higher than they are in the United States. The highly affluent oil-workers, land-owners, military officers and multi-millionaires in Caracas take most of the income, while the peasants and slum dwellers are as poor as those in Peru or Brazil.*

If *per capita* income was taken as a reliable index of progress in development, the Kuwaitis, with a national income *per capita* in the same year of $3,240, would lead all the rest, as the 'most developed' nation. If we look at the list of 'independent' Third World countries which follow Venezuela in the order of

* Peter Odell, in Edith T. Penrose, *The Large International Firm in Developing Countries* (London, 1968), p. 296. See below, pp. 98, 127, 128.

their *per capita* income, we notice more clearly the limited value
of the ranking:

Country	Estimated national income *per capita* in dollars
Argentina	699
Libya	682
Cyprus	620
Trinidad and Tobago	620
Uruguay	526
Singapore	517
Jamaica	491
South Africa	489
Mexico	484
Chile	465
Panama	452
Barbados	371

The 'high' level of achievement of Libya, formerly Italy's
colonial territory, which when it became 'independent' in
1951, with a *per capita* income of around $25, was a classic
example of a country extremely poor in resources, skills, educational opportunities and capital, and in 1967 had achieved a
per capita income of $802, would qualify it, rather than North
Korea or China, as the model for achieving miracles of rapid
development! In fact, the sudden boom in the petroleum
industry (in which US corporations claim a share of nearly
half a billion dollars and an enormous annual income) is
responsible for the change in Libya. Tripoli and Benghazi,
where the new rich and the foreigners live, have become
fantastically expensive cities like Caracas, but the mass of the
people remain poor.*

A list of this kind would have to be extended to include the
very lowest levels of *per capita* incomes before names of

---

* Their dissatisfaction led to the overthrow of the monarchy and the
ruling oligarchy in September 1969, and the request to foreign powers to
evacuate the military bases in Libyan territory.

countries in which the people are politically active appear: Colombia, Guatemala, Brazil, Peru, the Philippines, Iran the Dominican Republic, Ceylon, Pakistan, Kenya, Guinea, Indonesia, India, Nigeria, Mali, Burma, Tanzania and so on. The unsatisfactory nature of the comparisons giving Tanzania an index of development ($59) less than one tenth of that given to Libya or Trinidad is obvious. It is largely foreigners and a tiny ruling *élite* who enjoy the prosperity of Trinidad and Jamaica, while the people of the countries producing this prosperity lack the status and dignity, the power to run the country, and often even the material satisfactions available to the mass of the Tanzanian people.* India, with an income figure of $77, has, in spite of the corruption of its ruling *élites*, overcome difficulties and made progress which would be inconceivable to 'most developed' Third World countries like Singapore. Further, the gap between the United States and the Third World countries is not as wide as the artificially maintained status of the US dollar makes it out to be. Nourishing and tasty food, and comfortable housing of comparable quality may cost five or ten times as much in US cities as in those of India or China.

Some Western experts argue that a variety of factors other than income should be taken into account before progress in 'development' can be properly computed. Two of these, who have reputations as authorities on Education for Development, Professor Frederick Harbison and Professor Charles A. Myers, have in a well-known book ranked countries according to their levels of attainment in what they call 'human resource development'. In order to measure the level of development quantitatively they have worked out what they consider are appropriate index numbers, and classed countries as 'advanced',

* In an article on 'The Two Jamaicas' in the *Observer* (23 November 1969) Colin McGlashan reports Dr Philips of the University of Jamaica as saying: 'The sources of wealth are white and foreign, the sources of labour are local and black. We are back to slavery.' When the inevitable explosion occurs, as in Trinidad in April 1970, the prosperity of the privileged, threatened by Trinidadian people and soldiers, has naturally to be defended by US and British gunboats and troops.

'semi-advanced', 'partially developed' and 'underdeveloped' according to the index numbers they have scored. The ranking, calculated on data obtaining for the period around 1960, begins thus:

Country	Index number
United States	261·3
New Zealand	147·3
Australia	137·7
Netherlands	133·7
Belgium	123·6
United Kingdom	121·6
Japan	111·4
France	107·8
Canada	101·6
USSR	92·9
West Germany	85·8

The United States by these standards again far excels all other countries. Its index number is two-and-a-half times that of France, supposedly a highly developed country culturally, economically and scientifically. What is even more instructive in the Harbison–Myers classification is the list of countries, all excepting Argentina belonging to the group of territories which have attained the 'semi-advanced' level, which according to the criteria in use excel among the Third World countries. Here are the first twelve among them, with their respective index numbers:

Argentina	82	Costa Rica	47·3
Uruguay	69·8	Egypt	40·1
South Korea	55	South Africa	40·0
Taiwan	53·9	Cuba	35·5
Chile	51·2	India	35·2
Venezuela	47·7	Thailand	35·1

The data for Cuba is apparently mostly from the pre-revolutionary period. China (minus the province of Taiwan)

comes very low down on the list, with an index number of
19·5 – little more than one third the score of South Korea (the
leading Asian country) and one thirteenth that of the United
States. North Korea does not qualify for mention.*

To another American, Professor Samuel P. Huntington of
Harvard, it is the 'political gap' between the United States,
Britain and Russia, on the one hand, and the majority of
countries in Latin America, Asia and Africa, on the other, that
is significant. The gap between the European peoples and the
non-European peoples who are imitating them is also evident
in the work of another, equally representative, political scientist
who specializes in development problems, Professor Dankwart
A. Rustow of Columbia University. The Western countries,
according to his scheme,

continue to set the standards for a modernizing world not only in
economic production and material comfort but also in social
organization and political institutions. Universal suffrage, written
constitutions, presidents, cabinets and parliaments, an independent
judiciary, separation of the church and state, political neutrality of
the armed forces, and the vocabulary of nationalism, of egalitarianism
and of sovereignty – all these have been almost universally accepted
in principle, however widely they may be abused or disregarded in
application. They form as integral a part of the emerging global
civilization of modernity as do the telephone, the airplane, the
assembly line, the computer and other Western technical inventions.

He goes on to talk about 'the enormous and growing gap that
separates the West from the late-modernizing countries in
economic and political matters. To provide a suitable model, a
country must not only be ahead but also seem reachable. The
recurrent complaints of neo-colonialism in Africa and elsewhere reflect in large part the frustrations inspired by the
unreachable Western ideal.'†

* Frederick Harbison and Charles A. Myers, *Education, Manpower and
Economic Growth. Strategies in Human Resource Development* (New York,
1964).

† Samuel P. Huntington, *Political Order in Changing Societies* (New
Haven and London, 1968), p. 1. Dankwart A. Rustow, *A World of
Nations. Problems in Political Modernization* (Washington, 1967), pp. 249–50.

All this is very interesting. A number of the books, articles and reports written and published for the US Council on Foreign Relations, Social Science Research Council, Brookings Institution and similarly sponsored university centres for International Affairs research have established an orthodox conception of development according to which non-European societies, incapable on their own of creative achievement and progress in political organization, technology, science and political thought, are helped to make a guided transition to their proper place in a 'modern' international order. The process is one by which 'traditional' societies are turned into 'transitional' societies on their way to being 'developed' societies. 'The developed society is one made up of the social structures, technologies and life styles that exist today in the First and Second Worlds', according to a scholar who is more radical politically.*

There is in all this a fundamental contradiction which has not had the attention it calls for. If exclusively and peculiarly *European* qualities and achievements have given *modern* development its essential character, then its benefits can be enjoyed by the non-European peoples only vicariously, through the benefactions of the 'developed'. But if it was only because of a combination of identifiable social and ideological factors that the peoples of Europe happened to overtake other peoples during the eighteenth, nineteenth and early twentieth centuries, then their past achievements belong, like the pioneering

* I. L. Horowitz, *The Three Worlds of Development. The Theory and Practice of International Stratification* (New York, 1966), p. 59. Whether or not the sponsors of the notions referred to here, including the World Bank, want three billion Davy Crocketts trying to be Rockefellers and Kennedys is not clear. Emulation, it has been said, is the sincerest form of flattery. 'However coated this passion for emulation is with slogans about folk identity and national culture, the economic and sociological demands for better living conditions and better credit terms are dictated by standards derived from the cosmopolitan centers' (*ibid.*, p. 20). This, in his more folksy idiom, is what President Johnson said (see p. 24 above). On 'modernization' and 'models', see discussion in my *From Gandhi to Geuvera: The Polemics of Revolt* (London, 1970), pp. 27 ff., 61 ff., 70, 77 ff., 259 ff.

achievements of other peoples, to the common history of mankind as a whole; in that case, development from the middle of the twentieth century onwards is for *all* peoples the task of charting, and moving into, a future which has still to be made by living men and women. To assume that the peoples of Latin America, Asia and Africa are now entering the eighteenth and nineteenth centuries, rather than preparing to enter the twenty-first, is to imply that these peoples will *never* escape being backward, inferior and underdeveloped. (It is also to ignore the fact that these peoples did experience the 'development' of the past few centuries.) Since according to the racial theory the way to *modernity* in society, thought, politics and industry is necessarily pioneered by Western democracy, Western science, Western industrial know-how and Western leadership qualities generally, whatever the underdeveloped peoples do to develop their own societies and thus to modernize them will lead to something other than modernization. Equally, for them to anticipate what Westerners would do is futile, since Westerners alone, by this definition, can show how it must be done. Either way, the independent paths the poor take in order to reach the most advanced levels of science, industry, agriculture and political life will take them neither to developed status nor modernity! As development theory it is nonsense.

Asians, Africans and Latin Americans can achieve development through exclusively Western (that is, North American, Western European or Russian) political forms, science and technology in three ways: firstly, by assimilation or Westernization; secondly, by making servants or slaves of Westerners, taking possession of what they have developed, and of their unique capacities for modernization in an industrial and scientific age; thirdly, by entering into the kind of relationship which will enable them continually to benefit from the altruistic cooperation and service of the more advanced peoples. The first course may be relevant to a few individuals, but it cannot be the way of eliminating the cause of the oppressive poverty and misery of millions of towns, villages and homes. The second is equally unrealistic, and will itself be the cause of impoverishment and oppression. The third, which is in fact an argument for seeing Western aid and tutelage as essential to the development process, rules out any prospect of the equality of peoples and races; however, how able and willing the benefactors and tutors are to render altruistic service we must examine in its proper historical setting in Chapter 8.

The theories (with their racist assumptions and with the particular interests of dominant *élites* in mind) contradict themselves and clash with the realities. The people who seek to eradicate poverty do not even suspect that 'American society is an unique creation significant not only for the American people but also for all mankind', let alone hold it as a conviction. Apart from a few who have been assimilated, they know that it is only what might be said with truth to be possible for peoples anywhere and everywhere, and what has been achieved regardless of race, which is a realistic path to development. The 'gap' is fantasy. The development hierarchy is not a scientific concept, but derives from the ideology and interests of the class at the top.*

The peoples of the tricontinental south must no doubt take careful account of their development and modernization in the sixteenth, seventeenth, eighteenth and nineteenth centuries in the face of superior Western power and enterprise. They are, whether in the colonial city slums or the rural backlands, in the twentieth century. In so far as development took place *in the West* only because of Western, that is, indigenous, initiatives, efforts and achievements, learning and discoveries, such development as we can expect to see taking place in the future in the Third World can, as its most perceptive leaders recognize, be realized only by an *indigenous* struggle in thought and

* The quotation is from Theodor Geiger, *The Conflicted Relationship* (London, 1967), produced for the Council on Foreign Relations. A far more thorough and systematic discussion of influential assumptions and theories about development is to be found in A. G. Frank's brilliant 'Sociology of Development and Underdevelopment of Sociology' in *Catalyst*, Summer 1967. For J. S. Needham's remarks on the chauvinist character of some discussions of non-Western developments, see A. C. Crombie (ed.), *Scientific Change* (London, 1963), pp. 140–49.

work to progress well beyond the limits of existing social and political organization, productive activity, and knowledge of man and the world of nature. The income 'gap' is then an irrelevance, and so is the incentive value of affluence. It is not envy of high incomes that has given rise to the world-wide drive to eliminate poverty and oppression; it is, rather, the experience of the poor, and of their violated right to life, to human dignity, and to freedom. The 'passion for emulation' is there; but those being emulated are not the super-rich or even the well-fed in North American suburbia, but rather the poor who have fought successfully to break out of their poverty, and the sons and daughters of the rich oppressors who have renounced wealth, comfort and privilege. The development theories tend to turn the ranking order of countries upside-down. It is the most oppressed and poorest peoples, those most outraged, tortured and strangled in body, mind and spirit by the material and political conditions which prevail, who are at the top of the list – the list, that is, which indicates the nature of the drive for development which the colonial peoples began before and during the Second World War, and its goals. It is because of the action of the poor and ignorant peoples – nearly 2,000 million of them in the middle of the twentieth century – that the development process has become important. For they themselves decided, on their own initiative, to take action to make their own future freer and more richly human. And they did so at a time in human history when the poor and oppressed who desire to enjoy the good things of the earth need no longer subject others to impoverishment and oppression.* The majority of the men, women and children who entered the second half of this century lacking the material facilities for an independent and modern existence are also entering the age in which drudgery is no longer unavoidable, even in seemingly

* See discussion of 'Goals, Objectives and Values' summarized on pp. 259–61 of *From Gandhi to Guevara, op. cit.* Some examples of the characteristics of the 'new society' as seen by leaders like Li Ta-chao, Sun Yat-sen, Nelson Mandela and other popular spokesmen for the Third World are given in the same volume.

remote mountain villages. They are free to destroy because they can construct and create in a year what took a hundred years for their forefathers. Considering the immense resources which are there for the taking, as by right, the systematic and rapid development of material conditions for a richly human life is not merely a possibility. It is an imperative.

THE PRIMARY TASK IN DEVELOPMENT

People have always been attracted by the myth of man in a state of nature, enjoying fresh water, fresh air and sunshine, nuts, fruits and other things to eat, peaceful human company, and plants, birds and animals. But for many thousands of years 'nature's abundance' has been far from sufficient to meet the subsistence needs of men, women and children who make little contribution to it. *Man's* 'natural' powers are the most creative part of nature. The universe itself is always unfinished, waiting for man the revolutionary transformer, creator and discoverer to develop his full stature, ethically, artistically, scientifically and politically. It waits, that is, for the creation of the truly human city, which acknowledges its debt to the earth. People have to work for and produce what they need, even children and companions; or they can, perverting the whole process, get others to work and produce for them. But there is a world of difference in working for others as free men and women, and working for others out of necessity, fear, compulsion.

Man learnt the basic facts of economics very early from experience and practice, as we noted in the last chapter. He had the foresight to take time and trouble to produce whatever would enable him to enlarge the bounds of present existence, and to be prepared, when the occasion arose, to go beyond them. The greater the proportion of time, energy, thought, skill and other resources they devoted to making and building materially for an easier future, the richer and more secure men became. A river, for example, might be tamed after a great deal of effort. The people (the community, that is, and not the individuals) who achieved this (provided they were not driven out or enslaved by invaders) were immeasurably richer than they had ever been before.

One of the most striking facts about the peoples and nations who declined into the condition which at the beginning of the twentieth century characterized the underdeveloped world was their remoteness from simple economic realities. A significant aspect of the poverty which afflicted so many of them was the fact that the immediate material environment available to them was too poorly developed to provide more than the most meagre satisfaction. Its use for producing food, buildings, communications, play and defence against invaders was neglected. The stock of human knowledge on these matters had diminished. This decline and decay were arrested, and a new sense of economic and material realities was born, only when people were brought by the more perceptive among them to realize what they *must* have – the farms, mines, factories, irrigation channels, plants, metals, electricity, books, living space, guns, schools, computers, nuclear reactors, scientific knowledge, new organizations – and how to get them quickly, not by pillage, but by work. If these did not exist, or only barely existed, it was because they had decayed, been destroyed or taken from them or never been produced. If they had been producing these things for other people to enjoy and use, it was because their whole mode of work and organization had been wrong, and destructive of the opportunities for their own growth and development. The awakening to material realities is in fact much more confused at first than this summary indicates; but when it occurs, it can be decisive for the economic and political development of whole nations. Until the mass of the people act with correct historical understanding, development and modernization cannot begin.

Frugality has always been part of economic wisdom: those who live by their own labours know that to toil for wasteful consumption jeopardizes both the future and present satisfactions other than those of eating, drinking and dressing grandly; moreover, anyone who believes that the earth (or rather, the rest of nature) will tolerate prodigal living will discover how mistaken he is; for he is making life extremely difficult for his children. Would it be too fanciful to argue that the people who through the ages have worked hard as free men and women have eaten in order that they might live to enjoy what life would bring on the morrow? The wanting-to-be-alive-and-happy-tomorrow is what keeps people satisfied with frugal living. That the sun will shine the next day is not the fruit of the work of man. But that they are going to be there to enjoy the next day, and to see their children thrive, depends on how carefully, intelligently and resolutely they struggle against whatever blocks their development.

For millions of people existence has for years been such that readers of this book would find unbearable even for a day. Yet for men and women who have known only painful hunger and sickness and the premature death of those dear to them, and who, in order to survive, have had to submit their bodily powers, sexual functions and intellects to continual indignity and contempt, and to smother their awareness of their own worth, there is hope – as long as intelligence, foresight, ambition and daring are not lost irrevocably. When they are brought to the point of an uncompromising and courageous refusal to submit to what they perceive is a sub-human existence, they open up the prospect of a change for the better. They change their mute, passive, obedient posture to one of active struggle in thought and action. The prospect will be realized only by carefully planned use of whatever is available in the social and material environment for the recovery of their human powers. How the human spirit begins to burn with such anger, courage and hope as to overturn from below the structures which press down on it is a mystery. But it is not something imaginary. 'Poor people,' said Mao Tse-tung (who ought to have known better than anyone else) as he watched his fellow-countrymen's enthusiasm for the Great Leap Forward of 1958, 'want change, want to do things, want revolution.' Those who feel threatened by the first glimmer of its appearance bear witness to its reality by their terrified attempts to deal with the coming conflagration – whether in south-east China,

D

north-east Brazil, South Africa or Guatemala. People deadened in mind and spirit cannot animate the wilderness which poverty, oppression and apathy have created. But even in the 'lower depths' the masses can be stirred by some ultimate indignity. Josue de Castro relates how the now famous peasant leagues came to be formed in north-east Brazil: the workers at the Galilee Sugar Mill in Pernambuco organized to avoid the humiliation of being buried without a coffin. The plantation-owner, under pressure from other members of his class who feared that the league was a cloak for 'Communism', tried to suppress it. The peasants resisted. What began in 1955 as a concern for the dead and became transformed into a struggle of the living had by 1961 grown into struggle for social justice which aroused President Kennedy's fears of the Communist threat in Brazil.*

At the end of the last war there were scores of major historic communities and nations who did not possess the means of productive, creative and profitable work. The development process by which poverty is rooted out had to begin by the acquiring of a material base, from which further action could be taken. No significant change occurs in the underdeveloped society until the restoration of the poor and oppressed to human status is shown in a resolve to begin an economic programme, directed by the people themselves. For it is not in physical survival, but in having a free, mutually enriching and responsible relationship with the material environment that individuals and communities become human. If a number of villages and towns, or factories, or districts, or provinces took action simultaneously, it might be all the better. But essential to the development process is the intelligently directed and economical enlarging – and thus the modernizing – of an existing material base, however inadequate in the first place; without this push by the poor to break out of sub-human living conditions there would be no social dynamism generated. In effect, all those who work and are prepared to work *must* retake

* Josue de Castro's account of developments in Brazil appears in *Death in the Northeast* (New York, 1969).

possession of their rightful resources, in order to set them free to serve the needs of the people as a whole, as they are outlined in the pages which follow. The main obstacle to development, even to the understanding of what development is, is the wide, untested and fearful gap before them. On the one side is the authority and the power to resume the long-neglected process of development of all that roots out and destroys and transforms hunger, idleness, inferiority, subjection and ignorance. On the other side is the state of mind, the general culture, which consists in fear of, respect for, submission and obedience to the existing order which has deprived them of their rights. 'The initial step must be a complete break with the existing order,' as Jawaharlal Nehru recognized in British-ruled, semi-feudal India, but the distance to be covered required a leap, not a step.* It is impossible to see how, without this initial, active leap forward by the poorest and most dispossessed, they can conceive the development process and dare to take on the daunting, painful and highly demanding task of initiating in their lands, and in the tricontinental south as a whole, the process of economic and scientific modernization which in the capitalist countries was initiated by the bourgeoisie. It is by actually running or taking charge of the mines, farms, factories, banks, ports, laboratories, schools, military installations, printing presses, broadcasting stations, transport and communications systems, inland waterways and territorial waters, village, city, provincial and national administrative offices, courts, and their seats on international bodies – from which they have been forcibly or fraudulently excluded – that they can actually get on with the task of development and modernization.

To catch up with human progress in technology, science and social organization the people who have to do the work must

* Quoted in my *From Gandhi to Guevara, op. cit.,* p. 281. 'What a burden,' a future prime minister of India wrote to another future prime minister, 'our peasantry have carried these many years! . . . All of us, foreigners and Indian, have sought to exploit that long-suffering *kisan* and have mounted on his back. Is it surprising that his back breaks?' (J. Nehru, *Glimpses of World History*, London, 1962).

ensure a clean break with the oppressive past – no easy task. In the past the benefactors of the minorities who form the ruling class were allowed to take the initiative on their own account; they used the human heritage to build up their own power and authority and culture in an exclusive civilization of mansions and towns in which the muscle, brain and marrow of the increasingly dumb and torpid masses of men, women and children were consumed. In so far, therefore, as the 'damned of the earth' have faith in the human capacity to transform their lives and destinies, and in so far as they act on that belief, the authentic 'take-off' from underdevelopment to development begins. That, not neo-colonial status, is what marks the 'transitional' phase in development. For development proceeds as men, women and children who have been resigned and submissive are transformed into confident and revolutionary creators of a new material environment, learning more about themselves and the earth in the course of practical struggle. The new environment must, by definition, be one from which all the forces, habits and institutions which result in the exploitation and impoverishment of some people by others are eradicated. Man is himself only as he exercises responsible dominion over the rest of the earth directly through his efforts and tremendous powers. As long as the poor everywhere hesitate through fear or sloth to cross the threshold into a revolutionary human existence their material and social environment will accordingly remain underdeveloped. It will in fact continue to be 'developed' in forms which are destructive of their humanity and their potential. The large body of tested practical knowledge, which has either been left unutilized or been used by the rich against the poor, comes into proper use only as skill and mastery in its handling are acquired by struggle. Till then it remains the hostile and hideous science and technology of impoverishment and exploitation.

The practical experience of the poor critically and analytically summed up by them after they have successfully made the leap over the main gap is knowledge which is basic to development. To ignore what they have for generations paid dearly to learn, and to be taken in by the smooth rhetoric of the humanitarianism of the rich, is to court disaster. The willingness of the beleaguered rich to share out with a few leaders of the poor some meagre benefits from the existing order may confuse and demoralize. But the poor need not be told that those whom they displace from positions of power have not constructed an economy or created a heritage which the revolutionary poor can use or enjoy. For the forms in which agricultural and industrial activity, science and technology, education and the arts, housing and commerce are organized in any society are, as the poor well know, not neutral and flexible. The task of putting the scientific, energy and material resources to the most frugal and efficient use in relation to what they are aiming to create continually confronts the poor – once they are in power – with political problems of the utmost complexity. They cannot afford to tire or relax their vigilance and determination in solving the problems.

Political development on these lines is immensely more complex and demanding than that which development experts in this field tend to refer to by the term: the increasing approximation of the polity in 'emergent' nation states in the present world order to that which it is claimed the United States, and to a lesser extent the European countries, have developed.*

* Professor Lucian W. Pye of the Center for International Studies at the Massachusetts Institute of Technology, and one of those most active in promoting the 'free world' rhetoric on development, has given a very concise definition of 'political development': 'The key elements of political development involve first, with respect to the population as a whole, a change from widespread subject status to an increasing number of contributing citizens, with an accompanying spread of mass participation, a greater sensitivity to the principles of equality, and a wider acceptance of universalistic laws. Second, with respect to governmental and general systemic performance, political development involves an increase in the capacity of the political system to manage public affairs, control controversy, and cope with public demands. Finally, with respect to the organization of the polity, political development implies greater structural differentiation, greater functional specificity, and greater integration of all the participating institutions and organizations' (Lucian W. Pye and Sidney Verba (eds.), *Political Culture and Political Development* (Princeton, 1965), p. 13).

The lessons from experience of struggle in thought and action with all the complex and varied causes of poverty have continually to be formulated afresh in simple but precise terms; more or less far-reaching decisions of an unprecedented nature will have to be made and carried out in a variety of unpredictable situations; they will have to be made and carried out by people individually, in the exercise of public responsibility, or as teams in workplaces, as families, village units or as an entire nation. New loyalties come into force. Those undertaking revolutionary change and reconstruction and assuming power to do so are laying claim to great authority; mass action in exercise of this authority has to be ordered and structured, so that the lines of multilateral co-ordination and command, of responsibility and of supervision are clear. The difficult problems of social ethics and of organizational effectiveness which arise require a widely diffused and specific ideology of revolutionary aim and action.

Discussion of the development process here presupposes that the poor have acquired the authority and the power to effect the development of a society in which there will be no rich and poor. The process of acquiring that authority and power is not something about which it is possible to generalize. But once the poor have a base for development, it may initially be, as in China in the 1930s and Portuguese Guinea, only a small part of national territory. Until there is a structure of democratic politics in which the interests, objectives and needs of the poorest of the working people take precedence over those of the rest, the process of genuine development will tend to go awry. Without a core of politically very advanced people – these may be peasants who have a sound grasp of modern economic and political realities, rather than intellectuals or urban workers – the development process can be overwhelmed by the contrary pressures and demands of different sections of the community. It is not merely a balance, but the most creative and constructive form of reciprocity that must be discovered in the relationship between the interests and demands of developing towns and developing countryside, expanding industry and expanding agriculture, heavy industry and light industry, already developed and yet-to-be-developed parts of the country, what has to be destroyed and what has to be constructed, the economy as a whole and the regional economies, local productive units and the central planners, the well-educated, formally trained and the untrained mass leaders of real talent, individual workers and the community organization, racial or religious groups and the nation, the working population and the students in schools and universities, the poor in the nation and the poor in the whole world. The conflict of interests and aims with those who benefited by the old order of mass poverty, and who seek to restore that order, has also to be resolved politically, without repression.

The development of a political consciousness and political structures and processes (including international cooperation among the poor) which can cope with the ongoing tasks is fundamental for the war against poverty. Democracy of the kind described here, which involves and demands far more than 'participation' – after all, vote-casting every five years for candidates for political office is also 'participation' – as it requires personal responsibility and initiative almost all the time, and the continual making of political judgements; it depends on a very advanced form of community life. The kind of self-centredness which goes by the name of individualism, excessive family-consciousness, sectarian loyalties, abuse of authority, impatience and anarchism are likely to hold back the development process. A reluctance to discard practices or destroy institutions which have been useful but which stand in the way of new developments represents a state of mind which can obstruct the development process. The politics of development is clearly more complex, and more interesting, than anything which has been experienced in affluent societies.

Though the poor who opt to go all out to eliminate poverty and transform the material conditions of existence must be handicapped initially by the crippling physical, economic, social, and intellectual effects of long years of gross neglect and malnutrition, lack of skills and experience because of lack of

work, illiteracy because of lack of schooling, there is much that
they can do to build a better and more secure future. They may
be short of capital in the form of money which will buy goods
and expert services. But, once they are free to create, it would
be strange if they could not organize enough skills, energies and
resources to enlarge the scope of their life and productive
activities. The construction of new irrigation works and dams,
of schools, factories and hospitals, the clearing and cultivation
of new land and the training of new workers can expand capital
investment substantially. Quantity is not what counts most.
But investment which is sound from the point of view of
revolutionary reconstruction and growth will grow cumu-
latively like any other investment. An additional investment in
expanding productive opportunities may be no more than a
small percentage of the total economic activity. But, as economists have demonstrated, a steady rate of expansion of the
productive base can have most surprising effects in only two or
three decades. The impact on the development process of
political awakening, the rapid rise in the level of learning and
skill, voluntary economic and educational activity, innovations
in production, improved organization and other similar
consequences of political change are mutually reinforcing and
cannot easily be measured. It is clear that in favourable inter-

Cumulative effects of different rates of growth of the productive base

Annual increase percentage	Percentage growth at the end of				
	5 yrs	10 yrs	15 yrs	20 yrs	25 yrs
1	5	10	16	22	28
2	10	22	32	49	64
4	22	48	80	119	166
5	28	63	108	165	239
7	40	97	176	287	443
10	61	244	394	634	1,016

national conditions a developing country's 'leap forward' at
the rate of a steady seven per cent increase in productive

capacity will enable it to double its total productive base in ten years, and at ten per cent to multiply the original base tenfold in twenty-five years. With the resources of modern technology, and the revolutionary will, rapid economic development is conceivable for even the most populous of the poor countries.

The willingness of working people in the industrially and technologically developed countries to devote a small proportion of their working time and skill to providing the strategic needs of the poor peoples could speed up the development process considerably. International cooperation of this kind will enable modernizing countries which are short of certain needed resources opportunities of taking short cuts to rapid development. Cooperation in making trading arrangements which will help newly started industries to find foreign markets is another useful form of help.

There is a danger that this kind of discussion makes the development process seem much easier than is really the case. Have the forces making serious efforts to eliminate poverty had much *success* in the last twenty years? Has the international situation, and especially the attitude of the economically and militarily powerful nations, been favourable to these forces, and hostile to those which have been, and still may be, the cause of the poverty and ignorance? Why is there a fear of famine? Why is there evidence of severe malnutrition and illiteracy so many years after the poor made their presence felt in the 1940s? The evidence suggests that the struggle for development is not just against stagnation or excessive dependence of the labour force on agriculture. The main struggle is against active forces of anti-development.

Before we go on to discover the forces of 'anti-development' which create fresh poverty and misery, we must recognize how vast and complicated a phenomenon world poverty is. The estimates of nutritional requirements which in the post-war years placed two thirds of mankind in the category of those suffering from chronic hunger have no doubt exaggerated the problem. Even in the late 1940s less than half the world was suffering from serious dietary deficiencies. It was in the sense that they had been deprived of the minimum requirements for a modern industrial economy that two thirds of the world were poor. A deficiency of this size is not going to be made up, even in the most favourable conditions, in less than a century. There is, moreover, no precedent in past history for the systematic liberation of the poor and elimination of the material and institutional causes of poverty, and it is from the practice and experience of those who pioneer successfully that a systematic theory can be derived.

The self-reliant and politically developing poor who take on themselves their great historical task of creating a material environment, institutions, a body of indigenous knowledge and experience at the most advanced levels which will banish the systems and technologies which create poverty have to fight against their own ignorance, their lack of modern experience in scientific and technological matters, their tiredness, their meannesses and resentments and greeds; they have to cope with floods, droughts and pestilence, which can destroy work they have begun to do; they have to struggle against a backward environment, poor communications, authoritarian traditions.* But more serious than all these is the alternative version of development which is being promoted by the minority of their fellow-Asians, Latin Americans and Africans who in the old days had the good fortune to acquire an advanced education, wealth and professional training. The competing version of 'development' lays claim, by its radical rhetoric, to being revolutionary, anti-imperialist and socialist. And it tends to confuse and mislead the militants among the poor and oppressed who are impatient with backward colleagues. For the ruling *élites* of the world economy have recognized that in relation to the responsibilities which had to be undertaken and the roles which had to be played locally for 'international

---

* What the authentic development of the world's proletariat means in terms of new forms of education, for example, and the realization, long delayed, of the promise of the city in human civilization, we are only now beginning to understand as we observe what the poor have achieved in China.

development' to take place the colonial *élites*, landlords, merchants and intellectuals were backward and under-developed. What it aims to develop are the political power and sophistication of this class of person, and of the means of legitimizing that power: the effectiveness of agriculture, industry, communications, education, police and military organization and administrative methods, on lines which will in fact deny the liberation of the poor and their command of the development process. That version of 'development' has its 'mobilization' of the masses for 'participation' in the process of legitimizing the power of the 'modernizing' middle class. It capitalizes on the fact that unless creative revolutionary intellectuals join forces with the revolutionary poor who labour with their hands the ideological and educational work which prepares the latter for self-reliant action will be neglected. It will be instructive to observe how development and modernization of this type has affected the war on world poverty.

CHAPTER 4

The Process of Anti-Development

THE VIOLENT DEATH OF HISTORIC COMMUNITIES

The reader has been drawn into an exploration of the plight of entire nations and peoples whose destinies became subject to the will of the European peoples and their Japanese imitators from about 1500 onwards. These are the nations and peoples who, as the last withdrawals of the old-style colonial administrations began, came into a single focus as the Third World. In many of them poverty is on the increase. Why is this so? Why are nations and villages rapidly perishing?

Those are questions on which the impatient and angry poor outside the gates of the affluent enclaves insist. A grasp of the systematic working of political and economic processes and institutions in the contemporary world may take us some way towards an answer.

The suffering and salvation of men, women and children who are victims of political, economic and social *systems* which retard their development and dehumanize them should not be confused with questions of world famine in the 1970s, population explosions, or how terms of international trade may be eased for primary producers. Nor is it simply the gruesome spectacle of starving Biafran babies or of famine victims in Bihar. Our discussion is really about which group of persons does what in society, who rules, who is ruled over, what the system of production is, what it cannot be, what laws are in operation and whose laws they are, and whose values and interests prevail in practice.

How can the members of a highly affluent society approve of the values and international policies of their rulers and still understand the experience of the truly poor? How can they share, let alone encourage, the aspirations of those who view the affluent few not with admiration and envy but with rather different feelings? Statistical reports on conditions of poverty are sometimes eloquent. But they do not record the inner longings of the poor: their sorrow, their anger, their hatred, their daily sensations. They do not speak of the potential of the poor. And what the affluent write about the feelings and needs of the poor is, after all, what the rich think.

There are in the European cultural tradition compassionate and humane artistic creations which enhance one's sensitivity to and understanding of oppression and tyranny. Both drama and satire destroy the illusions and certainties on which the authority of the powerful and the rich is based. These works draw their strength from the clearsightedness and rebelliousness of the lowly; they are part of a tradition not lacking in insights into the real processes of oppression, and in which history has been made by the poor. That tradition has been submerged by the flood of trivial verbiage from newspaper offices, radio and television studios, pulpits and political platforms and the like. In an age of widespread literacy the highly centralized and bureaucratic control of the mass media does not favour the subversive activity of great art. The staple cultural diet makes high drama out of the trivial sentiments and agonies of philanderers and fortune hunters of court and boardroom and sees human destiny in the struggles and achievements of landlords and ranchers, shopkeepers and corporation lawyers, frustrated generals and ageing courtesans. It presents as Socratic wisdom the carefully staged discussion programmes and censored editorial pages which decry 'extremism' of all kinds – including an uncompromising loyalty to the truth, or the poor, or the oppressed. For the untutored poor to intrude with *their* sufferings into this conveniently sanitized and dehumanized world, amounts almost to treason. For when subject classes, races and peoples insist that due regard be paid to *their* rights, values and well-being they are threatening the ruling *élites* whose advancement and well-being is established on such flimsy rationalizations as *the* national interest, *the* guarantee of freedom or *the* welfare of all mankind.

It is a sign of the times that the complaints and demands of the poor all over the world have to be discussed. The poor have succeeded in intruding. In the first chapter the post-war 'discovery' of the militant poor was briefly described. It was in the community in which poverty was most extreme and in which the greatest political disasters threatened that ordinarily insensitive observers became most aware of the urgency of the problem of world poverty. That was China, in which the tremendous mass of the extremely poor exceeded the total population of Europe, including Russia. One of the wartime observers in China was an American journalist, Theodore H. White. He was not a particularly imaginative or radical person, and in later years he appears to have regretted the implications of the observations he made. But these are worth recalling, as an example of how direct encounter with the stark realities of social processes through which a whole nation is oppressed and impoverished can be instructive. White had seen enough from Chungking of what the US-supported regime of Chiang Kai-shek was doing to harm the Chinese masses. When news of an unprecedented famine in Honan province was denied by Chiang's officials, he decided to go and see for himself. Chapter 11 of the book he wrote with Annalee Jacoby contains his account of what he discovered. Its remarkable documentary value is increased by the fact that that winter, early in 1943, the Japanese were expected to launch a major attack from their territory into the as-yet-unoccupied province of Honan, immediately adjacent. The scenes of starvation and social breakdown White saw were horrible. After commenting on the corrupt and inefficient way in which famine relief was administered he wrote:

Stupidity and inefficiency marked the relief effort. But the grisly tragedy was compounded even further by the actions of the constituted local authorities. The peasants, as we saw them, were dying. They were dying on the roads, in the mountains, by the railway stations, in their mud huts, in the fields. And as they died, the government continued to wring from them the last possible ounce of tax. The money tax the peasant had to pay on his land was a trivial matter; the basic tax exacted from him was the food tax, a percentage of all the grain he raised, and despite the fine-sounding resolution of remittance in Chungking, the tax was being extorted from him by every device the army and provincial authorities could dream up. The government in county after county was demanding of the peasant more actual poundage of grain than he had raised on his acres. No excuses were allowed; peasants who were eating elm bark and dried leaves had to haul their last sack of seed grain to the tax-collector's office. Peasants who were so weak they could barely walk had to collect fodder for the army's horses, fodder that was more nourishing than the filth they were cramming into their own mouths. Peasants who could not pay were forced to the wall; they sold their cattle, their furniture, and even their land to raise money to buy grain to meet the tax quotas. One of the most macabre touches of all was the flurry of land speculation. Merchants from Sian and Chengchow, small government officials, army officers, and rich landlords who still had food were engaged in purchasing the peasants' ancestral acres at criminally low figures. *Concentration and dispossession were proceeding hand in hand, in direct proportion to the intensity of hunger.**

White went on to record how, driven beyond endurance by the oppression of their rulers, the surviving peasants armed themselves with birdguns, knives and pitchforks, and started to disarm the soldiers. Fifty thousand soldiers, he reported, were disarmed in this way, before the Japanese struck. White had on his visit met a peasant who was eating a concoction of buck-wheat chaff, leaves and elm bark; this man, he and his colleagues discovered, had actually produced 500 pounds of wheat on his bit of land the previous year, but all this, plus his ox and his ass, were forcibly taken from him. The obscene brutalities of Japanese imperialism could hardly have added to his sufferings.

* Theodore H. White and Annalee Jacoby, *Thunder Out of China* (New York, 1946), p. 174, italic added. It is not intended by this quotation to suggest that Mr White approved of the action of the peasants, together with the workers and intellectuals, in overthrowing the power of the landlords, officials and army officers, and putting their own government into power.

Of the thirty million people in Honan, two or three million had died and over two million were refugees. But the visiting journalists were given a farewell dinner by government officials which consisted of 'sliced lotus, peppered chicken, beef and water chestnut' in addition to 'spring rolls, hot wheat buns, rice, bean curd and fish'. The ruling classes, with whom the Americans and British identified themselves, were able to indulge in fine living not because they themselves worked harder and saved more than those who were impoverished. Some of the machinery for impoverishing a richly endowed country is there in White's experience: on the one hand, the peasants and their wives and children, and their livestock; on the other hand, the officials, the landlords, the merchants and the officers (playing interchangeable roles), and their regulations, guns and troops. The extent of the violence which created poverty – compelling people to yield their energies and skills in labour; seizing their produce, seed grain, cattle and land; terrorizing them, driving them off the land and the village, killing them and so on – is neatly summarized in the exchange of the rich and tasty food for leaves, bark and dirt.

There were other Americans like White whose strong feelings of outrage at the manifest humbug and wickedness of the Chiang regime for a while made them see what was plain to the angry poor in China. In a certain state of mind the barrier between rich and poor (whether one regards it as a growing gap between fiction and actuality or as a curtain of class prejudice) can be crossed. Truths which are conventionally denied may become the object of an active and challenging curiosity which is decried by the upholders of the established order as 'permissive', 'extremist' and 'subversive'. The intelligence begins to engage in troublesome inquiries. It asks about the specific ways in which the violence which once established and now maintains the social order brought about the impoverishment and ultimately the ruin of entire classes and communities of people. The discovery may begin of intangible, hitherto unimagined essentials of human well-being which have been strangled and cheated out of historic communities by the blows, rules and exactions of the powerful. The inquiring mind identifies anew the necessary ingredients of wholesome, untrammelled and responsible existence in the diverse villages, towns and countries of the modern world; and in doing so it begins to grasp the simple facts about poverty and development which elude the conventionally wise. The terms which are fundamental in any discussion of the facts of world poverty and of development taking place are freed of the cant and triteness which characterize their current use. The superficial and abstract discussion conducted in terms of 'the individual' and statistical surveys begins to give way to a more specific and concrete one based on the consequences of what happens in and to whole communities. Not only China, but India, Vietnam, Laos, Brazil, Guatemala and Korea provide basic lessons for the sociology and economics of development.

It is a struggle to reach through words alone the foundations on which people everywhere can play their independent part in building a world civilization free of tyranny and want. Men have had varying intimations of the ultimate goodness which must be attained. But whatever they make of the free gift of life, people must work out their destiny in a land and community to which they belong. The problems of their neighbourhood as well as its achievements are common to all. Personal growth is not achieved by an individual's self-love, cleverness and industry. Wholesome and truly human growth requires the familiar sensations which open doors to experience without which there will be no song, poetry or painting. One's land is shared with people who fulfil what is lacking in oneself – relatives, work-mates, and teachers. Without caring for the community context, there is no development. The poor are fighting not for the handouts of foreigners, but for their own country. One's well-being is inseparable from the presence, the words and actions, attitudes and expectations, bodily and mental states, achievements and failures, of compatriots of earlier, contemporary and succeeding generations. It is because of the health, skill and prudence of earlier generations that every new-born child can look forward to a personal future; for there is an orderly way in which fields have to be cultivated, houses and vehicles and machines constructed, goods and people transported, clothes and utensils made, ideas and plans understood and translated into action, the community defended against marauders. When 'body counts' and statistics of bombing, napalm or defoliation raids on the angry poor are gleefully announced by governments, it is the essentially *communal* nature of development and wealth which gives the statistics meaning. To think about the poor is to think about Pernambuco, Palestine, Calcutta, Song My and Tachai.

THE DISABLING OF THE PRODUCERS

Malnutrition: The Production of Malfunctioning Bodies

The fresh and increasing supply of healthy, deft, intelligent and hard-working men and women is crucial to the production process. Such people learn quickly and do not easily tire or lose concentration when engaged in skilled work; they work for many years, growing in experience and skill. In normally healthy physical and social conditions the supply of new generations of strong, clever and creative workers is never lacking. In these conditions, after several years of physical, mental and emotional experience the person attains the normal functions of manhood or womanhood. But a society which destroys the potentialities of its producers by depriving most of its members of fresh air, sunshine, nourishing food, human nurture and intelligent activity, retards its own development and in the long run produces its own breakdown. Violence done by chronic starvation and disease to the normal constructional processes within the living body of the potential worker hurts the body politic. In some villages in the state of Piaui in Brazil, where nearly every infant is destroyed by hunger, the death of the community is tragically swift. In other places, it is a lingering death. In societies where loss of productivity, because of strikes or illness, is a subject for concern, the progressive and irreparable destruction of priceless human resources is too fantastic to seem real.

But it is a fact that in most of the world man's natural urge to create a better life for himself is frustrated. From birth, and before birth, generations of children are given serious physical deficiencies to overcome. Millions either die in childhood or are so prematurely exhausted that they achieve little. Most never get to a start in life, since the adult members of the community who would have worked and cared for them perished either in life-long hunger or at the hands of foreign traders, airmen, soldiers or scientists.

In *The World Food Problem** a panel of United States scientists estimated that twenty per cent of the people in what are called the underdeveloped countries are undernourished, and that sixty per cent have diets inadequate in nutritional quality. Society not only starves people, but breeds diseases such as rickets and trachoma, as well as greater susceptibility to otherwise harmless diseases. Thus the rate at which people die as a result of getting measles is a hundred times greater in Chile than it is in the United States. But the diseases that ravage the poor are much worse than measles. Not long ago ninety per cent of Egyptians were estimated to be suffering from eye diseases. The millions who suffer from deficiency diseases like rickets are deprived throughout life of the full use of their bodies.

The politically and economically retarding effect of ill-nourished, malfunctioning and diseased might-have-been-workers has been argued here. The cause of this is, we have said, the lack of nourishment. Why, if the bodily health of the world's people is so important, have they been deprived of food? The explanation that it is a natural condition has been ruled out. The fact that deficiency is frequently due to faulty and unbalanced diet is not very relevant to people who often do not eat at all. People who eat expensive and lavish meals may not be taking a properly balanced diet; on the other hand, simple and (to the stranger) seemingly unpalatable foods may be highly nutritious.

* (Washington DC, 1967.)

An analysis of the reasons for the large-scale deprivation of food must form part of a theory of anti-development. The number of people in an area may for a time exceed the numbers for whom food supplies are locally available: a sequence of bad harvests, unprecedented flood and droughts, a sudden spurt in population increase, may be responsible. But the phenomenon we are considering cannot be explained on these lines. We are looking at the *systematic* denial of food on a global scale to a large part of mankind. Total numbers are not in excess of even existing supplies; as more was needed more could have been produced; and even in areas with a large food surplus, such as the United States, there is deprivation of the kind we have been describing.

The systematic destruction of fertile land is an important cause; and another is the reduction of food-production and the turning of the land to other uses. The productive resources of the land can, even in difficult climatic conditions, be husbanded for millennia, as in north China. On the other hand, exploitation like that which occurred in North America can lead to the destruction of animal life and the massive erosion of the richest soil. It can also happen that whole communities are forcibly driven off the land on which they grew food, and thereby cut off from their food supply. Food-producing land, or other resources which could be worked in order to pay for food, could be made unfit for production: methodical bombing of land and factories, defoliation and chemical or biological methods of destroying agriculture or industry has occurred in Vietnam. Irrigation and flood-control schemes built up over centuries have been neglected and allowed to deteriorate; as a result, drought and floods have reduced the land available for production. Stocks of food, or commodities that can be used to get food, have been destroyed. Finally the food that is produced is taken away by those who claim it as taxes, or rent, or just their private property.

The denial of food to the majority of the world's producers and potential producers then has a history. It has its political, sociological and ecological aspects, as the people who transferred from the kingdom of Kandy to the British colony of Ceylon discovered in the nineteenth century:

The basis of rural economy in ancient Ceylon was paddy cultivation. The social beliefs, customs and institutions were closely integrated with the system of paddy production. The Kandyan villages however, unlike the villages in other parts of the country, did not depend on artificial irrigation for the vitality of their economy. The terraced paddy fields, which were skilfully constructed by generations of cultivators, obtained their water from natural streams which rarely failed. The high land which could not be converted into paddy fields because of the lack of water was used by the villager to build his home, to plant fruit trees and to grow vegetables and other crops. The forests at a still higher level and the waste lands played a vital part in the village economy both directly and indirectly. They provided the peasant with pasture land for his cattle, with fuel for his household needs, and with leaf-manure for his paddy fields. Indirectly they helped him by ensuring adequate rainfall, preventing soil erosion, and maintaining his cattle which provided him not only with working power but also with manure to increase the productivity of his soil.

Thus paddy production was the pivot round which the economic and cultural life of the village revolved. The vital social values and relationships stemmed from this central activity of paddy cultivation and in turn supported the continuation of the economy. A well-integrated and self-sufficient social and economic system, well adapted to certain ecological factors, evolved.

The invasion of this system by the plantations struck a damaging blow to its stability; for it destroyed the balance that existed between high land cultivation, paddy production, *chena* cultivation and other uses of forest land. The story of the conversion of the forests into plantations, a process from which the village high land did not escape, is well known and need not be told here. What we want to remind the reader of is that the destruction of the forests not only affected the supply of water for the paddy fields, but also reduced the fertility of the soil by the double process of soil erosion and sedimentation and the reduction of the supply of vegetable and organic manure. Furthermore a number of irrigation channels having their source in forests were lost to the villagers when they became estate property.

The long-run effect of the opening of the plantations on the village was equally disruptive . . .*

The Poisoning of Life

A community produces and equips its producers only if it ensures them enough nourishment and space. It must also provide them with privacy and sanitation; otherwise they are not secure against crippling and fatal injury, and they are regularly denied the rest they need. Deprivation of sun and air in slums and tenements is a commonplace. Where there are eight people sharing a tiny, often windowless room, sleep does not bring rest and refreshment. The human body must be rid of its excrement if it is not to be poisoned; yet vast numbers of people are subject to social processes which poison them by forcing them to live in their own excreta. The air they breathe, the water they drink, everything they touch, is contaminated by it. The children are infected with parasites; and diarrhoea, dysentery, cholera and other bowel diseases reign where sanitation is lacking.

Personal cleanliness is as satisfying and conducive to a sense of physical well-being as the consumption of well-cooked food. People often do work which involves getting dirty and soiled – with mud, dirt or manure. When they get away from their work they bathe or otherwise clean themselves. They may in the pre-scientific age not have known about bacteria and viruses. But they had the sense to keep their cooking, play and rest apart from what they knew had to be eliminated. When they built cities they had sewage. The necessity for getting rid of dirt, excreta, other waste matter and foul smells and sights remains as constant as that for nourishment, whatever the environment. If millions of persons live in filth and dirt it is not because they have always done so, or because non-Europeans

* N. K. Sarkar and S. J. Tambiah, *The Disintegrating Village* (Colombo, 1957). Josue de Castro's discussion of Brazil's underdevelopment in my *From Gandhi to Guevara: The Polemics of Revolt* (London, 1970), pp. 205 ff., is worth comparing with this account of Ceylon.

have to learn from Europeans how to be clean, but because living in filth has been forced on people. Nirmar Kumar Bose, writing about Calcutta, notes 'the tremendous contrast that exists between what is public and what is private. The dwellings are clean and tidy inside, though they may be overcrowded.'* To have to live in filth is a regression; and a progressive destruction of the sense of well-being and enjoyment of what is clean does not lessen the fact that people are oppressed and destroyed by having to tolerate conditions such as those found in pre-revolutionary Shanghai, Lagos, Calcutta, Djakarta and in the *barriadas, favelas, callampas, villas miserias* and *cantigriles* of Latin America.

The United Nations Organization, in its *Economic Survey of Latin America* for 1963, estimated that Latin America (which in 1960 had a population of 205 million) had in 1951 a 'housing deficit' of 19,449,000 units. The shortages are estimated by modest standards. As the report says:

The calculation of deficits in Latin America has as a rule been confined to replacement requirements in respect of housing units considered to be unsatisfactory from the standpoint of their layout and the building materials used. Table 152 presents estimates of the shortage at various dates relating to eighteen countries. The principles used in formulating them have not been uniform, and generally speaking they reflect only the number of housing units that required replacement at the date of the last census. Thus, for example, in the estimates for 1951 prepared by the Pan American Union, the deficit, amounting to 19 million housing units, consisted in those 'buildings that are not in keeping with human dignity and that should be demolished'.†

The number of people living in each 'private housing unit', according to Table 152 of the survey, was in most cases about five. Not all the population was living in 'housing units' (which included huts). Percentage figures of those doing so for rural, urban and total populations respectively were interesting:

* *In Cities* (London, 1969).
† UN, *Economic Survey of Latin America* (New York, 1963), p. 166.

Percentage of population living in 'housing units'

Country	Rural population	Urban population	Total population
Chile (1960)	70	66	71
Guatemala (1949)	20	65	40
Venezuela (1950)	27	76	53

Such details were not given for Brazil, but its seventy million
population in 1960 managed with a housing deficit of eight
million units, which was possibly an underestimate. Referring
to the growth of shanty towns, the report gives some remarkable statistics: for example, 'the population of the *favelas* in
Rio de Janeiro, which had amounted to some 400,000 inhabitants in 1947, numbered 650,000 ten years later, and by 1961
had reached 900,000, representing approximately 38 per cent of
the city's total population. At the same time, the occupants of
favelas in Recife accounted for about 50 per cent of the total
population of the town' (p. 163). Lima's *barriadas* increased
their percentage of the city's population from ten in 1940 to
twenty-nine in 1961. Fourteen per cent of Mexico City's
population in 1952 lived in *colonias proletarias*.

What happens to the energies, imagination, senses and
relationships of people who are kept in these conditions? The
Indian economist, V. B. Singh, describes the counterpart of the
favelas in Bombay's *chawls*:

There are rooms so dark that even during the day the inmates
cannot see each other in passages, or in the single living rooms,
without the help of a light or fire. Fresh air is completely lacking.
Very often there is no passage of air from room to room, many of
which are built back to back . . .

It was estimated soon after independence that there were
eighty-six slums in Bombay, and that eight per cent of its
population lived with ten to nineteen persons per single-room
tenement.* The people who live in India's major city and port,

* Rangnekar, *Poverty and Capital Development in India* (Oxford, 1958), p.
181.

Calcutta (three million in the city, seven million in Calcutta Metropolitan District), are even more homeless. More than three quarters of the city population lives

in overcrowded tenements and *bustee* [slum] quarters. According to an official estimate 'two-thirds of the people live in *kutchka* [unbaked brick] buildings. More than 57 per cent of multi-member families have one room to live in. For more than half of the families cramped into one-room quarters there is only 30 square feet or less per family member.' One study showed that the indigent of the *bustees* share a single water tap *among 25·6 to 30·1* persons and a single latrine among 21·2 to 23.*

How murderous the living conditions in cities are is suggested by infant mortality rates for Bombay in 1925 given by Vera Anstey in her *The Economic Development of India*. The figures for deaths per 1,000 births for families living in (a) one-room tenements, (b) two-room tenements and (c) four-room and larger tenements were 503, 242 and 157 respectively.

If voluntary migrations to urban areas were an avoidable cause, all this would be a less serious problem. But in a number of countries living accommodation of even the simplest kind has for some time been lacking in the rural areas where the majority of people live. If we seek an explanation for the deterioration of living conditions in the countryside we find it in the social processes which were at work over centuries. In India there was a whole complex of developments which included the systematic destruction of manufacturing industry, particularly weaving, the pauperization of weavers and other skilled craftsmen, the introduction of private property rights in the land on which the cultivators lived and worked, the speculation in land and rising prices, the increasing use of densely populated land for commercial purposes, the export of food-grains and the destruction of the traditional economy and relations after the railway system was built. What it is important to be clear about now is the fact that the village communities were strangled or 'liquidated' during the colonial period by the same forces which built up and brought prosperity to the

* Bose, *op. cit.*, p. 70.

new mercantile and capitalist class in the towns and cities and to the members of the governing imperial nation.

Malnutrition, bad housing and sanitation and denial of clean air and water had severe effects in another important area, the Arab world. Between 1942 and 1947, according to one study, Egypt had five catastrophic epidemics: in 1942, 16,706 out of 80,619 typhoid victims died; in 1942–4, a quarter of a million suffered from malaria; in 1947, 10,277 out of 20,804 cholera patients died; and there were cases of relapsing fever and plague. Apart from this, bilharziasis, ancylostomiasis and pellagra were widespread.

Literally hundreds of millions in the Third World are homeless. Those who succeed in struggling to live beyond infancy not only waste away for lack of proper nourishment, but they are worn out in the struggle for the clean air and water, sunshine, rest, cleanliness and quiet which have been denied them. Healthy, vigorous, long-living and intelligent men and women are vital to the survival, development and security of any community. The system which positively cuts down the potential number of these, and then prevents the few survivors from achieving their best, is actively producing poverty and misery. Those who might have been born normal and healthy babies will, after twenty years of semi-starvation in a slum, produce sickly children; even though a mile away from where they eke out their existence the latest products of industrial technology and medical science may earn the admiration of the world.

The slums and shanty-towns are not only sources of infection for the whole body politic. The damaging and demoralizing effects of overcrowding and lack of housing on development are evident in other ways. Frederick Pike, referring to the serious housing deficit in Chile (where 'rentals take one of the highest percentages of income of any country in the world'), draws our attention to the effect of all this on family life. The high rate of illegitimacy, the high percentage of juvenile criminals (95) from sub-standard homes or no homes – indicate the bad conditions in which people are forced to live.*

* *Chile and the United States* (Notre Dame, 1963).

The anti-development function of the enormous deficits in housing and sanitation is not localized. That is, it does not only consist of the production of people who are inefficient and easily exhausted, and ignorant and indifferent partners in the direction of society. It is not a few individuals or even many individuals, but the whole community whose standards are lowered and features disfigured. Moreover, the poison of frustration, filth, disease and impotence of the *favelas*, slums and depressed rural areas seeps into the tissues of the whole society. In this way, people keep on producing what destroys society economically, politically and socially.

The Continuous Crippling of the New-born

It is in the young that the adult members see the future of the community. They inherit the cultural tradition and the fruits of the labours of their forefathers. They rebuild where it is necessary, and institute change. The economic and political resources for the future consist not only of their healthy bodies. Intelligent and resourceful minds are just as important. The 'poor' peoples of Asia and Latin America, and their descendants, together with the poor communities in North America, will by the year 2000 form eighty per cent of the world's producers or potential producers of machines, inventions, food, ideas, houses, books, scientific discoveries, etc. How well are the foundations being laid?

We are learning all the time about the ways in which children grow and develop. And what is known makes it all the more certain that there is a process of anti-development at work in many places destroying the valuable intellectual resources of the community where they are potentially most productive and creative. First, the development of intelligence is retarded; secondly, the educational process is denied and perverted. A healthy and intelligent person can meet with an accident or receive an injury in war which could damage his brain or his nervous system. The accident could be a personal disaster, if it permanently damaged his capacity for intelligent thought and action. We would see the accident, or the attack, as destructive of something of great value, especially if the victim was a person of unusual ability. It is much more difficult to identify the pre-emptive destruction, on a massive scale, of the mental faculties of a whole people, and still more difficult to measure the rate of erosion of a precious resource. Intelligence cannot, of course, be developed unless the brain is allowed to grow in a normal way. More significant for our purpose are the crucial phases in the development of the human brain, both in the mother's womb and soon after birth. Mistakes or deficiencies at these times are irreparable. In other words, the foetus or the infant denied at the crucial times the needed care and nourishment will as a person go through life with an underdeveloped brain. The process by which he is deprived physiologically limits the development of his intelligence.

Secondly, there is the importance for the productive and creative life of the community of learning at an early age. There are many countries today with a large proportion of children. This phenomenon occurs wherever there has been a very rapid rise in the rate of births. A number of Latin American countries have over 40–45 per cent of their population aged under fifteen. According to the 1964 UN *Demographic Yearbook*, Mexico and Brazil, together making up half of Latin America's population, had 44·3 per cent and 42·7 per cent respectively.

The fairly recent emphasis on starting school at five or six has obscured a long-known fact that children start learning and thinking in their first year, and have five or six years of intellectual development before they begin formal schooling. Their intelligence, which needs to be exercised and developed to the level needed for contemporary adult life, reaches much of its maximum capacity quite early. Half of the adult level of intelligence is reached by the age of four, and about 80 per cent by the age of eight. When large masses of children are forced by social processes to live in conditions which deprive them of the opportunity to develop their intelligence in early life, essential conditions for the rapid development of pre-modern societies are destroyed.

Human beings have a great capacity to adapt themselves to circumstances, and to survive in difficult conditions. They have survived in the slums, *favelas* and ghettoes. But intelligence is developed through the mentally stimulating effects of the variety and richness of what is seen, heard and touched, through intellectual contact between people, through a variety of play and work activities, through inquiry. For hundreds of millions of children the crucial early years are largely wasted. A comparison of present conditions in 'underdeveloped' societies with those in earlier periods, when from early infancy children started their training for living as responsible members of a human community, indicates how much children today miss. In some countries children have the opportunity to attend primary school. But education must be kept up as people grow older. Many children who are statistically counted as getting an education in fact go to school for only two or three years. According to a report issued in 1963 by the Organization of American States, out of every 1,000 Latin American children enrolled in the first grade of primary school only 136 survive to complete the five-year (in Brazil four-year) course. (Only one out of that thousand completes high school.) The respective figures for some individual countries are – Argentina, 493,7; Peru, 342,3; Chile, 305,2; Venezuela, 214,0·6; Mexico, 189,1; Brazil, 169,0·3; Colombia, 124,1. It must be remembered that in some of these countries large numbers of children never get even a year in school. In some Asian countries the record is somewhat better. According to calculations made in Gunnar Myrdal's *Asian Drama** for the 1960s the percentages of primary school entrants successfully complating primary school and high school respectively are as shown on the table on the next page.

The quality of what is taught and learned in primary school varies considerably. But it is true to say that the early 'dropouts' might as well not have gone to school as have (a) enrolled without attendance, or (b) left after a year or two of irregular 'attendance'. Like those who never even enrol in school, the

* (London, 1968), pp. 1792–3.

Country	Number of years to complete primary school	Percentage successfully completing primary school	Number of years to complete high school	Percentage successfully completing high school
Ceylon	6	85	13	7
Malaya	6	70	13	3
Indonesia	6	40	12	2
India	5	30	11	6
Philippines	6	35	10	15
Thailand	7	20	12	4
Pakistan	5	15	12	4
Burma	4	20	9	3

majority of them have no chance of getting an education in the congested, broken-down, unproductive population centres in which they eke out their lives. The process by which they learn to adapt and survive in their environment atrophies their human powers – blinds, deafens and mentally stultifies.

There is tremendous variation in the Third World in the proportion of school-age young people who complete secondary or advanced-level courses. There is also great variety in standards of academic performance. Some 'underdeveloped' countries offer free education to a pre-university level which is academically as advanced as the best *lycées* and sixth forms in affluent countries. The impact on political and economic development of the educational curriculum is of great relevance, though. For in colonial and post-colonial societies the truth may be that the more perfectly a certain type of educational system works the more of an anti-developmental force it is. Why this is so is considered later.

THE ENRICHMENT OF THE LORDS

The Ethics of Underdevelopment

The book *The Geography of Hunger*, by the distinguished Brazilian scientist and humanist, Josue de Castro, still deserves to be read, though it was written before the deprecation of world poverty and hunger had become a popular cause. De Castro was a native of north-eastern Brazil, which was as good a laboratory in which to observe the systematic operation of impoverishment as any other human community. His home state of Pernambuco had at one time been part of a fairly prosperous area, but for years it had witnessed a wasting heritage of starved bodies and miserable spirits. Though he came from the Third World in the vaguely idealistic and optimistic years just after the war, de Castro had been elected Director-General of the Food and Agriculture Organization. He described the subject of his book as 'the plague of universal hunger, that prevailing social calamity of our time'. And, as studies have shown, he was not exaggerating. Nor was he mistaken in describing universal hunger as a *social* calamity. 'Is it possible,' he asked in the book, 'to consider hunger as a phenomenon inherent in life itself, a natural and inevitable contingency like death, or should it be regarded as a social evil, a plague of man's own making?' And he went on to examine the 'explosive political and social implications' of the subject. If de Castro was correct in saying that the discussion of the solution of *the* major problem of mankind would offend and disturb, he was pointing out yet another obstacle in the path to development.

What is it that prevents people getting the nourishment they need? If the earth were too barren to feed those who live on it, then inevitably some would starve. But, as we argued earlier, the earth is certainly not barren. The nourishing plant and animal life, fresh air and water, material for dwellings, workplaces and the tools of work and raw materials it provides are adequate for many more people than the world's total population for a long time to come. Since recurring food shortages will normally tend to encourage people to increase the availability of food, we have in the fostering of this very tendency a practical solution to the initial problem of development. Several things can be done. Distribution of food can be improved, for even under the present inadequate arrangements world output of food products compares favourably with world food needs. There can also be more research into unrealized possibilities in irrigation, methods of cultivation, use of fertilizers, animal breeding, fisheries, food preservation and processing, pest control and storage. More can then be produced by the extended knowledge and practice the producers have thus gained. Yet there are obstacles in the way of those who want food which they can cook and eat to satisfy their hunger and to give them the strength and the energy to work.

One of these is the fact that foodstuffs are unobtainable by most people unless they are paid for in money or services or by the surrender of the freedom to use the energies and powers it releases. Hundreds of millions are denied their right of access to sustenance because they are denied *any* rightful access at all to the earth. They are, by the working of man-made historical forces, treated as though they are outside the human community, and are therefore compelled to renounce their claims to a share in the productive resources of the earth and their responsibility to tend, care for and develop those resources. Given the situation, what is anomalous, even scandalous, is that they are born at all. Logically speaking, it is their being alive which is the source of the problem. The basis of what has been described in this essay as 'development', on the one hand, and the rationale and ethos of the prevailing economy, on the other, are totally contradictory. Once it is assumed as 'normal' that there are people alive who have no earthly inheritance apart from their own bodies (sometimes not even that) it is understandable that those whose labours, under permission, produce the world's food are, in many societies, not free to replenish the energies they have lost, and the bodies they have worn out, in producing the food (or what can be exchanged for it). Food has been turned into a commodity, to be bought and sold for profit. This commodity character supersedes its authentic role as a means of sustenance, growth and enjoyment for human beings and animals. It is produced on orders only in so far as it can be traded or used for the profit of those who are in command. It can be destroyed on the same principle.

What starves people is not the shortage of food supplies, the infertility of the earth or their unwillingness to grow food. It is not the fact that when shortages occur in particular areas, owing to drought, flood or pestilence, food supplies do not reach them from other areas. What causes starvation is the existence of unwanted people, people without human status. This accounts for the four things that prevent starving people from acquiring or producing more wealth for their survival.

First, measures for the rational and equitable distribution of available food supplies among the living are defeated by social forces and institutions which take food supplies beyond the reach of the hungry and the starving, and the food deficit areas generally. The distribution channels flow away from the producers and the poor. Since agricultural products are to be bought and sold for maximum monetary gain, those who want to eat (partly to work) must produce the money which sellers of food and other vital materials demand. Only ownership of money, and the consequent ability to pay the price demanded, entitles one to eat, if one is not in possession of productive land. The historical emergence of the new capitalist rationality can be seen in India with British rule, the growing status of the money-lender, the town-dwelling owner of agricultural land and the domination of the countryside by the market economy. Thus it was primarily in the interests of the person who 'made the money' that food and other goods were produced, not in the interest of those who made the goods.

The social causes of starvation are indicated by the spectacle of people dying without a fight outside food shops and granaries where food is stored in plenty. In some cases people dying of hunger, and watching their children dying of hunger, actually use their last energies to deliver grain and foodstuffs they have themselves produced to landlords, grain merchants or rulers. What happened during the famous Bengal famine in India and the Honan famine in China – both during the Second World War – illustrates this. The poor are apparently ruled by some 'law' more overriding in its demands than the necessity of survival and their duty to feed their starving children.

The Bengal famine of 1943 was one of a series of famines in

z

Bengal, but it got a good deal of publicity at a time when north-eastern India was under threat of attack from Fascist Japan, and Indian opposition to the continuation of British rule was very bitter. The worst period of the famine was the second half of 1943. K. P. Chattopadhyaya, a professor at the University of Calcutta, estimated on the basis of a careful study that three-and-a-half million people died as a result of famine. The official (British) Famine Relief Commission gave the figure as one-and-a-half million.

It is interesting that during the famine, which stirred people to send money and supplies for relief from all parts of the world, the grain merchants and government agents were estimated by the Famine Commission to have made a profit of 150 crores (1,500 million) of rupees. B. M. Bhatia, in his account of the famine, writes:

Natural shortage, together with dislocation of normal channels of distribution of supplies and a tendency on the part of consumers, producers and traders to hoard the supplies, sent prices of food grains to unprecedented heights. The rise in prices began in November 1942, and continued till May 1943. There was a short respite of two months after that and prices stood still till July, when they resumed their upward course. During the next four months, which comprise the worst period of the famine, prices touched astronomical heights.

In the Burdwan district, the price of medium rice rose from Rs. 7·5 a maund on 18 November 1942 to Rs. 10·5 per maund seven days after, and Rs. 11·5 per maund on 2 December 1942. On 7 January 1943, the price stood at Rs. 14 and by May 1943 it had reached the high mark of Rs. 29·7. *This was an extremely oppressive price for the poor*, but things did not stop at that. By August 1943 rice in most of the districts was quoted at Rs. 40 to Rs. 50 per maund, while in Chittagong and some other parts of Bengal it was quoted as high as Rs. 80 per maund in October 1943.

The high prices rendered rice beyond the reach of the poor who began to starve. . . . Speculation, hoarding and profiteering in grain were regarded by the Commission as the main factors responsible for the spectacular rise in price . . .*

* B. M. Bhatia, *Famines in India 1866–1965* (Bombay, 1968), italic added.

During this period the entire leadership of the nationalist movement was in gaol for its opposition to British rule.

The Bengal famine was no exceptional phenomenon. The famine of 1896–7, the most severe in India in the nineteenth century, is also described by Dr Bhatia. Over ninety million people lived in the area affected. Crop failures owing to drought had come at a time when 'heavy exports of grain in the previous years had drained away whatever surplus there might have been'. There were grain riots in Delhi, Agra, Nagpur, Muzaffarnagar and Mhow, and protests against the continued exportation of grain. The imperial government refused to change its policy. Prices rose steeply. The poor suffered most. During the two years of the famine the normal rate of deaths in the country was exceeded by 4·5 million.

The social structure which produced the spectacle of famine in the midst of plenty remained intact after the withdrawal of the imperial rulers. As recently as 1965–6 people were dying in India because of 'famine'. A news item in a British newspaper on 17 June 1966, headed 'India's Crisis of Plenty', told a familiar story.

Paradox has always been a principal ingredient of Indian political and economic life, but the strange problem the country is now facing on the food front is bewildering beyond belief.

Two years ago millions of Indians were in the grip of famine, and mass starvation was averted only by massive imports of wheat, mainly from the United States, often at a heavy cost to national pride. Today an abundance of home-grown food has plunged India into a crisis no less acute than that caused by the worst drought in history.

Two factors have created this crisis of plenty: the heartless cupidity and greed of traders in food grains and the heart-breaking inefficiency of the Government machine.

All over North India the grain markets – called mandis – are choked with wheat brought by cultivators for what amounts to distress sales. But the grain merchants, hoping to beat down prices even further, are refusing to buy wheat; and the Government, although morally committed to take over all unsold stocks at prices previously announced, has failed to discharge its duty . . .

Since heavy rains have set in all over the country, wheat stocks have either piled up in the markets or in transit by rail, and are in danger of being damaged . . .

Much more damaging than the destruction of large stocks of grain in the immediate future is the likely effect of the present situation on next year's crop. India has been on the brink of an agricultural revolution – the use of improved seeds and fertilisers as well as modern techniques were catching on like wildfire – but now the whole impetus behind the breakthrough might collapse . . .

Unless the Government reverses its lackadaisical policies – it is not clear why the restriction on the movement of wheat between States is not lifted immediately – farmers may be driven to cutting down their production, and so force a return to the days of food shortage and humiliating dependence on America.*

Poverty Beyond Remedy

Secondly, those who can and are willing to satisfy their food and housing needs by increasing the area under production discover that they are in conflict with institutions, practices and values which keep land and other resources out of the hands of the producers of food and houses. One obvious escape from starvation is to produce more food by cultivating fertile land which is not being used. But those who grow food-crops have in some cases been driven off the land, or had their fields or crops destroyed. Where they have sought to work uncultivated land they have been prevented, even attacked. The use of food-producing land for plantations of commercial crops and the private enclosure of communal land are features of modern society.

In Southern Rhodesia the colonial government's policies had reserved forty-one million acres of the best land for less than a quarter of a million white settlers, while over 3,600,000 black Rhodesians were allowed only forty-four million acres. A select committee of the colonial legislature reported in 1957 that only 1,100,000 acres of the 31·7 million in European ownership were actually under crops. When hungry (and land-hungry)

* *Guardian*, 17 June 1966.

Africans began cultivating unused land they were driven off and their houses and villages razed to the ground. Over 100,000 Africans were reported to have been expelled in this way in the decade ending 1960. In Guatemala, Peru and several other countries the denial of land to hungry people willing and eager to grow food has been common. For example, in the Pasco province of Peruvian Andes Ayllu Indian communities, whose fully legal land-rights had continually been encroached by the US Ferro de Pasco Corporation, decided to reoccupy their own land peacefully. They were attacked and driven off, and some of them killed.

Thirdly, the world is divided into an international order of nation-states which strive to get maximum power and advantage for themselves. However murderous the competition to secure exclusive advantages and powers, it is justified in terms of national interest. The division of the world into competing national economies accounts partly for the fact that hungry people who are willing and eager to work to produce what they need are unable to do so. This phenomenon, now taken for granted, is the monopoly by the ruling classes of much of the world's fertile agricultural land and its products. People who want to migrate from famine areas to food-rich or potentially food-rich areas come up against boundaries of race or nation which they are not allowed to cross.

The earth has much more land capable of producing wheat, rice, coarse grains, dairy products, cattle, pigs, poultry, sheep and goats, other edible birds and animals, fish, nuts, beans, vegetables, fats and oils, sugar, fruit (fresh and dried), cotton, wool, jute, sisal, leather, rubber, timber (for fuel, construction and pulp), minerals and other similar products than is being put to careful use. Frugal, hard-working, ingenious and adaptable peasants, such as those in China and Japan, have never been unwilling to pioneer in new lands or to eliminate the shortages of food and fibres which have given rise to malnutrition, deficiency diseases and premature death.

Even land which can be classed as 'marginal' for agricultural purposes can be turned to good use. The peasants of Tachai, in China's north-western province of Shansi, were fired by a highly political determination to revolutionize the material conditions in which they had lived. Their achievements show what could be done in the most difficult natural conditions.

The greater part of mankind is, in fact, shut out of vast areas of the earth. The rulers in Moscow control access to nine million square miles of land, some of it seized from China; to all but the Soviet Union's 240 million (and restrictions apply even to them) the use of this vast territory – a good part of the earth's surface – is denied. Yet the Soviet rulers continue to encroach on foreign territory. North America's population, also about 240 million, has exclusive use of seven million square miles. The European peoples settled outside Europe prevent the normal and rational process of migration by cutting off millions of square miles of land from the non-Europeans; for there are also areas of Latin America, Africa and even Asia from which they exclude the potential native producers. Food production in the United States is actually kept down, through government-granted financial incentives. Within countries, apartheid and other forms of racial segregation define the geographical boundaries which must not be crossed.

Fourthly, any rational comparison of the ample quantities of food stocks and living space with unsatisfied people is contradicted by the prevailing systems of moral and economic reasoning. The consumption and waste of food and living space by a few takes precedence over the needs and the right to life of the hungry and homeless. Even in communities where people are dying of starvation a good deal of 'normal' economic activity is going on. Meat, grain, fruit, etc. are being produced or imported, building is going on, drainage being laid, roads being built, metals being mined. The hungry who may seek to solve the problem of hunger by working to produce more – food, perhaps, or minerals which they can sell for food – find that they are involved in a fustrating process. They are working to produce what is going to be wasted by the affluent. They can build, but what they build are large mansions, swimming pools, casinos, even cathedrals, from which they will be excluded. What they grow may, if they are lucky, come back to the poor in the dust-bins. It has been the experience of peasant cultivators that if, driven by the needs of their families, they have worked harder to increase productivity, what they get is still the left-overs of those whose profits or luxuries have first priority. This obstacle to development is rooted in the social structure and the class values and attitudes which go with it.

'Hungry people,' according to Professor Harrison Brown, 'are combustible' (see Chapter 1 above). The instinctive reaction of anyone who is being strangled is to struggle for breath and to fight off the assailant. The reason for the reaction is not aggressiveness or love of violence, but the fact that a living person does not want to perish. The struggle to break the stranglehold is as much an unavoidable response to a warning of grave danger as is the avoidance of pain. It is in order to live, and go on living, that people have worked hard in more or less difficult circumstances. People know that the chances of ending chronic debility and starvation are increased if the social order which systematically destroys them is changed. Revolt as a solution to the problems of desperate poverty and hunger has been common in the past. Aliveness is expressed partly in the way in which people respond to the crushing of the human spirit and human dignity (something different from aristocratic or bourgeois notions of 'dignity') and to the reduction of themselves to levels far below those enjoyed by other people. This inherent characteristic of man appears to be one of the guarantees of historical progress and of peace.

It did not need book learning for people to be aware that change, decay and renewal characterized historical existence. Those who work, and on whose work the continued existence of rich and powerful classes depends from day to day, were able to understand the economic facts of life. If in return for their taxes and labours they got some security for themselves and their families, and some services, such as irrigation, water, education and the administration of justice, they might tolerate some abuses and even some loss of their freedom and their human status. But when injustices, land-seizures and taxation become intolerable, then they were ready to revolt.

'The people are forced by the officials to revolt' was the slogan of the White Lotus Rebellion, which began in 1796 and lasted eight years. The White Lotus were a sect in China's Shantung province, where the consequences of the breakdown of order and justice were being felt by the peasantry. In the mid-nineteenth century there was the prolonged rebellion of the Niens, for whom 'robbing the rich and relieving the poor' was the ideal. They were defeated in 1868. Above all, there was the great Taiping Revolution, the greatest of its kind in the world in the nineteenth century. These and other revolts were endemic in China. They were a regular feature of its political life. In India, too, popular revolts were much more frequent than is usually supposed.

The 'underground' which comes into being in times of great oppression and economic decline includes elements which are not political. Enterprising and adventurous types of people, who cannot get access to officially sanctioned positions from which they could live by exploiting the labour of others, take to making a living by banditry and extortion. They rob rich and poor alike. In periods of decline in China, India, Indonesia and other countries the people had to suffer the exactions of bandits and dacoits, and not only of landlords, money-lenders and officials.

Oppression in all its forms is part of the impoverishing process; it crushes the human spirit, whatever is free and creative, whatever is daring and full of hope. It gives rise, however, to countervailing forces which may in time bring it to an end. To weaken and disarm these forces, which alone can bring dying communities back to life, social and psychological devices have to be employed to make people insensitive to the human worth outraged by oppressive institutions and practices and to make them feel guilty about their desire for changing the system under which they suffer. The mass of the people can be made to accept their condition as something necessary and immutable, divinely ordered, just, or more bearable than the consequences of self-reliant efforts to change things or to revolt against them. This acceptance is a major obstacle in the way of progress towards economic development. There are forces hard at work in many countries to 'modernize' this obstacle and increase its effectiveness. They use bogus religion and anti-Communist brainwashing to keep people in order; to tranquillize the oppressed and to prevent the creators of wealth from removing what stands in the way of increasing production and welfare. Religion and ideology often condone the terrible violence for which the oppressors are responsible. They produce spiritual torpor and deaden the sensibility. They are then anti-human and anti-development.

THE OPPRESSIVE HERITAGE OF THE OLD COLONIALISM

In Chapter 2, both underdevelopment and rapid development were discussed as fairly recent phenomena. The widely spread notion that non-European societies were traditionally backward, that they had stagnated for centuries as primitive agricultural communities, is false. It still gets in the way of one's understanding of the present-day dynamics of a poverty-creating system. The legal, economic and social changes forced by the victorious imperialist powers on the countries they conquered and ruled – the British in India, Ceylon, South Africa and Nigeria; the French in Vietnam, Cambodia and Algeria; the Japanese in Korea and parts of China; the Americans in the Philippines and Puerto Rico; the Portuguese in Brazil and Angola; the Spanish in Peru and Mexico; and several of them in China – determined the colonial foundations of politics, law, property, communications, education, industry, agriculture, trade and social life. The way this colonial heritage took shape can be illustrated in the case of the British impact on India, beginning in Bengal.

The wealth of Bengal about a century before British conquest [writes M. K. Sinha] has been vividly described by Bernier.

According to him Bengal produced rice in such abundance that it not only furnished its neighbours but many remote places. Bengal's surplus rice was transported by sea to Masulipatam and to the ports of the Coromandel coast, Ceylon and the Maldives. Its sugar was exported to Golconda, Arabia, Mesopotamia and Persia. Of commodities of value, cotton cloths and silk stuff, Bengal was the great magazine, not only for the empire of the Great Moghuls as far as Lahore and Kabul, but also for the neighbouring kingdoms and for Europe.*

The reputation of Bengali manufacture and trade in silk and cotton cloths was very high. Bengal's chief exports to the Coromandel coast through Calcutta included 'grain, pulse, sugar, saltpetre, molasses, ginger, long-pepper, clarified butter, oil, silk wrought and unwrought, muslins, turmeric and borax' and other articles such as hempen rope. The East India Company changed this. After the battle of Plassey, in 1757, they were the victorious power in Bengal, and their employees were able to arrange the administration of production and trade so as to amass and extract fortunes from India. Material conditions in pre-British India cannot be inferred from the conditions that obtained *after* the British began their own development of India.

Even at the end of the eighteenth century economic conditions in India were advanced, and her 'methods of production and of industrial and commercial organization would stand comparison with those in vogue in any other part of the world', according to Mrs Vera Anstey. No doubt the conditions in the interior, where lack of communications was an obstacle to trade, and where the decadence and corruption of the ruling castes held sway, were not what they were in more progressive areas like Gujerat, Bengal or Malabar. Educational levels and literacy were far from what they became in Europe. But owing to the financial and trading organization of enterprising Indians their manufactures could compete with British goods in the home market of the most advanced European nation, and there was a drain of gold into India. To counter this, Britain erected high

* M. K. Sinha, *Economic History of Bengal* (Calcutta, 1956).

tariff barriers against the import of Indian goods, just at the time when European prosperity was beginning. The effect on India's economic development of the restriction of the European market for her manufactures was severe. Her government and economy were also restructured in ways favourable to those who aspired to imperial rule and world markets. Textile exports to India began as a trickle early in the nineteenth century; by the middle of it they had become a flood. British remoulding of India helped to stifle material and spiritual forces which might have brought about indigenous development, which in turn might have initiated much-needed social and political renewal.

Given the political circumstances, neither the high-quality products nor the coarser cloths made locally for the ordinary people could compete with the cheap Lancashire machine-made cotton goods.

The value of British cotton exports to India shot up from £0·11 million in 1813 to £3·86 millions in 1840, £5·22 millions in 1850, and £6·30 millions in 1856. In 1814, the quantity of cotton goods exported to India from Britain was 818,208 yards; in 1835, the figure had risen to 51,777,277 yards. The British manufacturers had already made sufficient inroads into the Indian market before the railways began to traverse the length and breadth of the country. After the revolution in means of transport, the flood of cheap imports from abroad not only undermined the competitive power of the urban weaving industry producing finer silk and cotton fabrics, but it also made its way into the rural areas thereby threatening the livelihood of the village weaver.

Though the most important the cotton textile was not the only industry which suffered as a result of foreign competition. Urban industries producing silk, woollen cloth, brass, copper and bell-metal wares, enamelled jewellery and stone-carving, embroidery and manufacture of papiermâché met a similar fate. *Industrial labour was thrown out of its traditional occupations and in its search for livelihood turned to agriculture.* The village artisan, except the weaver, did not have to face any direct competition from abroad. But the gradual change in tastes and modes of living of the people that came in the wake of the opening up of the village to the influence of foreign modes of living and consumption led to the gradual replacement of locally made products by cheap machine-made substitutes.*

We see in this process the reverse of the transformation of the pre-industrial economy in Europe. Society regressed into a more primitive condition. Nineteenth-century India was further from the threshold of industrial modernization than eighteenth-century India. The percentage of the workforce engaged in non-agricultural production declined. In addition, the newly developing urban capitalist class had the advantages for accumulation of wealth that British-imposed laws and notions of property provided. But they had no interest in setting up rival new industrial enterprises in the rural areas to compete with industry in Britain. Such meagre opportunities for technical and medical training as were provided by Company and imperial authorities before the 1914–18 War were suited only to a pre-modern economy.

Even further-reaching changes were taking place than the ruin of Indian handicraft industry and the consequent destruction of the economic and social balance in the village communities. These changes were the results of decisions of policy of India's new rulers, and had a great deal to do with the size and seriousness of the problem of world poverty which appeared in the years when machine industry became a world-wide feature. The reader will be familiar with the conventional features of an underdeveloped economy – the high proportion of the population dependent on the agricultural sector for employment, and the uneconomic organization of agriculture. These items cannot be explained either by the traditional practices and institutions or, in India's case, by the consequences of India's suddenly being turned into a captive market for cheaply produced British manufactures. How, then, is one to explain the high percentage of the population in a low-productivity agricultural sector, or the lack of diversification? How did the obstacles to development which have been

* Bhatia, *op. cit.*, p. 17, italic added.

discussed come to be so firmly planted that the restoration of the land and the people to their proper productive functions appears almost impossible? How is the low production *per capita* and per acre to be explained in a country which for millennia has known the art of agriculture? Questions of this kind (relevant to China, Indonesia and Vietnam as well) can be answered only by reference to historical developments which the economic historian, Surendra Patel, has called, with good reason, 'the most dramatic social transformation in the entire history of Indian rural society'.*

The view that 'overpopulation' is responsible for the large numbers of landless and impoverished in pre-partition India is untenable because it is made with no reference to the far-reaching developments which followed India's subjection. An arbitrary decision of Lord Cornwallis in 1793 made the *zamindars*, the men who used to be responsible for collecting and remitting revenue from the cultivators to the ruling authorities, private owners of the land which had belonged collectively, in the traditional sense, to the cultivators who paid the taxes. This *zamindari* system, designed to increase revenue for the British from the cultivators, was a radical change in the economic and social system, destroying the status which the producers, even in the far-from-ideal conditions of pre-British India, enjoyed. In the southern parts of the peninsula, in the Madras and Bombay areas, another system was imposed, just as arbitrarily, with regard to British and not Indian interests. Here too, with the elimination of the land-holding system, long-established institutions and practices which secured the land for those who lived and worked on it were swept away. This came to be called the *raiyatwari* system, as the individual cultivator of a plot, the *raiyat*, had private 'ownership' of it attributed to him by the new law-makers. The land on which people had taken it for granted that they could live and work was made transferable at the will of the new owner, and could be inherited, mortgaged and generally treated as a commodity. Previously, the services rendered to

* *Essays on Economic Transition* (Bombay, 1965), p. 5.

the community by the cultivators and the village artisans and manufacturers, and the satisfaction of their wants, had not required the possession of wealth in cash. The cultivator was now required to supply an expensively maintained foreign government with the cash it wanted. But his skill was in producing grain or other food products and fibres – the substance of what the community needed – not money. The alien rulers had introduced complicated laws and institutions which he could not understand, much less control or adapt to; and they insisted on seizing the land if tax-assessments were not met. The pace at which rural indebtedness increased and at which cultivators became landless labourers was a testimony to the way in which the new systems worked.

In his valuable essay, 'Agricultural Labourers in India and Pakistan', Dr Patel reviews the information available on 'the major economic changes that took place in the agrarian society during the nineteenth century and how they affected cultivation and handicrafts, the supporting pillars of Indian rural economy . . .'.* He refers to the difficulties the cultivators had in paying the compulsory twice-yearly fixed amounts for which they became liable, whether or not there was a crop. In his analysis he relates how the 'unholy trinity' – 'heavy cash revenue demands, famines and world price fluctuations' – afflicted the producers and assisted the rise of the money-lenders to a dominating role in agrarian society. Figures for rural indebtedness in British India are not available for the nineteenth century. But between 1901 and 1938 the total multiplied sixfold. The selling by the government of the property of vast numbers of cultivators for the collection of land-revenue, the dispossession of the peasants, the concentration of land-ownership in the hands of a few money-lenders and absentee landlords, and the rapid growth in the class of landless labourers were accompanied, in the nineteenth century, by numerous rebellions by the peasants.

The establishment of colonial rule committed India irrevocably to the pauperization of those who worked on the land.

* *ibid.*, pp. 11–12.

Since land had become a commodity, money invested in buying it would bring in rent as income. Money-lending would help in the acquisition of more agricultural land. The burden of taxation imposed by the expensive government apparatus was borne by the rural areas, not the towns, in which the British, too, lived. Artisans and cultivators, who had become wage-labourers, and peasant cultivators who were progressively pauperized and driven off the land, could have little hope of being productive. For nothing like the more-than-compensatory construction of a new material order taking place in capitalist England could take place in this imperial possession.

The overpopulated rural areas were deprived of some of their food-producing land for the cultivation of commercial crops. Moreover, since a country which had once exported manufactures was brought to a state where it was needed to supply only raw agricultural commodities, part of the diminishing food-stocks had to be exported. Rising food prices played their part in reducing the standard of living. The mass of Indian people eventually could survive only at an uncivilized, or even subhuman, level. A whole complex of social, economic and political policies and practices had brought a considerable part of mankind to a condition of gross poverty, malnutrition, ignorance, unemployment, technological backwardness and social disintegration.

The decisions which helped to bring all this about were the consequences of the policies of financiers, businessmen and politicians who used India for the economic development of capitalist Britain. Society, as J. S. Furnivall said of similar developments in Java, 'relapsed to a lower level'. In Java it was the Dutch who were the foreigners mainly responsible, and, for good reasons, policies did not favour the emergence of a class of newly affluent natives who lived in the towns, and acquired communal land and other economic resources as 'private property'. But the Indonesian people too had developed what were by pre-Industrial Revolution standards complex economies, and found themselves turned by the economic forces which were given free rein under colonial rule into 'a nation of cultivators'.*

The condition of poverty at the time of 'independence' was not an ancient, pre-colonial, inheritance; it was not simply 'traditional'. It was created; it was a social product. The class formed by those in India who inherited the power and influence of those who had adapted to the British system and enriched themselves during the period of British occupation and rule understandably desired the preservation of the deformed social order. The prevailing assumptions and laws about 'property' and 'rights' protected a social system in which the means of life and the resources which alone could permit creative activity and economic progress among the people had become commodities. As in other countries – Brazil, for example – the tradition of development was one which created underdevelopment, as Josue de Castro and others have demonstrated. It was a tradition of false modernization. The state of mind which conforms to, accepts and preserves the colonial inheritance is more backward than that of pre-civilized man. This helps to explain why, while the middle classes were an innovating, revolutionary force at one time in Europe, the Third World peoples were burdened with extremely backward, reactionary moneyed classes in what were travesties of civilized centres – the disintegrating cities of Latin America, Asia and Africa.

* See J. S. Furnivall, *Netherlands India* (London, 1939), pp. 39–45. The native *élites* had a large store of responsibility for Indonesia's decline.

CHAPTER 5

Anti-Development: Malignant Forms of Growth

HUNGER, overpopulation, disease, homelessness, disintegration of family life, misery, insecurity and violence are on the increase among mankind because they are demonstrably being bred or produced faster than ever before in world history. The argument that poverty is inherent in a certain type of social system is not complete. The demonstration of the way the social system (and technology) of anti-development works (or used to work) in practice in various parts of the Third World must continue in this chapter and the next. This essay has come to the point of considering why the incomes of most of the people in the poor countries are so meagre. Why, indeed, is the little that the poor have being taken away?

THE DYNAMICS OF THE WORLD-WIDE GAP IN STANDARDS OF LIFE

The Status-Gap: Few Rich and Many Poor

The processes of anti-development are assisted by the concentration of political and economic *power* in the hands of a small minority seeking the advances primarily of itself or the class to which it belongs. The monopoly of power which is exercised in the control and direction of what is produced also effectually prevents the mass of the people from increasing what they create and produce for themselves. If they seek to mobilize the community's productive resources in order to increase human welfare, they discover that they lack the necessary power. The monopoly of power also deprives them of the initiative in inventing new and better techniques. The poor may know what they lack, and how they may begin to get it; but they are powerless to get the economy moving in the proper direction. The minority who have taken possession of the land, and who control agricultural, industrial, tax and other related policies, will direct the productive process, at minimum cost to themselves and their allies and associates at home and abroad, to the satisfaction of their wants. For they are linked, as we must discover, to powerful foreign and supra-national forces, which have identical interests. Further, in countries like Brazil, Indonesia, South Africa and Thailand the small group in power uses scarce national resources to maintain powerful armed forces and police, and other modern devices for surveillance and repression, in case the psychological and ideological devices mentioned earlier fail to disarm the poor.

Let us look at Latin America and the Caribbean islands, an area of seven million square miles of land, with a population in 1966 of just over 240 million – roughly the same as the area and population of North America and the Soviet Union.* In those provinces of China which cover the area lived in and cultivated intensively for many centuries, not very long ago 524 million lived in an area 1,124,100 square miles in extent. The Latin American continent, therefore, is not over-crowded. But it manifests the extreme inequalities of income which characterize Third World countries before they start the development process.

One United Nations estimate for the years 1949–55 showed that the 'top' five per cent of the people in Latin America (not all natives) received thirty-three per cent of the total income, while the bottom fifty per cent of people enjoyed sixteen per cent of total income. The differences are greater than they are in some other areas where poverty is produced for the mass of the people. The *per capita* income of the first group was 600 per cent of the continental average, that of the second thirty-two per cent.

* With 7,470,000 and 8,650,000 square miles respectively.

*Distribution of Income: a Comparison**

Relative differences in the distribution of personal
income in Latin America, Western Europe and the United States

Income brackets	LATIN AMERICA			WESTERN EUROPE			UNITED STATES		
	Population (per cent)	Income (per cent)	Differences with respect to the average of personal income (average =100)	Income (per cent)	Differences with respect to the average of personal income (average =100)	Income (per cent)	Differences with respect to the average of personal income (average =100)
High	5	33	600	22	436	20	400
Intermediate	45	51	113	56	124	57	127
Low	50	16	32	22	44	23	46

This same pattern is to be observed in the different countries. The Chilean economist and agronomist, Jacques Chonchol, cites the following figures (published in 1963) in an article on land tenure and development in Latin America.† In Peru 'large land-owners and capitalists' (o·1 per cent of the active population) and 'technicians, top executives, and small capitalists' (o·4 per cent) obtained 19·9 and 6·3 per cent respectively of the income. Contrasted with this o·5 per cent who took 26·2 per cent of the income, there were the two groups at the lower end. They were the 'proletariat' (22·8 per cent with 14·2) and 'mountain-dwelling peasant class' (56·7 per cent with 12·9 per cent): 27·1 per cent of the income of a poor country among 79·5 per cent of the 'active population'. The differentials in *per capita* income are staggering even when the poorest are lumped

* From *Economic Development of Latin America in the Post-War Period* (New York, 1964).

† The greater part of the article is reproduced in my *From Gandhi to Guevara: The Polemics of Revolt* (London, 1970). The original is to be found in Claudio Veliz (ed.), *Obstacles to Change in Latin America* (London, 1965).

together. Peru's 1966 population was twelve million. Therefore
a fifth of the total income went to the 12,000 land-owners and
capitalists; while any group of 12,000 among the peasant class
was allowed on average about 1/4300 of the total. The comparison between the 'top' 0·1 per cent and the 'bottom' 0·1
per cent could be unimaginable.*

Figures for Chile and for Venezuela are also of interest. The
figures, given in the report, *The Economic Development of Latin
America in the Post-War Period,* do not distinguish people by
classes but by size of income.

Chile: Distribution of personal income, 1960

	Percentage of total population		Share of total personal income		Average income per unit in relation to the national average	
Category I	50		15·6		31	
Sub-category I A		31·7		5·6		18
Sub-category I B		18·3		10·0		55
Category II	45		59·0		131	
Sub-category II A		37·3		40·8		109
Sub-category II B		7·7		18·2		236
Category III	3		11·7		390	
Category IV	2		13·7		685	
Total	100		100			

In very rough terms, a third of the people in Chile and in
Venezuela, too, form a class with a *per capita* income one
fortieth or one fiftieth that enjoyed by their rulers, the top two
per cent. Private ownership of the agricultural, industrial and
other material resources of the community by the small group
in power is directly related to this unhappy coexistence of
super-rich and super-poor. In Mexico, where an urbanized

* Peru's *per capita* income was given in 1964 as $240. The dominant
class of landlords and capitalists would get 199 times the national average.

Venezuela: Distribution of personal income, 1957

	Percentage of total population		Share of total personal income		Average income per unit in relation to the national average	
Category I	50		11·0		22	
Sub-category I A		35·5		6·0		17
Sub-category I B		14·5		5·0		34
Category II	45		58·5		130	
Sub-category II A		18·0		11·7		65
Sub-category II B		11·0		12·2		111
Sub-category II C		16·0		34·6		216
Category III	3		12·8		427	
Category IV	2		17·7		885	
Total	100		100			

oligarchy gradually took control after the revolutionary years, the share of the national income available to the 'bottom' fifty per cent of Mexicans fell, according to studies made by Ifigenia Navarrete, from 19·1 per cent in 1950 to 15·6 per cent in 1957.

The situation which produces growing inequality is also manifested in the percentage of people who, on account of the social structure, are prevented from acquiring the knowledge and power commanded by the advanced literacy and 'numeracy' necessary for modern living. According to the 1950 figures for Latin America, (a) the proportion of the total population illiterate at the age of fifteen and over was very high; (b) the proportion of those aged 5–14 who were enrolled in (not necessarily regularly attending) primary schools was low; and (c) the percentage of the 15–19 age-group enrolled in secondary schools was small. Education is kept as the privileged preserve of the classes in power, who, like the prudent colonial rulers, allow a share in it to those whose services and loyalties they need: managers, clerks, police, accountants and the like.

We can conclude that, (d) regardless of the statistics of what is spent by the state on education, the policy is such as to modernize and strengthen the dominant classes, and to retard, impoverish and debilitate the vast mass of manual workers.

Country*	Percentage of population aged fifteen and over who are illiterate	Percentage of 5–14 age-group attending primary schools	Percentage of 15–19 age-group in secondary schools
Argentina	14	66	21
Bolivia	68	24	07
Brazil	51	26	10
Chile	20	66	18
Colombia	43	28	07
Costa Rica	21	49	07
Cuba	22	49	—
Dominican Republic	57	40	07
Ecuador	44	41	09
El Salvador	61	31	04
Guatemala	71	22	07
Haiti	89	15	—
Honduras	65	22	03
Mexico	43	39	04
Nicaragua	62	23	03
Panama	30	54	24
Paraguay	34	51	09
Peru	58	44	—
Uruguay	15	62	17
Venezuela	48	40	06

Those attending secondary schools in 1950 as a percentage of the 15–19 age-group for certain other countries are: Canada

* From Table on p. 50, *Economic Development of Latin America in the Post-War Period*. The illiteracy figures are probably understated in some cases. Guatemala's, for example, are believed by some students of its economy to be higher. It is instructive to examine Venezuela's high *per capita* income figures in the light of these statistics.

forty-three, France seventy-six, Italy fifty-two, Japan eighty, Netherlands sixty-two, Sweden fifty-seven, United Kingdom sixty-nine, United States sixty. These percentages have increased in recent years. But Cuba has virtually eliminated illiteracy, and nearly doubled the number in primary and secondary schools.

There have been schools and universities in Latin America as good as the best in Europe and North America. Some of them (in Córdoba, for example) have in the past played roles of great historical importance, and they still could help either to widen or to narrow the gap in power and modern resources. But, in the main, university faculties tend to be literary and philosophical, rather than technological and scientific, and to cater to a small, leisured and affluent minority which seeks access to European and North American upper-class society. Latin America's intellectuals are second to none. But when educational opportunities for most of the young are negligible, the large amounts spent on Western-style universities for a few are wasteful. In Guatemala, where according to Professor Alonso Bauer Paiz, ninety-seven per cent of the population will soon be illiterate if present demographic trends continue and present structures remain intact, the universities can hardly be said to be in the same country as the stricken peasantry.*

The shape which increasing poverty takes geographically is to be noticed in the diverging and grossly unequal development of coast and interior, city and countryside, and different regions or provinces within countries. The United Nations study from which we have been quoting worked out, in regard to Brazil and Colombia, the ratio of the income of the richest and the poorest of the states. Brazil's richest state is Guanabara (which includes Rio de Janeiro). Its poorest is Piaui, in the north-east. Colombia's richest state is Cundimarca, while the poorest is Choco.

These figures make sense only if they are correlated with the complex analysis of sensitive and intelligent students of Latin

* See Eduardo Galeano, *Guatemala: Occupied Country* (New York, 1969) p. 95.

Extreme disparities in regional income per capita *in some countries* (per capita *income, average of the country* = 100).

Country	Year	Average *per capita* income of region with highest level		Average *per capita* income of region with lowest level		Ratio
Brazil	1960	State of Guanabara	291	State of Piaui	29	10
Colombia	1953	Dept. of Cundimarca	185	Dept. of Choco	17	11
USA	1960	Delaware	126	Mississippi	53	2·5

American society.* We can make only a cursory study of them. Before noting some of the implications of these figures, however, we should mention the situation in other parts of the world. For the existence of great prosperity and affluence amidst the worst poverty is to be found not only in Latin America. It used to exist in China not many years ago. It is to be seen in south-east Asia, in countries such as the Philippines, Indonesia, Laos and Thailand. Some people are getting a large enough income to become millionaires in Bangkok and Manila as easily as in Lima and Caracas. But in the countryside in north-east Thailand and Central Luzon men, women and children cannot get even a meagre diet with their income.

The Power Gap: Few Rich over Many Poor

How can we explain the enormous disparities in income and standards of living? Clearly, the vast majority of the people in the low-income countries are not simply careless about the material conditions of life. The hunger and the thirst (for in some of these areas even drinking water is scarce) are as un-

---

* They need therefore to be interpreted in the light of the systematic and comprehensive political and economic analyses made by Latin Americans like Celso Furtado, Josue de Castro and Orlando Fals Borda.

bearable for them as they would be for anyone else. The Latin American figures show that millions of people have a *per capita* income one sixth or one fifth of the already low national average. This estimate is confirmed by United Nations studies that show that, excluding Argentina and Uruguay, more than sixty per cent of rural families have a *per capita* income below $60 – a very low figure, considering high prices in several countries. Conditions in Thailand and the Philippines appear to be similar. In terms of food, clothing, housing, amusements, etc. – their income must be fantastically low.*

For producers in the modern world, in which national communities have to be well-informed, 'tough' and shrewd in order to make their way, education is vital. (It was not so in more isolated, rural and traditional societies of pre-modern times which satisfied their own needs and had enough of a cultural tradition to enrich the mind and spirit.) Today, without the ability to read and write a modern language, and an elementary training in the arts and sciences, there is almost absolute intellectual and cultural poverty. The misery, indignity and impotence of poverty is made all the more obvious when increasing prosperity is immediately visible. Both because the spread of modern knowledge would tend to equalize opportunities and because literacy would in some countries earn the right to vote, education, as we have noticed, is a source of power (and hence economic advancement) which must be denied to the people.

The monopoly of the powers of government is thus an economic asset. Frederick Pike, writing about Chile's 'culture of poverty' a few years ago, described the redistribution process between 1940 and 1953 which worked to the disadvantage of lower manual-class labourers, who formed fifty-seven per cent of the active population. Their income increased by seven

* The Inter-American Development Bank in its Fifth Annual Report in 1966 noted that 'most of the increase in production recorded' in Latin America was in commercial export crops, while '*per capita* domestic output of nutritionally important products such as meat, milk and eggs seems to have actually declined'.

per cent. The 'top' group, consisting of proprietors, self-employed and workers in the various services increased their income by sixty per cent. This kind of 'regressive redistribution' forms part of the dynamism of anti-development, even in a country in which, according to a 1942 estimate, '77 per cent of the working force did not earn sufficient income to provide a single man with a decent and respectable mode of life. Only 0·3 per cent enjoyed income adequate to provide the minimal standards of respectable living for a family of four.'* Conditions such as these, according to Pike, can be accounted for by an 'outmoded, non-productive, semi-feudalistic land and social structure that denies to the serf (*inquilino*) any right to a share in the riches of society beyond what his master may paternalistically dole out to him'. Pike writes of 9·7 per cent of agrarian property-holders owning eighty-six per cent of Chile's arable land, while 76·4 per cent owned 5·2 per cent of it at the time of which he was writing. While differences of income and living standards cannot be attributed entirely to the pattern of land-ownership, the connection between the two is strong. Throughout Latin America, 'operators of "sub-family-sized smallholdings" and landless farm workers' together make up a high proportion of families in agriculture: out of every hundred 60·9 in Argentina, 68·4 in Brazil, 70·7 in Chile, 70·2 in Colombia, 86·1 in Ecuador, 88·2 in Guatemala and 88·4 in Peru.† The concentration of wealth in the hands of a few and in urban areas or provinces where the land-owners live, is understandable. Given the denial of economic opportunities, there is almost nothing that most of the people in the rural areas can do to increase their income. Chonchol shows that 1·4 per cent of

* *Chile and the United States* (Notre Dame, 1963), pp. 273–4. Mrs Navarrete's study of Mexico showed that while business executives and the self-employed increased their incomes over a period by seventy per cent, wage-earners achieved only a thirteen per cent increase.

† From Solon Barraclough, 'The Agrarian Problem', Table 1, p. 49, Veliz (ed.), *op. cit.* The figures are for 1950 in the case of Brazil, Chile and Guatemala, 1960 in the case of Argentina, Colombia, Ecuador and Peru.

the total holdings of land (105,000 out of seven-and-a-half million) accounted for sixty-five per cent of Latin America's 723·6 million hectares of agricultural land. Some land-owners own more than one 'holding'. But, leaving that fact out of calculation for the moment, we have to see the consequences for production, expansion of production, investment and even industrialization in this major region of just over 100,000 persons owning 470 million hectares. A group of people, no larger than the population of a small city, own an area of the best land in Latin America equal to 1·8 million square miles, when the total area of India is 1·3 million square miles. (That is an area equal to twenty times the total area of the United Kingdom.) The same people are likely to have owned most of the urban land too.

Much of the land in *latifundia* (large holdings) is utilized below capacity or is not in cultivation at all. Yet, as we shall see, the acquisition of land by the rich continues. Brazil, a country of about the same area as China, had only 3·35 million agricultural holdings in 1960. The decisions of a few people therefore have enormous importance. Figures from the 1950 census help to explain this phenomenon. There were then *latifundia* in Brazil each covering a quarter-of-a-million acres (100,000 hectares).* On the other hand, 500,000 *minifundia* occupied only 0·5 per cent of the farm land. Guatemala, one of the poorest countries in the Third World, is very much smaller in size and population than Brazil. A study of the 1960 Census† revealed that twenty per cent of the *fincas* (farms) occupied ninety per cent of the farm area. Twenty-two of the largest *fincas* covered 13·4 per cent of the total area, and belonged to three owners. The United Fruit Company, which owned 650,000 acres, was the largest *latifundista*; only eight per cent of its land was cultivated. Whereas the *minifundia* were 100 per cent cultivated, only 5·7 per cent of the large properties were cultivated. The high rents are not a sign of a shortage of land,

* For those not mathematically inclined, this area of 1,000 square kilometres is about 386 square miles.
† By Mario Montefiore Toledo in *Guatemala, monografia sociologica.*

but a measure to force the mass of people to accept the status of landless labourers.*

The *latifundistas* have no reason for increasing production. The fact that hundreds of millions in the world are going hungry is not reason enough for them. Just as their political monopoly is a source of enrichment, so their monopoly of land and other productive resources is a source of growing power. In Brazil only two per cent of the land has been cultivated. That is as much as the Brazilian land-owners and allied groups need to cultivate for economic and political reasons. What labour they want they get almost free from people who are in no position to demand adequate wages or land. Here, as elsewhere, the only other social groups of any account are the small numbers of independent farmers, the industrialists, a few organized industrial workers, professional people and officials, and the army. The land-owners can generally get the state to build the roads and irrigation works they want, keep down taxes and protect their interests. Their power is used to see that labour is cheap. The cheapness of labour and their own affluence act as disincentives to mechanization or investment in progressive methods. It is only when the labourers show a marked unwillingness to tolerate the conditions in which they have to live and work that it becomes politic to expel them and

* Some figures of landholdings in the Arab lands can be compared with those for Latin America.

Distribution of landed property in the Arab East at the middle of the twentieth century

Country	Year	per cent of total registered area in hands of		
		Small-scale owners	Medium-scale owners	Large-scale owners
Iraq	1951	15·7	17·2	67·1
Syria	1952	13·0	38·9	49·0
Egypt	1950	35·3	30·4	34·2
Transjordan	1950	36·3	49·5	14·2

From Gabriel Baer, *Population and Society in the Arab East* (London, 1964), p. 146.

use labour-saving methods. The management skills which the land-owners have are those which enable them to devise various means to tie the peasant to the existing structure. Heavy land-rent and low wages, often below even the inadequate legal minimum, are paid in chits redeemable only at the land-owner's store at reduced value, and credit is made available at very high interest rates. René Dumont, investigating the status of Chilean *inquilinos* around Santiago, found that 'rent' for grazing, plot and 'house' amounted to forty-five per cent of daily wages. He also observed in Pernambuco a *fazenda* shop which sold inferior goods at specially high prices and in short measure. The system of *cambão* in north-eastern Brazil obliges the workers to provide one day of free labour every week. This way of increasing the indebtedness of the peasant increases his inability to improve his condition or to leave the land-owners' domains. The methods and organization of the existing political system is such as to make it the easiest thing in the world to squeeze the poor and make big profits; in its own terms it is highly efficient.

Where communities exist outside the framework of the system various means are used to integrate them into this economic system. An ILO report describes this process in relation to an indigenous tribe in Colombia, 'where there was originally common ownership of land and tools, and collective work'.

Encroachments and alienation of land in various guises (exchange for commercial goods, foreclosure, enforced liquidation for debt, or authority with excessive powers) led to the aboriginal groups being deprived of their traditional rights and reduced to the status of landless labourers, or tenants sharing their produce with a landlord. A great many of the surviving collectives are in remote, sterile, mountainous regions where they can barely subsist. Neighbouring properties have monopolized water and wood supplies and arrogated control of essential rights of way, with the result that the aboriginal communities are obliged to work on the estates to obtain use of these resources and rights.*

* René Dumont, *Lands Alive* (London, 1964), p. 12. Refusal to cooperate, in other words, had come to mean imprisonment without even water.

This example from Colombia is typical of the politico-economic process of free enterprise. The costs do not have to be counted, the work is the exercise of genuine political skill, the increment of land, serf-labour and status is pure gain. Speaking of Brazil, the great sociologist and economist, Celso Furtado, who was once Brazil's Minister of Economic Planning, wrote for a North American audience:

This development of which we are so proud has brought about no change at all in the living conditions of three-fourths of the country's population. Its main feature has been a growing concentration of income, both socially and geographically. . . . The majority of the Brazilian population has reaped no benefit. . . . Economic development has produced social results of an extremely negative character. Because of the anachronistic structure of Brazilian agriculture, it has led in many regions to a relative increase in the rent from land, thus rewarding parastic groups. Similarly . . . a variety of subsidies – in the name of development – have very often put a premium on investments which . . . favoured a still greater concentration of income in the hands of privileged groups.*

The very show that is made by the ruling *élites* of a concern for economic development strengthens the foundations of a poverty-breeding society. We have noticed already what the situation in Peru was in the early 1960s. The structures which made productive resources and created wealth flow in the direction of a tiny group of landlords and capitalists were very marked. What 'modernization' does for the people of Peru is indicated in an accurate account, published in *The Times*, of the economic development in Peru in 1964 and 1965 which is creating a new urban middle class:

* *Foreign Affairs,* April 1963. As Frederick Pike put it in relation to Chile: 'The ruling class, the amalgam of upper and middle groups, has consistently resisted any move aimed at incorporating the lower masses, those who depend exclusively upon manual labour for survival and who are at best barely literate, into society. Frequently, middle groups have committed themselves more passionately than the upper class to preserve the gulf between those who guide and benefit from the course of national development, and those who are supposed to accept and suffer from it with resignation' (*op. cit.*, pp. xxii–xxiii).

Income is growing faster than population. The industrial sector has registered very satisfactory growth and there has been a shift from food processing and textiles towards a modest heavy industry with some interest in chemicals and engineering, notably ship-building and vehicle assembly.

The benefits of economic growth have been very unevenly distributed among the various sectors of the economy. Wealth and income are highly concentrated. The top 10 per cent receive 60 per cent of the disposable income; the top 0·25 per cent get 35 per cent. Land-ownership is concentrated to a degree which is extreme even for Latin America, and foreign investment has played a very large part in the recent growth of industry as well as in export-orientated plantation agriculture.

But at the other end of the scale there has been little or no progress towards more adequate levels of income for the peasantry, the landless rural labourer or the unskilled urban labourer.

The regional inequality of wealth and economic growth is just as striking . . .

Coastal Peru as a whole has seen steady expansion and growing prosperity. Its population increases at a rate of 3·3 per cent a year; income levels, averaging about £200 a head, are six times greater than in the sierra; literacy rates are higher than the average for the country; roads and public utilities are better developed than in the sierra, for example; and there is more skilled labour. All Peruvian towns are small compared with Lima, but Chiclayo, Trujillo, Chimbote, Ica and Tacna are beginning to emerge as nuclei o regional growth.

But 52 per cent of the population of Peru live in the mountains, the majority over 10,000 ft above sea level. Many are Quechua-speaking Indians living at the margin of subsistence and often at the margin of a money economy. The provision of education, public services, roads and electricity is sadly inadequate. Illiteracy is high and housing and nutrition poor.

Average income is said to be of the order of £30 to £40 a head, but such calculations are often unrealistic in an area such as this.

The predominance of absentee ownership frequently implies an immense and immediate drain of estate profits to the towns, and above all to Lima.*

* 'Peru Pushes Ahead' by C. T. Smith, *The Times,* 13 September 1967. A few weeks earlier *The Times'* Latin America correspondent wrote from

The Management of Threats to the System

Humanitarian attempts have been made from time to time to reduce the gap between the thriving rich and the poor. Guatemala, a country of great interest in the study of anti-development, provides an example. The liberal President, Juan Jose Arevalo, in spite of many attempts to get rid of him, tried during the years 1950–54 to pay some attention to the needs of the poor.* His successor, President Jacopo Arbenz, instituted some mild land reform which gave idle land to landless peasants. His government was overthrown, after an invasion organized by the US Central Intelligence Agency, in 1954, and about 100,000 families who had benefited by the land redistribution had to restore their land to the former land-owners.† Guatemala

---

* The Colombian writer, German Arciniegas, quotes Arevalo, and outlines his programme: see my *From Gandhi to Guevara, op. cit.*, pp. 360 ff.

† David Wise and Thomas B. Ross, who allege, without any supporting evidence, that Arbenz was a 'Communist', provide a racy but detailed

---

Lima a despatch published under the heading 'Peru runs risk of an Indian peasant revolt': 'What surveys have been made by economists suggest that while coastal and urban Peru of recent years has got richer, the rural *sierra* goes backward or stagnates. This explains the staggering growth of cities like Lima and Arequipa situated on the edge of the *sierra*, over the last decade. . . . Since the drift to the cities can only siphon off a part, the land question is probably crucial. In President Belaunde's first 100 days there were widespread invasions of the often vast Peruvian haciendas by Indians. But they wanted only to take a part, disputed for ages, and only in those organized by Hugo Blanco (the Communist [*sic*] leader now under permanent arrest) did they seek a complete take-over. With hunger, almost no lands being handed out, and serf-like conditions continuing, there is a real risk of a build up of Indian feeling leading to an explosion. Who will then control it? The parallel with pre-1832 England is apt in a number of ways. There exist today in Peru industrial and business groups which have an interest in ending the mestizo-dominated system in the *sierra*. Unfortunately instead of making themselves the representatives of the modernizing national interest they put their efforts solely behind getting exemption for the cotton and sugar plantations on the coast from agrarian reform, although their solidarity with the *sierra* land-owners is often only verbal' (*The Times*, 17 August 1967).

continued to have some of the worst poverty in the whole of Latin America, as figures given elsewhere in this book indicate (see p. 129). The richest land-owners live in the capital and travel abroad, while the military and police act with the utmost firmness on the slightest hint of active or overt discontent. They do not have to worry about the training and upkeep of these forces, since direct taxation is small. A great deal of foreign help in the maintenance of order has been available. The groups who continue to make economic progress under-standably repress any movement to change the existing order of things by attempts at agricultural cooperation, or the formation of rural trade unions. Father Thomas Melville, at the time he was a missionary of the Roman Catholic Maryknoll Order in Guatemala, described organizations which the governing *élites* found it necessary to use. There was the 'National Liberation Movement' (MLN) which ran the right-wing terrorists called 'Mano Blanco' (the White Hand) who had their headquarters in the main police building in downtown Guatemala City. NOA (the New Anti-Communist Organization) was a group of terrorists used to keep the peasants and their supporters in order. It was headed by army officers on active duty. A third terrorist group, CADEG,* was composed of land-owners; this also dealt summarily and brutally with 'trouble-makers'.

In the past eighteen months [according to Father Melville's report], the three law and order groups together have assassinated more than 2,800 intellectuals, students, labour leaders and peasants who have in any way tried to organize and combat the ills of Guatemalan society. The 'Mano Blanco' itself admits that no more than one in ten of these is probably a Communist.

I personally know a good friend and benefactor of the Maryknoll Fathers, a daily communicant, who accused a Christian labor leader who was trying to organize a union on his big sugar plantation of Communism, and had him shot by the army. This man today, like so

* Anti-Communist Council of Guatemala.

account of how President Eisenhower and the CIA achieved their *coup* in *The Invisible Government* (London, 1965), pp. 165 ff.

F

many other landowners, maintains army guards on his farm to avoid the repetition of such an occurrence in the future.

When the cooperative I started among the destitute Indians of Quezaltenango was finally capable of buying its own truck, the rich tried to pay the driver to run the vehicle off a cliff. When the truck driver wouldn't be bought, at least four attempts were made to run it off the road, one of them successful. In the parish of San Antonio Muista, where my brother, also a Maryknoll priest, was pastor, the president of a land cooperative was killed by the town's wealthy including the mayor.*

Father Melville was not exaggerating. And, incredible as reports about the working of the political system in Guatemala may seem, the practices they describe are not peculiar to that country. The degree of violence required to keep the system working in the face of opposition is increasing, and becoming more and more destructive of the economic base.

However crushed in body and spirit the unprivileged majority are, as in Guatemala, the possibilities of development remain a threat as long as the people are alive, and love and care for one another. But the more quickly they are killed, the more unstable the order becomes. The growing awareness among the impoverished and acquiescent majority of their human dignity and of the realities of the political-economic-social processes which oppress and impoverish them ('politic-ization' or, as the Brazilians call it, *conscientizacão*), is a threat to order and stability which, in its turn, must be got rid of, if genuine development is not to be allowed to create new patterns of power and wealth. Even in its mild and timid forms it interferes with the smooth working of the prevailing economic system. The machinery which keeps the rural areas in order and outside the political system cannot deal with the conscience-stricken among the well-to-do – the liberal and radical intel-lectuals, whose political analysis, philosophy, theology, ethics and theories of economic development have a subversive influence. This was the group of people, in Latin America's

* Article in *National Catholic Reporter*, reproduced in *I. F. Stone's Weekly*, 19 February 1968.

major country, Brazil, who posed a serious challenge to the established authorities in Brazil and, as we shall see later, the United States. For they had among them Brazilian men and women of great distinction in São Paulo and Rio de Janeiro.

Brazil's recent history is very complicated. There were a variety of factors which accounted for the developments of the late 1950s and 1960s.* The vigorous (if not always sound) and forward-looking civilian leadership of Kubitschek, Quadros and Goulart was possible partly because there was in the top army leadership a man, General Lott, who prevented a military *coup* in 1955 in the interests of the conservatives. During this period Brazil might have broken out of the rigid mould in which its political and economic structure had been set. Groups which were more genuinely revolutionary than the Muscovite Communist Party began to be active. In the northeast, 'Peasant Leagues' had begun to take action, partly under the leadership of the socialist Francisco Julião. These, together with other bodies representing the rural masses, dared to call a strike in 1962, for improvements in the working conditions and wages of peasants. The Rural Workers' Statute was passed by the government. President Goulart, somewhat of a demagogue, but in increasing conflict with the military, land-owners, foreign-orientated industrialists and other *élite* groups who were concerned that unrest and mass political activity had upset the smooth working of the country, became a serious threat when he tried to extend the vote to illiterate Brazilians. That threat increased when it became obvious that there would be support for a government action to recover the vast holdings of Brazilian resources expropriated by foreign corporations. The danger of a government outside the control of Brazil's ruling class was considerable.

The *coup* of April 1964 was the inevitable outcome of the subversively egalitarian and populist policies of those years. It was not Goulart who was dangerous, but those, like the radical

* See accounts by Helio Jaguanibe and Celso Furtado in Veliz (ed.), *op. cit.*

Christian organizers of the Basic Education Movement, whose work was awakening the rural masses. For, once awakened, they would certainly not abide by the customary economic and political conditions. Under the military dictatorship of Marshal Castelo Branco and his successor, Marshal Costa e Silva, a return to the stability of the old days has proved to be impossible, in spite of solid United States backing. Increasing resort to terror, secret police methods, imprisonment and even torture has become necessary. The Latin American military bureaucracy, with the large share of the national budget which gives them a high standard of living, their relatively easy life (since there is little physical risk in bombing, shooting or napalming peasants, strikers and students), political power, prestige (which enables them to hobnob with the prestigious military top brass of the United States) and supra-legal status, have a big economic stake in the systematic enrichment of the small ruling class. Military organization for the control of state power is a social device for appropriating a large share of the gross national product.

In Pakistan, too, the need to secure and extend the power of the landlords and owners of large businesses led the way to military dictatorship and the rule of martial law. The declining efficacy of covert and institutional forms of coercion made the growth of overt forms necessary. The military were needed as a police force. Anti-Communism helped provide international approval.*

The larger the military apparatus, the more scope there is within it for able and ambitious men. The wider the disparity in numbers between those who enjoy the benefit from the economy and those who only work and pay taxes as they are ordered, the more the state has to be organized on military lines.

* See Hamza Alavi, 'Army and Bureaucracy in Pakistan', *International Socialist Journal*, March–April 1966. 'More than any other political leader in a modernizing country after World War II Ayub Khan came close to filling the role of a Solon or Lycurgus or "Great Legislator" on the Platonic or Renaissance model . . .' writes Professor Huntington in *Political Order in Changing Societies* (New Haven and London, 1968), p. 251.

Even in India, where the political campaigns of Nehru and Gandhi brought the rural masses into national politics, similar tendencies have been at work. In the anti-imperialist struggle the military forces, police and feudal elements had served the British. But after the egalitarian phase of the first post-independence years, it is the wealthy who have been getting wealthier. The subversive effects of India's close friendship with revolutionary China, and the economic logic of the poverty-breeding system have made necessary tactics designed to put India firmly on an anti-development basis. The political manoeuvring which led to the Indian military attack on Chinese forces in disputed territory in 1961* and the steep increase in the military budget, make political and economic sense. The conditions for the poor in India are very bad indeed. The education and literacy statistics alone, twenty years after Independence, suggest how great the need is for a rapid increase in the provision of teachers, schools and books. Illiteracy in 1961 was 71·7 per cent, and the school attendance figures have already been noted.† Yet forty per cent of the national budget in 1967 was allocated to the military.

The Necessity of Poverty

In maintaining stability, justice and order according to prevailing standards the well-to-do have made their advantages more enduring. For example, again and again it has been the experience of low-caste communities in Latin America that perfectly legal titles to land desired by the ruling castes have been proved invalid. Fundamental human rights, it turns out, stand in the way of 'progress'. The opportunities for productive activity and for enjoying its fruits increase and even multiply when there is economic activity. The unequal distribution of these opportunities is connected with the expanding monopoly of power to legitimize the retention and appropriation of

* Incredible as this may seem in view of American and British references to the war over the disputed boundary, this is in fact what happened.
† See above, p. 128. Illiteracy in the state of Kerala was 44·9 in 1961.

productive resources by a section of the community. Political authority and the power to enforce it is thus an essential economic resource, and the great inequalities of power in caste-ridden societies like those of Latin America and Asia are decisive in concentrating wealth in the hands of a minority. The kind of development which we have been commending in this book – that which eliminates the sources of the poverty and oppression of the people – would be the opposite of what development means to the land-owners, 'owners' of industry and mineral resources, and the high civilian and military officials who administer and safeguard their system of owner-ship. It would reduce their power, their income and the extent of their property. For the productive process, in that case, would be directed towards the enrichment of 100 per cent instead of five or ten per cent; initially, and for a period, power and productive resources would be directed to the repair and restoration of what has been damaged and emaciated by the denial of the freedom to govern, to produce and to discover. But what happens is that the people are forced to pay the cost of police and military forces, and of international police and military assistance for those who maintain the existing anti-development process. South Korea provides an instructive example. Its government in 1969 commandeered the services of 620,000 South Koreans to provide it with what is, if we leave aside the Saigon regime's army, the world's biggest military establishment in relation to size and population. Some of these troops are provided as mercenaries to be used to torture, terrorize and kill another Asian people, the Vietnamese, earning valuable foreign exchange from the United States for South Korea's rulers.*

What this book calls 'the development process' must, for the sake of the stable and peaceful working of the *other*

---

* Till 1945 Korea had been part of Japan's imperial possessions. It had been the policy of the Japanese colonial administration to recruit the most disreputable elements among the Koreans to the Gestapo-like *Kempetai*. The campaign of terrorism and unspeakable tortures carried out by the South Koreans had been well tried in Korea itself.

'development' process, be forcibly prevented. And that is what explains much of the repression in the world.

Countries which have not gone far in modernizing their economies need to use their existing resources to maximum effect. The expenditure of time and money and training and the use of men in the apparatus of repression is therefore doubly wasteful of economic resources. Terror and torture as practised in Brazil, South Korea, South Africa and other countries are not only deliberately aimed at disrupting the forces leading to development; they use up a large part of the material resources of the country and destroy valuable traditional assets while providing rather uncertain security for the existing system.* Men and women who ought to be trained and employed as engineers, scientists, teachers and industrial workers are employed as executioners, torturers and prison guards. Napalm is no substitute for fertilizers. Further, the greater the intensity of the terror and repression the fiercer and more destructive tends to be the inevitable revolt. Such a revolt may not succeed, but at the end of it economic conditions will be worse than they would have been if the military, police and secret police had not been used to 'solve' development problems.

The economics of anti-development are demonstrated in post-war Thailand as well as anywhere else. The well-to-do in Bangkok have had to deal with an easy-going, placid people. But military and police dominance has been necessary as well as long periods of martial law, even though the Thai people have been under no military threat since the defeat of Japan in 1945. The work of leaders like Pridi Panamyong had, since the 1930s, tried to bring economic development into serious political discussion. But since his overthrow Thailand has been paying the costs of a society organized in such a way as to prevent the economic and political modernization of the

* The *fact* that the populations are kept in 'order' by exemplary terrorism, torture and imprisonment is often denied. The evidence of these has not, however, been successfully suppressed, e.g. in Brazil, South Vietnam. The tortures practised by the US-trained Brazilian officer corps have been documented in some detail.

country. The Ministry of the Interior has been the dominant ministry. Monopoly of administrative power by a small bureaucratic *élite*, civilian and military, in Bangkok is remarkably complete. Cabinets have been almost exclusively formed by the same group. 'Civilian' in an authoritarian country like Thailand is not too distinct from 'military', especially since neither under the dictatorship of Field Marshal Luang Pibun Songkram (1947–57) nor under that of the man who ousted him, Field Marshal Sarit Thanarat (1958–63), has the Thai army had to work to defend the country against foreign attack.*

The career and administrative actions of General Phao Sriyanand are instructive. A Director-General of Police, and Deputy-Minister of the Interior, Phao subsequently became Minister of the Interior under Pibun. Phao's work consisted in organizing opium smuggling and in maintaining twice as many policemen in the poor and economically neglected north-eastern provinces (which are plagued by usury and landlordism, and were a base for a wartime anti-Fascist resistance) as in the Bangkok area; political opponents and dissidents were either illegally detained or (including in 1949 four former Cabinet Ministers) assassinated; he ran an extortion racket, misappropriated state funds, allowed (for payment) the running of unlicensed brothels, and gambling and opium dens, faked elections and bribed members of the legislature. Phao was one of the leaders of the regime which, in the name of 'anti-Communism', agreed to the South-East Asia Treaty Organization devised by John Foster Dulles. When the regime was overthrown he fled to Switzerland in 1957 to enjoy the fortune which he had worked hard to earn.

Sarit continued the same policies. To justify the repression and the international alliances which brought foreign forces into Thailand to repress troublesome Asian peasants, his regime spent the scarce money, skills and time in concocting the stock excuse, the 'international Communist conspiracy'. 'Creative' activity of this kind – which consists in playing an elaborate charade to mask the increasing exploitation of the

* Thai citizens have been sent into Vietnam for use against Vietnamese.

people – is wasteful. The Sarit regime's 'repressing' and 'suppressing' were 'constitutionally' allowed. But the production or purchase of prisons, executions and military hardware does not provide rice and expand economic opportunities. The kind of arrangement which made General Prapart, Minister of the Interior, and General Thanom, Minister of Defence, rectors of the two major universities, also was destructive in its economic consequences. The sequel to the free enterprise regime of Sarit is both amusing and instructive. For some time after this exemplary leader died a woman who claimed that she was his wife went to court with Sarit's relations over the sharing of his fortune. Because of the legal dispute it transpired that Sarit had stowed away $25 million of Thai public funds for his use in numbered Swiss bank accounts.*

It has been argued earlier that a ruling class of a few hundred thousands, or even a million or two, in a nation of several million, have little difficulty in achieving remarkable rates of development for themselves. For they have the resources and labour of many millions working for their enrichment and security, and the right also to tax and conscript. They can also use some of these resources to purchase from similar classes in foreign countries industrial, military and counter-revolutionary technology. But costs, in terms of real development, are high (even when we take into account the assistance that has been given to the realization of Thai territorial ambitions in Vietnam, Cambodia and Laos). In Thailand the provision of land and labour for bases from which the people of China, Laos and Vietnam can be attacked by United States forces has brought a sudden flood of wealth into Bangkok. Two consequences

* General Khanh, who rocketed into international fame when he was tried out for a while in Saigon as the Vietnamese chief of the regime there, once admitted to having amassed $10 million (*I. F. Stone's Weekly*, 10 February 1964, quoting a report in *NYHTI*, 3 February 1964). One can understand the fear the Sarits, Thieus and Parks have of the poor, with their 'subversive, Communist' ideas about corruption and tyranny. The contribution they have made to the analysis of modern politics is discussed in the Latin American context by German Arciniegas (see my *From Gandhi to Guevara, op. cit.,* pp. 186–7).

may be mentioned. First, the element of stability in Thailand achieved by the reforms of King Mongkut will be lost if the new rich invest in land. Secondly, the impetus given to the growth and dynamism of the existing society may be difficult to control. The injection of new money facilitates investment in enterprises which, because of the existing system, cost little and bring quick profits. What Pote Sarasin, a pro-Western businessman and a fervent anti-Communist, said is worth noting. 'Finance Minister Pote Sarasin noted that ... most Thai capital had been put into quick-return projects in Bangkok – notably hotels and massage parlors – rather than projects that would increase long-term productive capacity, for which foreign capital still carries the burden. ...'* What 'hotels' and 'massage parlors' mean when every month 3,000 US troops from Vietnam visited Bangkok for 'rest and recreation' is obvious. A dispatch by United Press International (an organization above suspicion of being friendly to the masses anywhere) from Bangkok reported the massive promotion of prostitution in Thailand. It said:

> The number of prostitutes and cases of venereal disease in Thailand are increasing at an alarming rate, the National Research Council said today. It said there were 2,417 brothels in the country in 1968.
> The number of prostitutes working in these houses was 151,244. Both figures are expected to be higher by the end of this year, the announcement added.†

The provision of brothels and women is only the most conspicuous example of what Thailand's rulers are doing to develop the freedom of the rich. The provision of one's wife, daughters and sisters for foreign troops occupying bases in

* *NYHTI*, 27 January 1967.

† There is much profit, of course, to be got by playing the procurer in other ways, and meeting the desires of needy foreigners. But a great deal can be learnt from the role which women are made to play in foreign-occupied lands. The distinguished French journalist, Robert Guillain, who wrote a series of articles in *Le Monde* in May 1966 after a study of US-occupied areas of Vietnam, described prostitution as the 'biggest industry' in Saigon. The physical attractiveness of live males is that they can be offered as mercenaries or assassins.

one's own country or invading a neighbouring country must be subject to economic analysis. For it is impoverishing in the worst sense of the term. It is a very high price for the community to pay for the enrichment and security of a handful of land-owners and businessmen and *their* families. We must consider it as much a form of disinvestment as the letting in, in exchange for money and other favours, of foreign troops to lay waste the country and kill and maim its people. (Even as a form of 'consumption', prostitution in its colonial forms is much more exploitative and wasteful than it is in its indigenous form.) The decline of the moral traditions of a society with its great Buddhist heritage certainly does not represent modernization. In an economy of the Thai type the liberation of women, so essential to the development process, is denied. Where there is no moral choice, where sexual attractiveness is made a commodity, the impoverishment of the community is immense.

Thirdly, the price of the 'boom' for the wealthy and middle classes in Bangkok is not only the progressive impoverishment of most of Thailand. It is also the gearing of Thailand's political and economic structure to the systematic impoverishment of Asian peoples beyond the boundaries of Thailand. Anti-development certainly has a dynamism of its own. We have noticed already how Thailand has become a serious threat to the industrial and power plants, irrigation works and other parts of the economy which the Chinese and Vietnamese peoples have painfully constructed for their own and others' use. We can take, for example, the new 'growth areas' outside Bangkok – the areas of United States bases. 'The biggest single boost to the Thai economy,' the *New York Times* claimed, 'came from United States military spending, expansion or operation of six bases for the air war against North Vietnam.'*
In fact, the bombing of poor Thai villagers in the north-east, the massive destruction of recently constructed Vietnamese factories, schools, dams, towns and people in the north, the defoliation and pulverization of Laos and Vietnam in the south, have actually been far more destructive of the potential for

* 27 January 1967.

development in the Third World than any other single campaign since 1945. A great rice-surplus area has thus been made into a rice-deficit area, hundreds of thousands of Asian children in a single generation have been orphaned and crippled – these and other similar economic consequences of the use of Thailand far outweigh the 'boost to the Thai economy'. In return for the amassing of wealth (and foreign exchange) by a few Thais the crucial and world-historic process through which civilization began in south-east Asia – the beginnings of settled cultivation and the elimination of malaria in the Red River delta – is deliberately being reversed.

DISINVESTMENT

Unproductive Expenditure

We have touched several times on the processes which drain away or destroy precious resources which are essential for development. Again, trying to be brief rather than systematic and thorough, we should take note of the ways in which *disinvestment* occurs. We have mentioned the cumulative and accelerating growth which occurs when work is regularly invested in the creation of new and more productive opportunities for the people. A small increment in the community's capital resources and expansion in its productive apparatus can rapidly multiply both opportunities for productive work and products to be enjoyed. On the other hand, there is the reverse process. A considerable proportion of what is produced or otherwise available for investment in a less developed economy can regularly be taken out of it. The process of impoverishment is thus accelerated.

Within a national economy this may work, as we saw, in the extraction from the rural communities of their skills, labour and products for the enrichment of urban centres which do not offer enrichment of any kind – cultural benefits, cheap manufactured products, political leadership or security and order – to the working people of rural areas. The impoverishment of the national community as a whole in some cases continues the process – the cities being the outlets for the extraction of the 'surplus', and much more than the surplus. When a large proportion of the working people are concentrated in primary production there is little left over after the basic subsistence needs of the community have been met. The outflow of resources from the productive sector can have an enormously adverse effect on the rate of investment for better development.

There are several ways in which economic resources are siphoned out of the economy. One which is peculiar to 'underdeveloped' countries is the private hoarding of wealth or its exporting for investment abroad. The opportunities and incentives for investment in existing or new projects are not very extensive in economies which need to keep the educational level low and economic power concentrated in a few hands. In some societies the possession and display of wealth in its nonproductive forms wins great power and prestige. Cultural and social factors may account for this. In some cases those who are earning large incomes may not have much confidence in the long-term future of the economic and political system; the legitimacy as well as efficiency of the system may be under attack, and the continued loyalty or obedience of those who provide the work and accept low living standards may be uncertain. It would be impolitic to stake too much wealth in the existing system. In other cases, it might be part of the rules of the game that the period of ascendancy of the families or individuals in power must be used to amass wealth while the going is good. People who expect to be ousted in a *coup d'état* by one of their colleagues or rivals must hoard their wealth in movables or cash.

The numbered Swiss bank accounts perform a necessary function in the type of economy which we have been discussing. The control of foreign exchange regulations and of export of capital for private investment overseas is no problem to those who control the government or have power over civil servants. Sometimes the money that is made is earned abroad as payment for lucrative contracts or concessions or services to foreign firms or governments.

India, which is short of investment capital, is estimated to have the world's largest supply of privately hoarded gold. One rough estimate is that the value of India's total hoard in the mid-1960s may have been in the region of $8 billion.* Latin America, according to estimates by the Inter-American Economic and Social Council, loses approximately $1·5 billion of flight capital a year with something like $15 billion held abroad. Uruguay alone was estimated by an Uruguayan weekly to lose $300 million every year in this way – an amount equivalent to a quarter of the national income, and the value of two years' exports.† The amounts that are taken out of Guatemala are also impressive.

The accumulation of reserves of hard currency is particularly valuable because it enables a poor nation to command resources for development which are unavailable or in short supply locally. With the deteriorating terms of trade for primary producers every year foreign currency becomes more difficult to earn. Cultivators and miners have to undergo increasing hardships so that freely convertible currencies may be accumulated. Therefore when a small *élite* makes use of hard-earned foreign exchange for the import of luxury goods or unnecessary foreign travel for themselves, we have another example of disinvestment. In the French-speaking African states the import of perfumes costs almost as much as the import of fertilizer; and import of alcohol accounted for almost as much as that of agricultural machinery, farm tools and tractors combined.‡ The way of life of the millionaires takes them to the expensive resorts. The tendency is for them to cease to belong to the local society. A report on the Guatemalan ruling class by the Inter-American Agricultural Development Committee (not a radical body) said in 1965:

* Fred Hirsch, *Money International* (London, 1967), p. 210.

† In spite of her high *per capita* income statistics, Uruguay has seen much discontent in recent years.

‡ Keith Buchanan in *Monthly Review*, April 1967, p. 55.

They seek to maintain a life of colonial aristocracy, while at the same time trying to idealize and imitate the North American standard of living. They have a big house, with many servants, luxury automobiles . . . modern domestic appliances, etc.; at the same time they frequent social centres distinguished by their high cost, and keep up to date with the fashions. . . . *They frequently travel abroad and have a marked tendency to internationalize their social relations . . .**

An aspect of the economic significance of maintaining large military establishments has already been discussed. Another aspect comes into view when we note that the proceeds of taxation are frequently absorbed in non-productive government expenditure. The administrative civilian as well as military bureaucracies provide regular sources of income for the ruling families and their retainers. For example, sixty-five per cent of the national budget of Dahomey was used up in 'administrative expenses'. René Dumont pointed out that in East Africa a parliamentary deputy earned for one-and-a-half months of work as much as an average peasant in thirty-six years – a life-time – of hard labour. Houphouet Boigny, President of the Ivory Coast, built his presidential palace at the cost of four billion francs. According to reports hundreds of tons of malachite were imported by air from Russia for its construction. Those who have control of poorly developed small countries with small populations are not necessarily badly off. Rafael Trujillo, dictator of the Dominican Republic until 1961, was found when he died to have a hoard of fantastic proportions. Among other things he had $235 million in foreign, mainly Swiss, banks, twenty-two per cent of local bank deposits, thirty per cent of the land and twenty-five per cent of the country's livestock.

In countries (e.g. India) in which the economic base is narrow, and opportunities for productive work are limited, the costs of 'administration' tend to go up. Those considered trustworthy enough to be heads or sub-heads of departments

---

* Quoted in Galeano, *op. cit.*, italic added. These words describe the 'universalism' of the *élites* of scores of countries in the Third World.

very understandably add the names of relatives for whose welfare they are responsible to the payroll. The salaries bill gets inflated as new jobs of no economic or political value are created. One consequence is the additional weight of oppression that bureaucratic methods impose on the less fortunate members of the community. For the most lowly underling is vested with some authority over the cultivators, workers, teachers, scientists, other working people and their families; he may determine their access to officials who must be waited upon, or have the function of handing over a valuable document – a ration book, an identity card or a licence. What may begin as a slightly corrupt use of power and patronage leads to the multiplication of opportunities for idle people to harass and humiliate ordinary working people, to control their lives and extort bribes from them. The increasing arrogation of powers over the activities and movements of the public by those in the higher echelons of the bureaucracy puts the people at the mercy of a powerful minority.

In countries which for one reason or another escaped the extremes of mass poverty, the covert oppression and exploitation of the people may be mainly bureaucratic. In Ceylon, it used to be said, the main industry was the government services. Bureaucracy was one of the main features of the colonial inheritance. The ordinary citizen knew well the arrogance and power-consciousness of the politician in office and the public servant. His precarious daily work would be held up as he answered the imperious summons to attend the drab office of some official, hung around outside the door for a whole day waiting to be summoned, and was then ordered to come back the next day. The land-owners, businessmen, ministers of state and public functionaries, whose livelihood depended on the productive activities of submissive plantation workers, cultivators, stevedores and others, could always use 'influence' with officials.

Of the 2,268,740 Ceylonese 'gainfully employed' according to the 1953 Census, more than half were engaged in agriculture, livestock production and fishing. But 'government services', not counting the educational, medical and transport services, used up a large part of public revenue. In many cases these were the people whose occupation it was to ask people to fill in forms, or actually to give them orders of various kinds which could be ignored or disobeyed only at considerable cost; they permitted and prohibited, demanded and decided; a small number of men, from 'ministers' down to peons, who could not put down a single creative or original idea on paper, ruled and mystified the rest of the population with paper; with permanent salaried posts, they sat in their offices and oppressed the working masses. In a country in which there was a considerable demand for a wide range of manufactured articles, and with the tremendous task of industrialization before it, the numbers engaged in manufacture were ludicrously small: for example, 1,577 were engaged in the 'manufacture of rubber and rubber products', 7,810 in that of 'chemicals and chemical products' (in a country in which the teaching of the sciences to advanced secondary level was widespread), 1,004 in 'the manufacture, installation and repair of non-electrical machinery', 2,094 for electrical machinery, and so on. An 'industrial' base of the size indicated was inadequate for the wants of the government personnel and the rich whom they served, let alone the rest of the country!

The British rulers had 'transferred power' in such a manner that the main developed resources remained in private hands: the tea, rubber and coconut plantations. It was not because of 'backwardness' that the profits earned by the tea and rubber plantation workers was not invested in the economic modernization of Ceylon. The expensive government apparatus was designed precisely *not* to encourage or assist the forces working for the transformation of the material conditions in which the people lived and worked. The plantation workers, workers in transport services and industry, lower-middle-class radicals in the rural areas and revolutionary intellectuals pressed for change. Together with the cultivators, fishermen and other similar rural workers, they formed the vast majority of the population of a nominally democratic country. But the concentration of their leaders on the parliamentary process served only to enlarge the area of bureaucratic governmental activity which kept the existing colonial order in working condition, and kept the mass of the people from taking an active part in making their own history. Among the tactics used by the ruling *élites* to render the opposition ineffective was the disfranchising of the most highly exploited section of the working people – the plantation labourers. By working on racialist feelings and attitudes this was achieved with little protest from among the major communities, the Sinhalese and Ceylon Tamils; for the plantation workers were of Indian origin.

The expensively maintained bureaucracy has been self-perpetuating. It has demonstrated that an enormous bureaucracy at the disposal of reactionary and incompetent politicians only serves to multiply opportunities for corruption, venality and oppression. It is the structure of Ceylonese society, and its established institutions, which enable a handful of individuals to arrogate to themselves the power of both feudal lords and colonial masters. If the working and creatively active people administered the productive process directly, it would not only be cheaper, but also more conducive to the elimination of the causes of poverty, unemployment, malnutrition and oppression of all kinds. Ceylon has had, from 1943 onwards, laws providing everyone with the right of free education from primary school to the university. In spite of discrimination against certain social groups, the high rates of school attendance have been impressive. But bureaucratic interference has been the curse of the educational system. The insistent demand for increased educational opportunities forced governments to build more schools and to raise the academic level of teaching in the provincial centres nearer to that which had been enjoyed in Colombo, Kandy and Jaffna. But whereas the need was for a new educational system, democratically run, and stressing creativity, originality, self-reliance, inventiveness and experiment, and other revolutionary qualities needed for development, the deadly grip of officials in 'education offices', jealous of all who endangered their authority, has made government-controlled education a waste of the large amounts spent on it. Parents, teachers and others who could have taken pioneering action to liberate the young from the sterile thinking and practice of the colonial tradition, made education a force for true development and inculcated revolutionary ideas of service to the masses, would have been a threat to the established *élites*. To keep or, rather, make the young uncritical and docile the government, whichever faction of land-owners, businessmen and officials has been in a majority in Parliament, has used the schools, colleges and universities to prevent the young from becoming too aware politically.

The Export of Valuable Skills

The transfer of funds, jewellery, bullion and cheap raw material from a poorly developed economy is one way in which the poor are made to contribute to the economic growth of already developed countries. Another is the systematic export of able, enterprising, professionally trained and industrially skilled men and women. In Britain the 'brain drain' has often been described as the loss to Britain of scientists, doctors and engineers. But the export of public-spirited persons with modern skills from countries with retarded economies is relatively a far greater loss.*

When Irish and continental Europeans emigrated to the United States, it was the impoverished rural population which tended to seek new opportunities. In Latin America, Asia and Africa maintenance of political and economic rigidity in the interests of 'order and stability' suitable for oligarchies and foreign enterprises favours the emigration of enterprising and radically inclined people, especially intellectuals, who do not belong to the land-owning or industry-owning families. A similar situation has been developing in south Asia. If people who see neither profit nor dignity in serving under the existing

* The emigration of middle-class politicians, lawyers and businessmen who have lost political dominance is entirely different.

system of authority have no prospects of work, they would incline to consider action to make the system more tolerable. Students, scientists, economists, writers, engineers and doctors could, if they remained in a frustrating and oppressive situation, in which the only practical opportunities bred attitudes of revolt, be better off abroad. In countries in which this problem has been foreseen, and educational opportunities restricted, the dangers have been reduced.* It is when the discontented people with modern techniques and ideas and critical attitudes remain within the country, and express solidarity with the rural malcontents and urban proletariat (as in Pakistan early in 1969 or Brazil now) that law and order is in danger. Good doctors, research scientists, original thinkers in the economics and politics of development, and others like them are normally unwilling to work in menial positions, or under mediocre and old-fashioned superiors who owe their position to political favouritism, corruption, age or loyalty to the established order, or under imported 'experts' who know less than they.

A good part of the resources of a poorly developed economy given to modernizing and developmental activity is used up in the 'production' of engineers, teachers and doctors. But when, for want of employment opportunities, people are idle or emigrate, the cost of training is a contribution to the working of a more developed foreign economy. (In many cases, the training fits people for work not in the highly populated rural areas but in conditions similar to those in Europe and the United States.†) In 1968 the number of trained engineers unable to find employment in India was reported to be 36,000.

It is estimated that from 1961 to 1965 30,000 Latin American

---

* The existence of educated natives who seek ways to modernize and develop their countries democratically is seen as a 'problem' by some experts on development. See below, p. 262.

† Doctors from some Commonwealth countries are as highly trained and skilled as any in Britain, and often more experienced than those of comparable age. Third World universities and colleges, hospitals and clinics, research institutes and laboratories, are paid for by the backward natives to train skilled and experienced workers for the affluent societies.

professionals emigrated to the United States. The extent of the loss to Latin America of the skills represented by these people must be considerable. Central Africa, short of doctors, suffered a decrease in the total number of doctors of about 300 between 1962 and 1965. The emigration of Puerto Ricans in large numbers to the slums of the 'mother country' is an example of the way in which pressure for revolutionary change is conveniently relieved by emigration.

Debt Repayment

The servicing and repayment of national debts incurred by the ruling class is another way in which what is or might be saved from current consumption by the producers is lost to the economy. The function played by the money-lender in the rural areas is often played in the nation and between nations by foreign creditors. The way in which in the nineteenth century the Khedive of Egypt was made to pledge the public funds of his country against his private debt is well known. A similar nineteenth-century practice was that by which whenever China failed to resist an attack on her she was made to pay 'indemnities'. The administration of her customs revenue was taken out of Chinese hands.

More recently, the amounts which have been paid as interest by the 'developing' countries is enormous. Early in 1969 the New Delhi correspondent of *The Times* reported that the Indian government was finding its foreign debt burden too great. In the report, headed 'India may refuse to repay huge loan burden', he wrote:

Indian economists are beginning to fear that the country will face acute financial embarrassment in coming years when it might be preferable for the Government to renege on its massive aid debt and forego further international economic assistance.

This pessimistic picture is painted by economists and backed up by current statistics on India's debt on international aid loans recently published by the Finance Ministry. Figures show that unless prospects and terms of international aid improve rapidly, India's annual debts commitment on past hard currency loans will soon exceed the diminishing quantum of external assistance.

In short, officials in the Finance Ministry predict that India may soon become an 'exporter' of inflowing aid which will virtually have to be returned to donors to meet debt commitments . . .

Total debts on aid, including payments in hard currency, in rupees and through exports, have risen to £180m. this year. In 1972, India's annual repayment to both the west and the Soviet block will exceed £210m. of which £120m. is payable in elusive hard currency.*

Loans and credits from foreign governments provide valuable opportunities for the small dominant minority who have an eye for their own economic advancement and security. They are in effect a means by which present generations (who pay the interest in the form of taxes) and future generations (who are liable to pay off the 'national debt') subsidize the industrialists and financiers who are in control of the developed economy of the donor nation. Some forms of foreign aid are requested by the families and classes which enjoy the monopoly of wealth, influence and power since they help to develop *their* own businesses, landholdings, industries and banking institutions, or the schools and universities which are maintained for *their* children. Technical assistance and training schemes are requested, at no cost to themselves except their share of increased taxation, as long as they help develop *their* business and industry. Aid which is used to build up military and police forces, and also the apparatus to ensure their 'security' is, like the rest, a public debt, to be paid for by the community as a whole; it may provide opportunities for them to seize power in the face of popular and nationwide opposition.

Poverty is thus far from being a condition of 'stagnation'. The dynamism of the anti-development process continually creates it. Whereas economic growth requires the steady investment of a proportion of a country's resources of manpower, raw materials, etc., to construction *for* development, the anti-development process is one by which meagre human skills

* *The Times*, 13 January 1969.

and energies, and natural resources of fertile land, minerals, power, industrial plant and money are transformed, through the functions and roles which people are made to play in the political and economic system, into forms in which they can permanently be taken out of the economy and society of the homeland. The cumulative effect, when every year twenty per cent, say, of agricultural, industrial, production, construction and other work are disinvested in this way, is immense. In the social monstrosities begotten by colonialist and indigenous ruling classes 'growth' only enlarges the gap in power, ownership of productive resources, status, freedom and physical well-being between the few rich and the many poor. The dynamism of anti-development drives the oppressed people further and further away from the world which rightfully belongs to them, and even from knowledge of it.

CHAPTER 6

Anti-Development:
International Partnership

THE COST OF THE BENEFITS OF
FOREIGN INVESTMENT

THE preceding discussion has drawn attention to the set of consequences by which foreign economic control exploits the whole or part of an undeveloped economy. The anti-development process is then at its most destructive. The deformed and distorted structure of Third World economies deteriorates as a result of the neo-colonial relationship. As Adolf Berle, who was later to be head of President Kennedy's Latin American Task Force, once stated:

Preachments about the value of private enterprise and investment and the usefulness of foreign capital, were, to most students of the situation, a little silly. . . . Foreign and/or private investment may industrialize, may even increase production, and still leave the masses in as bad a shape as ever.

It would, in fact, leave them in considerably worse shape.

Rigid political structures must be loosened and the disparities of ownership and power removed if the productive opportunities for the population as a whole are to expand. The entry of the powerful foreign corporation into the local scene, and its concern for maximum profit and stability, only increases the rigidity and the inequalities. Entry is secured by invitation, and not by conquest, when the small ruling groups who open the door expect both to benefit by superior military and police assistance against the restless majority of the population, and to accelerate the rate of their own economic development without a democratization of the system which would, inevitably, impoverish *them*.* Conservative rulers can offer opportunities for speedy enrichment to foreign groups at the expense of the mass of people still denied their share of the agricultural land, minerals, schools, food supply and machinery; they can also guarantee to provide legitimacy for the operation. The political management in this is all of a piece with that which makes possible the concentration of the wealth and power of the whole community in the hands of a few thousands or hundreds of thousands, and the 'freedom' to proceed with policies of disinvestment. Since the few in power 'own' the country, they are exercising their rights even when they give away parts of national territory, together with the people living in them.

Foreign interests will tend to develop those sectors of the economy that yield the quickest and biggest profits and in which there has been previous investment. They will also go where most of the investment in the substructure for foreign profit-making will be undertaken without compensation by the local community. In the 'underdeveloped' countries these will tend to be the extractive and plantation industries rather than manufacturing. The most frequently discussed aspect of this is the extraction of minerals and oils in distant lands and off-shore areas. But such activities as the attempts at maximum and speedy exploitation of Peru's off-shore fish must also be included. While by 1964 54·3 per cent of United States investment in Europe was in manufacturing, percentage figures for the Third World were: Africa 13·8, Asia 17·5, Latin America 24·3,† some of this being in the assembling of foreign-manufactured parts – a practice by which any contribution to the development of indigenous industry is avoided. The trend is towards increased concentration on the extractive sector. One of the surveys by the McGraw Hill Economics Department estimates that US overseas mining companies raised capital spending by thirty-one per cent in 1968 and expected to double 1967 investment by 1970, while US overseas manufacturing

* Feudal-type elements fearing indigenous capitalist developments find foreign opponents of local development useful allies.

† *Survey of Current Business*, September 1965, quoted in Magdoff, 'The Age of Imperialism' in *Monthly Review*, October 1968.

companies planned only a three per cent increase in investment in 1968 and a reduction of six per cent in 1969.* The foreign companies in extractive industries do not, of course, provide materials for use in the local economy; they extract it from the economy as a whole. Local sales in 1965 of US mining firms in Latin America represented 17·8 per cent of sales compared with local sales of manufactured products which represented 92·5 per cent of sales.† Thus foreign capital by its policy of investment and sales tends to preserve and enforce the colonial status of countries which are merely raw-material exporters and captive markets for foreign-manufactured goods. Foreign economic activity, alert to quick profits and long-term political uncertainties, may run down the resources of a country by overproduction. American 'investment' in Latin American oil, for example, is highly profitable to the production companies. In 1967, while there was a net outflow of capital investment from Latin America of $46 million, oil companies' earnings were still $532 million.‡ However, on the basis of 1963 production and reserves, it has been worked out that oil could be exhausted by 1978.§ It was not surprising that careless political and economic 'management' alerted some members of the Peruvian oligarchy to the danger in which they themselves stood from the enthusiasm of the International Petroleum Corporation. The quarrel between the two forces which had collaborated in the economic exploitation of Peru brought to light a great deal of the process which was responsible for impoverishing the Peruvian people.

The way the material resources essential for industrialization in the Third World have been extracted in a massive, world-wide operation by foreign corporations is conventionally discussed, in fact, from the anti-development stand-point. The resources which with modern science and technology are waiting to be put to use for the economic modernization of

* *Time*, 6 August 1968.
† *Survey of Current Business*, November 1966, quoted in Magdoff, *op. cit.*
‡ *Survey of Current Business*, October 1968.
§ UN, *Economic Survey of Latin America* (New York, 1963).

Asia, Latin America and Africa are immense. Unfortunately, it is for the rich that the climate and soil for plantation industries, the oil and gas, copper, manganese, cobalt, tin, chrome ore, antimony, lead, zinc, gold, diamonds, bauxite, phosphates belonging to the 'poor' peoples of the world have been a source of great wealth. The production figures show how valuable they might have been if they had been extracted not *from* the Third World, but *for* its peoples.

THE USEFULNESS OF PEOPLE AS COMMODITIES

The discussion of these matters suffers because of inadequate attention to a more basic form of exploitation by foreign capital than the appropriation and use of the non-human material resources on which the poor must depend for their livelihood and economic growth: it is the using up of the *people* in these 'territories'. Whole peoples become commodities. It was not long ago, when the obstacles to the international mobility of capital, profits and labour were directly in the control of the international capitalist forces, that the most hardworking of the poor were indentured as 'coolies' to perform pioneering tasks in the areas marked out for plantations: the poor are still useful in the same way. The very precariousness of their existence – nowhere to live, nothing to eat and no work of their own to do – adds to their usefulness in the anti-development system. That is why, underfed, sickly and uneducated though they generally are, they are still sought after by the foreign corporations. The more they are terrified, made submissive and acquiescent by the law and order of the local oligarchies, the more the latter have the power of life and death over them, the more, paradoxically, they attract the 'investors'. Some members of the native *élite* find profit in acting as procurers. The status accorded the non-white masses of South Africa by the racially-restricted regime in power is a well-known example. British, United States and other foreign corporations make enormous profits out of South Africa. *The Times* Banking Correspondent wrote on 4 November 1968:

Britain and the United States are the heaviest investors in South Africa and their rate of return on these investments is substantially higher than that on similar investments elsewhere, according to a United Nations survey. These findings of a UN unit dealing with the economic aspects of apartheid are substantiated by figures given by the South African Embassy in London. Indeed, the UN estimate that the United States and Britain together account for 70 per cent of total foreign investment in South Africa may even be an underestimate because the South African embassy puts the figure at 80 per cent. . . . South Africa has, however, recently become a capital exporting as well as a capital importing country. In southern Africa, this policy has a political motivation. . . . But such is the wealth of South Africa, founded largely on the twin pillars of gold and cheap labour, that the South African Reserve Bank is now able to move into making investments abroad which have primarily a business motivation.

South Africa has the largest concentration of highly skilled 'blacks' anywhere in the world, and it is not strange that the head of the family which has made the best use of their skills and of apartheid, Harry Oppenheimer, is praised as the 'richest man in Africa'.

Another contemporary example of available and cheaply expendable humanity is to be found in South Korea. A full-page advertisement inserted in *The Times* by the 'Office of Investment Promotion Economic Planning Board' of Seoul was headed 'CHOICE COUNTRY FOR A GROWING INTERNATIONAL BUSINESS'. It offers foreigners 'rapid economic growth and political stability', and 'attractive investment opportunities' and recommends 'profitable areas for investment'. Some of the details make their points clearly:

> Liberal way of establishing business. All the usual types of business organizations are possible in Korea, including proprietorships, unlimited and limited partnerships, and corporations. A business may be 100 per cent foreign controlled. There is no requirement for Korean participation. However, many foreign investors have found it to their advantage to choose joint ventures

with Korean partners. The same rights, privileges and protection enjoyed by Korean nationals are extended to foreign individuals and firms.

Attractive investment incentives.

The Government recognizes the importance of foreign investments. Generous investment incentives and safeguards – the most liberal and attractive in Asia – are offered to foreign investors:

A five year holiday and a 50 per cent reduction of income tax, corporation tax, property tax and property acquisition tax for the ensuing three years.

Exemption from import duties and commodity taxes on machinery and materials necessary to set up a manufacturing plant.

Exemption for six months following the completion of the plant from import duties and commodity taxes on raw materials.

Permission to remit capital, earnings and royalties from the investment in foreign currency.

No restriction for foreign investors on ownerships of shares in establishing a business organization.

Sure guarantee against expropriation or nationalization of a private industry or business.

'Labour-intensive industries,' the Korean government adds in more prosaic terms, 'are particularly profitable because of the low labour costs in Korea.'*

* 18 June 1968. US financiers and businessmen have, according to a report headed 'Low Korean Wage Draws Investors' in *NYHTI*, 27 January 1967, benefited not only from cheap and docile labour. 'Equally attractive is the adaptability of Korean workers to new skills. "If we had looked only for low wages, we could have gone to Africa," James Stokes, president of the Signetics Korea Corporation said. . . ." After only a couple of weeks of training," he said, "these girls are ready to work on a machine completely new to Korea. . . . Another thing I like about Koreans is that they're very hard workers. They're used to hard work and they don't mind working long hours." A responsible official at the United States Operations Mission said he had seen Korean women learn to operate intricate garment-making machines in three days while it might take an American woman three weeks.' But according to *US News and World Report* (3 February 1969), 'Korea's lure to many US manufacturers – low labor costs – may be losing some luster [*sic*]. Wages have averaged less than $1 a day, but workers have been organizing for wage increases.'

Hong Kong is another politically congenial place providing conditions of cheap and efficient 'manpower' for foreign enterprises seeking quick profits. Singapore's rulers have been ambitious to make their island another such attraction, though the political repression necessary presents problems.* It does too in Brazil, a major Third World country, with a third of Latin America's population. Recent policies have led 'experts' like Rustow to point to it as a model of 'modernization'. Its Amazon region has been attractive to foreigners. *US News and World Report* in an article on 2 September 1968 in which the huge foreign stake in Costa e Silva's Brazil was itemized – $1·3 billion US private investments, $3 billion US government 'aid', $1·25 billion Western European, $618 million Canadian and $147 million Japanese investments – referred to the land of the Brazilian Indians as 'paradise' and 'Eden'. The article complained, however, about the obstacles to free foreign capitalist activity. Yet a Rio de Janeiro despatch in the *New York Times* of 18 February 1968 had said:

An international industrial boom is taking place where it might least be expected – in Brazil's big state of Bahia, whose quaint charms and customs are celebrated in song and story. Boom and charm are being kept apart, though, so that one does not clash with the other. Powerful incentives are fueling industry at Aratu, 10 miles from the charming Salvador, the state capital, with goldlined baroque churches, voodoo rites and a sleepy atmosphere. In little more than a year, 50 foreign and Brazilian concerns have signed up to build plants at the Aratu industrial centre. Magirusdeutz of West Germany is making bus chassis. Eternit of Scandinavia is making asbestos building supplies and the American Cyanamid Company is planning a $20-million investment to make insecticides and plastics. Alcan, Allis-Chalmers and Celanese are coming in. Federal and state governments join in offering the incentives. Rivaldo Guimaraes, superintendent of the Aratu industrial centre, a Bahia State agency, lists such examples as these: A 10-year exemption from income tax. A 10-year exemption from the new-products-turnover tax, which took the place of the old state sales tax. The deduction, however, must be reinvested. Financing by the federal

* See 'New Tides for an Island Nation' in *Fortune*, 15 August 1969.

Government's Superintendency for the Economic Development of the Northeast. The agency may provide up to 87½ per cent of financing for favored projects. Factory sites at nominal prices with power, water, sewers and paved highway connections. A new deep-water port big enough to accommodate manganese ore ships. Guarantees of compensation, monetary convertibility and single taxation to United States investments under an agreement between the United States and Brazilian Governments. The state has set aside 165 square miles for the center on the shore of All Saints Bay. Areas have been marked for light and heavy industry, a business center and residential districts, streets are being paved, trees planted, water and sewer pipes laid. Aratu is connected with Brazil's main highway running southward to Rio de Janeiro and São Paulo, and northward to Recife. A line will connect it with the country's chief railroad system – the Central do Brasil. Aratu will have its own airport to supplement Salvador's.

Bahia is part of the north-east. The resources of Amazonia are incomparably greater. The military government, advertising 'investment opportunities', in February 1967 announced 'Operation Amazon' in terms which remind one that those who secure a measure of power and profit by selling their country and their countrymen to profit-hungry foreigners must, like all procurers, have a sense of the attractiveness of what they are offering:

'Operation Amazon', a bold and forward-looking program to develop the vast potentials of the immense Amazon Basin, which occupies 60 per cent of Brazil, is the latest gigantic task undertaken by the Brazilian Government. Encouraged by the success of its development program in the Northeast through incentives to private enterprise, the Government has now called on the nation to turn its attention to the importance of a similar development program for the Amazon area. The two-million square-mile Amazon region . . . contains the most extensive system of navigable rivers in the world. . . . Forest resources are considered among the largest in the world, yet only an infinitesimal fraction of the potential has been exploited. Though the region is a traditional exporter of rubber, lumber, Brazil nuts, babassu and other oleaginous seeds, it was only recently that the application of agricultural methods produced jute and black pepper in sufficient amounts for shipping to other areas. No one could even guess what the forestry resources of the region would yield if modern technology were applied on a large scale.

Mineral Resources

Even with only the very modest amount of surveying already undertaken, rich deposits of iron ore, cassiterite, limestone, bauxite and lignite have been discovered. Large-scale manganese mining and export operations are already being carried out by Bethlehem Steel Co. and the Brazilian Antunes group in Amapa. More mineral wealth will no doubt be discovered when a master survey of the region is conducted in the near future by Brazil in cooperation with the US Government.

Incentives to Investment

Private industry, however, is already moving into the Amazon region even before complete information is available. Federal and state incentive programs are already proving an attraction to new enterprises. Together with these programs, a major step was recently taken when SUDAM (Superintendency for the Development of the Amazon Region), a central planning and co-ordinating body organized along the lines of SUDENE, was set up. Credit facilities for free enterprises are provided by FIDAM (Fund for Private Investments in the Amazon).'*

The easing of terms for profitable private exploitation of the Amazon's rich resources was part of a general *policy* which the Castelo Branco and Costa e Silva regimes announced regularly in advertisements and political statements. For example, early in 1966 the *New York Times* carried a large advertisement headed: INVEST IN BRAZIL. It began: 'More than 600 American companies – and 3,500 European and Japanese firms – have invested in Brazil:

In Brazil, the expression is 'my house is your house'. Now our house is in order. Now within the context and under the inspiration of pure capitalistic economic philosophy, we welcome and encourage investment from other countries. Brazil has adopted legislation on foreign capital that is undoubtedly among the most liberal

*NYTI.

in the world. Its philosophy is to create conditions sufficiently favorable to stimulate investment and reinvestment of foreign capital, rather than adopt negative restrictions on remittance of profits and dividends abroad. These incentives comprise an extensive span of activities. Examples: total exemption of import duties for equipment and accessories in certain key industries; 50 per cent income tax deduction for firms investing in the Northeast and Amazon regions; an investment guarantee agreement signed by the governments of the US and Brazil is already in operation, similar agreements are under negotiations with other countries; US and Brazil are presently working out new arrangements to exempt income of US investors in Brazil from duplicate income taxation; other specific advantages, too numerous for inclusion here, have been formulated and put into effect to facilitate the widest possible range of investment. New 1965 regulations have given extraordinary impetus to the capital market. It will now be possible to quickly raise resources in cruzeiros through normal stock market practices in addition to ordinary banking facilities.

Who is investing in Brazil today? The American government, the International Monetary Fund, the World Bank, the Inter-American Bank and other credit institutions have demonstrated their confidence in Brazil with new credits and loans of more than 1·3 billion dollars in the last twenty-one months. What about private enterprise? Here are just a few of the American and other companies who have recently embarked upon or announced new major investment programs in Brazil. Gulf Oil Corporation has entered in partnership with Refinaria e Exploracão de Petroleo União for the construction of a petrochemical complex in the state of São Paulo. Union Carbide has announced an investment program of 40·5 million dollars for the expansion of its activities. Plans call for doubled output of polyethylene and the installation of the world's most advanced facilities for the production of ethylene and acethylene. Significantly, only 6 million dollars of this figure represents reinvestment, 34·5 million dollars will be new investment funds. Ford Motors, hitherto engaged only in truck and tractor operations in Brazil, will enter the consumer auto field with an expansion investment program of 30 million dollars. Hanna Mining Company has merged with the Brazilian Antunes Group in a 50 million dollar investment program for the exploration, processing and export of iron ore. Phillips Petroleum Company and Cincinnati Chemical and Industrial Corporation have

G

entered a partnership with a group of Brazilian refiners to create a multimillion dollar industrial complex for the production of ammonia and fertilizers. Brazilian Traction Light & Power Company, of Toronto, is adding 100 million dollars to a loan from AID to expand its network of power distribution in the burgeoning industrial area of São Paulo and Rio de Janeiro. With annual auto production in Brazil averaging 200,000, Volkswagen and Willys-Overland have each announced important expansion programs to increase their productive capacities. Right now, under the sheltering provisions of the investment guarantee agreement between Brazil and the US, there are at this time 77 projects under advanced study representing an outlay of 230 million dollars. History is on Brazil's side. Its future is rich and promising. Brazil needs and invites foreign investors to share in the development of that future in an atmosphere of mutual benefit and cooperation.

Under Costa e Silva (who took office in March 1967), the attempts to open Brazil to foreign capital were stepped up. In addition to calling for investments in industries, land was advertised at give-away prices. Eduardo Galeano, the Uruguayan editor and author, reported that after the 1964 military *coup* in Brazil, United States Ambassador Lincoln Gordon had asked for Amazonia on a ninety-year lease. Popular opposition in Brazil, however, was too strong for this to be granted. But advertisements that Galeano quotes indicate that, regardless of the needs of land-hungry Brazilians, immense territories were being offered to North Americans.*

The massive report of the official inquiry conducted by an Brazilian lawyer, Jader de Figueiredo, and published in 1968, documented what the Brazilian 'Service for the Protection of the Indians' and the much-invited foreign 'developers' were doing to the people of the Amazon region. There was clear evidence of genocide carried on in the most brutal fashion. The

* One 'farm' of 98,000 acres was being offered at $2 per acre. 'The Biggest Land Bargains in the World' happened to be 500-acre ranches or farms for $1,200. 'You will help carve a civilization out of this wilderness that is actually God's country. A vast new empire with new cities, new highways, new industries will dawn before your eyes' (*Monthly Review,* December 1968).

role of the missionaries, foreign corporations, the Pentagon and other foreign government agencies, in the systematic extermination of the native Brazilians and the looting of the area was brought to light in the discussion provoked by the scandal.*

What was going on was more than Costa e Silva's Minister of the Interior could tolerate, as the following news report indicates:

General Albuquerque Lima, the Brazilian Minister of the Interior, has voiced the country's suspicions that 'foreign interests' may at present by showing too much interest for Brazilian taste in developing potentially rich regions like Amazonia. The General spoke of 'international avarice' to transform the natural resources of such regions into gain for the benefit of various interests, which the Government had to watch against. He accused 'groups of prospectors' of provoking incidents last year in the Rondonia region with the Brazilian territorial police.

The Times correspondent understandably concludes his report thus:

What foreign researchers are doing in the area, no matter how eminent their reputations in North America or Europe, is the subject of recurring suspicion among Brazilians. The present Government often strikes a nationalist attitude, but it also understands that

* Galeano also reported that according to estimates of the Brazilian military authorities 10,000 foreign scientists and 250 North American religious missions were in the area, engaged in activities of which some members of the government and public knew almost nothing. It is known that valuable minerals are flown out of the country from private airstrips. Conrad Gorinsky, reporting on 'The Amerindian Situation' in *Race Today* (August 1969) wrote: '... Indians are being machine-gunned, bombed, dynamited, napalmed and even systematically poisoned by the agents of banks and investment companies anxious to clear the land so that it can be sold to speculators. Ranchowners often hunt the tribespeople for sport, or round them up and force them to work for them in conditions of near slavery. Mineral prospectors and rubber tappers shoot them on sight, introduce "doctors" who inject them with smallpox and have been discovered distributing gifts of sugar laced with arsenic ...'

foreign expertise and capital are essential to develop the out-back.'*

In the nineteenth century, Asian and African colonials proved useful in wars of colonial conquest and in putting down unrest and disorder. The cheap manpower of these countries (where life is asserted by outsiders to be held cheap) is still useful in the acquisition and the political and economic management of profitable investments. The increasing difficulties foreign interests had in maintaining order in post-independence Asia led naturally to the policy of 'Asians kill Asians'. Instead of direct recruiting of mercenaries, or forced service, as in colonial or semi-colonial situations, 'cooperative' oligarchies were persuaded, in return for suitable political and economic rewards, to provide the necessary cannon fodder. Their mercenaries are not soldiers of fortune, but conscripts sent abroad to serve foreign international economic interests, or even to destroy local nationalists. In Latin America the way in which a nondescript force formed by the most oppressive dictatorships took over from US troops to prevent the emergence of a liberal–democratic regime in the Dominican Republic is typical.

While the running of foreign-owned enterprises is increasingly being financed from local sources (eighty-four per cent of United States foreign 'investment' in 1968 was locally financed, according to a *Times* report),† the profits of these enterprises are primarily intended for export to the home territory of the corporation's effective owners or management. The export of dividends, repatriation of capital, profits and interest of the earnings of the few industrial or semi-industrial enterprises deprives the local economy of an obvious source of investment in development projects. The drain on the meagre surplus of the 'underdeveloped' economies is an irreparable

* The US Air Force has already made an aerial survey of what is on the surface of northern Brazil, as well as under it. US corporations are no doubt more 'expert' about Brazil's mineral resources than Brazilian scientists.

† 6 August 1968.

loss, for what is exchanged for the outgoing funds is negligible in terms of its value for the construction of an economy and society with adequate opportunities for creative and productive work. There is no increment in the local economic substructure to correspond to the increment in the wealth and power of the profit-making corporation. 'Investment' does not necessarily mean the actual transfer of dollars or sterling to the value of the amount invested. Even if it did, the figures for direct investment by United States corporations from 1950 to 1965 are instructive:

($ billion)	Europe	Canada	Latin America	All other areas
Flow of direct investments from US	8·1	6·8	3·8	5·2
Income on this capital transferred to US	5·5	5·9	11·3	14·3
Net outflow from US	2·6	·9	−7·5	−9·1

That is, in the underdeveloped countries almost three times as much money was taken out as was put in. Furthermore, direct investments owned by US business corporations increased over this period for Latin America from $4·5 billion to $10·3 billion, and in Asia and Africa from $1·3 billion to $4·7 billion.* The outflows from the Third World economies are in fact underestimated; for foreign companies use a variety of devices to reduce the declared profit and profit rate, and therefore the tax paid to the country in which they operate. Declared capital and outflow from the investing country may be increased by paper loans from the parent company to its subsidiary abroad which appear in the books but do not represent any actual investment, while the capital can be artificially increased, for example, by issuing bonus shares – shares issued free or at reduced rates for shares already held.

* Magdoff (*op. cit.*), citing US Department of Commerce, *Balance of Payments, Statistical Supplement* and *Survey of Current Business*.

Sophisticated accounting procedures and legal manipulation are part of the management process by which the deformation of the economy progresses. It obviously will be considered subversive and treasonable if the mass of the poor are shown how the corporations which work freely across several national boundaries operate. It is relatively easy for declared profit in one place to be decreased and the balance transferred to regions of lowest tax.* Corporations like Standard New Jersey and Shell, it has been pointed out, own fleets of around 150 and 120 ships respectively, and those like United Fruit Company owned whole towns. Excessive charging by the transportation sector of a corporation increases deductible expenses and reduces taxable profits, but does not affect the earnings of the corporation as a whole. The profits of a subsidiary may be 'loaned' to its parent in the developed country, where it is used as capital, while the subsidiary pays no taxes on an unrepaid debt. These are some of the legitimate ways in which the skills of corporation managers, accountants and lawyers are employed.

Once the highly resourceful and politically skilled forces in control of an industrialized foreign economy get a base within a weaker and less developed economy and society, they act with a dynamic of their own. The collaborating indigenous minorities, with little bargaining power, must assume a subordinate role in exchange for security of tenure in the ruling palaces, and sometimes for support against rebellion which has been intensified by the determination of their subjects to get rid of 'imperialist' and 'neo-colonialist' powers. The international implications of the developments which follow we must survey in a later chapter. Among the domestic implications are the increasing restriction on the power of the local oligarchy, and a blocking of the development of any forms of local capitalism. The laws, regulations, values and culture of the host country become assimilated to the requirements of the foreign corporations. (After the 1964 *coup* in Brazil US 'experts'

---

* An understanding of the structure, resources and power of the 'international' companies which have come into being is indispensable for a grasp of what is going on in the world today.

began to alter the subversive education system.) The policy-making bodies have to accept foreign patronage. Argentina is an example. The Ministers of Defence, Foreign Relations, Economy and Labour, and Industry together with the Deputy Minister of Commerce and President of the Industrial Bank were all reported early in 1969 to be holding high positions in US-owned and German-owned firms operating in Argentina. Similar associations, which blocked policies unfavourable to foreign interests, obtained for a long time in Peru. The dispute between the International Petroleum Company (a subsidiary of a Canadian New Jersey Standard-owned Company) and the Peruvian government over unpaid debts resulted in the nationalization of IPC holdings and the suspension of US 'aid'. It can be traced back not only to international arbitration in 1924, when the Company started operations in Peru by violating long-standing local laws, but also to a 1945 decree allowing the amount of profit to remain strictly confidential. There was a 1950 mining code giving vaguely defined exploitation rights and allowing fifty (later amended to 33·33) per cent tax exemption for depletion. IPC subsequently occupied a monopoly position, by 1959 handling ninety-eight per cent of all oil refined in Peru. The oil-fields were later returned to Peru, leaving only the refining in IPC hands. But IPC wielded tremendous influence in the country. The chairman of the national oil company was accused of altering a price agreement with IPC in the latter's favour. The military-backed political opposition to President Belaunde found the scandal a convenient occasion to overthrow the government and nationalize the oil. Western European financial interests have been trying to break the virtual US monopoly in Latin America, and General Velasco skilfully exploited the widespread Latin American opposition to the high-handedness of the US government and US corporations without allowing the privileged position of the Peruvian oligarchy to be lost.

Foreign capital, it is well-known not only in Latin America but also in Indonesia, India, Pakistan and South Africa, demands stable conditions and security for investments. These

are not conducive to development. The Brazilian Minister of
the Treasury was to say in 1953, 'I have to declare that foreign
capital ... demands guarantees to enter the country, greater
guarantees to remain in it, and still greater ones to withdraw
from it. Therefore, it does not seem desirable for any country,
and still less for Brazil.' The path to development through
indigenous capitalist development is closed, if laws and
regulations discriminating in favour of foreign capital are
passed. The President of the Federation of Industries in Brazil's
São Paulo state was reported to have commented on import
restrictions: 'Foreign firms can bring their entire equipment
at the free market price ... national ones, however, have to do
so through exchange licences established in import categories.
In this way there was created veritable discrimination against
national industries. We do not plead for preferential treatment
but for equal opportunities.'* The Capital Investment Guarantees which the powerful US government was able to get the
Brazilian government to sign after the *coup* against President
Goulart were a severe blow to Brazilian capitalist enterprises.
A cooperative Brazilian enterprise, the Vale do Rio project,
was developing Brazil's rich deposits of high-grade iron ore.
This indigenous venture, undertaken by private and public
capital, had to yield to the Hanna Mining Company (an
affiliate of Republic Steel). The US company was also given the
concession of a private sea-port.

The conditions in countries where the mass of the population
are put to work or starve for the sake of a minority, and in
which a small, isolated *élite* or class has the power to make laws
and regulations, are highly favourable to the economic expansion of foreign enterprises. The officials and politicians in the
capitals are in no position to withstand the pressures of major
powers, and their decisions are not subject even to formal
democratic procedures. The activities of foreign capital tend,
even in a country like Canada, to predominate in the 'host'
country, and to assume a monopoly position in various sectors
of the economy. The United Fruit Company (now largely

* *Monthly Review*, September 1964.

owned by AMK) markedly exhibited this characteristic. As the US Department of Justice was to state in the 1950s: 'With the exception of land in Ecuador, United owns, leases or otherwise controls 85 per cent of the land in the American tropics suitable for banana cultivation.'* The way in which economic dominance of Third World economies by foreign capital is developed is also illustrated in Liberia. According to a 1964 United Nations Report, two fifths of Liberia's total national income goes to foreign firms (notably Firestone and Bethlehem Steel). Foreign capital also controls about half of India's economy, while foreign exchange banks control about four fifths of India's foreign trade.† Under conditions such as these it is the obstacles to a reorganization of the economy of poverty, and to the creation of a democratic productive base, which are actively and systematically being developed and strengthened. New channels of disinvestment come into being.

THE DEFENCE OF FOREIGN INTERESTS

The political consequences of foreign investment are many. Among them is the unique status of foreign firms from particular countries. They have all the rights to draw on or dispose of the national resources and traditions of the host-communities, and all the privileges that the indigenous people ought to have – but they have more, for they have special concessions and privileges. They have the services and security which the government, police and army should provide for the people whose country it is – but they are exempt from bothersome obligations, having the protection and assistance of a far more powerful government, able to deal diplomatically and militarily with those who would interfere with the international freedom of private enterprise. The 'power gap' is thus greatly increased because of 'international partnership'. The distance to be crossed politically to reach a genuinely developing productive base increases.

* J. Gerassi, *The Great Fear in Latin America* (New York), p. 171.
† C. Bettelheim, *India Independent* (London, 1969), pp. 56–62.

The traditional or other conservative forces in societies can, as we have observed, produce the running down or decline of the economy. The vast majority of the population can continue to be impoverished while the flow of wealth and services can be concentrated in the direction of a few. Part of the social and political management by which this process is made to work depends on the use of traditional forms. But indigenous traditions have elements which can be used as resources for the modernizing forces, and as restraints on those in power. However wide the gap in well-being and power, the members of the ruling class are never out of reach of the forces struggling for change. There is also a limit to the devastation and destruction they can achieve short of cutting the ground from under their own feet. But for the poor to size up, contain or defeat destructive forces the bases of whose power and domination are far distant, requires an effort which calls for resources which lie much deeper than the already available or traditional resources. The political struggle needed for modernization in that case requires the development of new powers. Foreign corporations (for reasons which we need to examine at some length in the next two chapters) are not limited by the considerations or restraints of the kind which work on the local rulers. What works with a Trujillo or even a Chiang does not work with 'international' companies. Imperialists out to make money or ruin the opposition can devastate and destroy far more thoroughly.

Where the short- or long-term interests of foreign capitalist businesses and enterprises require it, resort is made to drastic political or military action which depresses the economic level of the people. Foreign political intervention acts to complicate, slow down, retard or even reverse political advance towards the creation of a sound base for the rapid emancipation of the poor. 'Political management' for the benefit of the 'international developers' is more oppressive than that of the local oligarchies.

THE DISRUPTIVE CONSEQUENCES OF PARTITION AND DISUNITY

It has been argued here that, as oppression impoverishes the people, their resourcefulness, power of organization and creativity are brought into play in the revolutionary struggle to achieve a richer quality of life. Thus, as peoples arrive at the threshold of a new, more advanced, stage of technological and economic development they must, for survival and the realization of richer productive possibilities, create a new, more democratic community life, involving all working people. The national territory, which contains the material and cultural resources which belong to the people, becomes the basis for development. At this point political manipulation of the international order by outside powers may instead bring about economic and political changes which distort and inhibit economic activity and growth. Boundaries may be given or denied 'international' status, territory taken away or partition imposed in such ways as to make the newly developing territory economically unviable. This is the cold logic of another, contradictory, economic rationality, which is part of the dynamic of a highly distorted world economic system, which is legitimized and protected by what is called 'international law'. Where conditions permit, peoples who need to cooperate in developmental activity may be induced to engage in mutual competition, rivalries and hatreds; these not only prevent the cooperation and solidarity of the whole Third World, and of its component regional communities, essential for development, but also engage them in a process of mutual, even fratricidal, destruction. If a key country in that part of the world can be brought to the point of arming for action against a neighbouring friendly country – particularly one which is ready for international cooperation across traditional boundaries – resources of both countries are being diverted from genuine development activity. And the poor become more vulnerable to invasion and conquest by their real enemies.

Unity and cooperation among the peoples of Latin America,

the Arab lands, south Asia and east Asia are vital for economic development. The overthrow of colonial rule in Latin America in the nineteenth century was accomplished by a variety of local uprisings, as a result of the alien or oppressive nature of Spanish or Portuguese rule. The forces under Simon Bolivar and San Martin which converged on the main South American centre of Spanish rule, Lima, had a great deal in common. The final defeat of the Spanish, at Ayacucho, was accomplished by a republican army drawn from the whole continent. But when independence was secured by 1825 (in all of Spanish America except Puerto Rico and Cuba) neither economic nor social development was ripe enough for continental unification. The area stretching from Mexico to Argentina was much more extensive than that covered by the North American colonies which became independent. Only small patches of it had been developed economically, and communications were poor because the roads which in the pre-colonial period had connected the different areas to centres in the interior had been neglected. Francisco de Miranda's dream of 'Colombia' – a great nation stretching from the Rio Grande to Cape Horn – was as impractical as his belief that Spanish America could be liberated with British help. Bolivar's 'Gran Colombia' itself did not last, and the pan-American (that is, Latin American) conferences he and others called* were only partially successful. The new republics did not have statesmen to rule them, they were not democratically run, and in spite of the common threats they faced, from time to time they warred against one another. Authoritarian attitudes and colonial social structures persisted (as in Africa today), and there was little sense of achieving economic development and trade among themselves. Bolivar himself had blamed 'different climates, diverse situations, opposing interests and disparate temperaments'. In later years the need for cooperation and unity in Latin America became very evident. But Latin American

* The Congress of Panama (1826), the First Congress of Lima (1847–8), the Continental Congress in Santiago de Chile (1856) and the Second Congress of Lima (1864–5).

'nations' have remained or been kept divided, even while outsiders engaged in exploiting Latin America's people and resources have acted in the name of supra-national bodies.

Despite the common historical and cultural background the colonial past bound the different parts of colonial Latin America to outside interests. In the post-colonial period the *caudillos* and middle-class and feudal *élites* were less interested in Latin American nationalism, which is essentially 'of the people', than in foreign ties which might be advantageous to them. In the early years of the twentieth century it had become clear to those who recognized the vital importance of unity and integration that the plan for a confederation could not begin at the level of governments, since, as these Latin Americans saw it, the governments were under Yankee control. The absorption of the Latin American peoples into a pan-American system dominated by the United States made Latin American solidarity even more difficult to achieve.

The divisions and antagonisms in south-east Asia, in the Arab lands, between India and China, in tropical Africa and elsewhere are demonstrably destructive of actual possibilities of and tendencies towards development. One could fill a book with accounts of how forces outside the Third World have tried to prevent unity and cooperation among the peoples in various regions of this vast area.

The anti-development consequences of internal disunity must not be underrated. The post-war partition of Korea, newly liberated from the oppression and exploitation of half a century of Japanese imperial rule, has been disastrous for the Korean people. If the solidarity of the industrious Korean people had formed the basis of a modern Korean nation, which excluded all intervention by the superpowers, Korea's history would undoubtedly be happier than it has been. In India, the political ambitions of middle-class leaders, together with British policies, allowed Hindu–Muslim differences and rivalries to be exaggerated. The mass of the people, who should have seen poverty as their main enemy, were persuaded to turn on one another rather than their actual oppressors; those who dominated them were able to establish a false solidarity on a communal basis, and thus to control and manipulate the backward and illiterate poor, while the communal fanaticism not only made political and economic rationality impossible but also added to the suffering and breakdown which had been the lot of the Indian people. The Hindu–Muslim clashes and pogroms, the breaking up of the weak economy of the subcontinent, and the deliberate maintenance of artificial tensions between India and Pakistan, provided opportunities for foreign interference and helped governments hostile to independent Asian development to establish footholds within the subcontinent. These have all been destructive of south Asia's tremendous potential for development, and of a realistic political consciousness in a subcontinent of peoples whose contribution to the progress of mankind and of peace is as indispensable as that of the Europeans, the Chinese and the North Americans.

Even in the small island of Ceylon, where Sinhalese-speaking and Tamil-speaking people have coexisted for over a thousand years, a 'communal' problem was artificially created. Ceylon is a country with a small population and a limited area: the same population as the Netherlands, but with twice the area. The mobilization of all its people on democratic lines is vital for its economic and political survival; but it is not vital if the prosperity of a small land-owning, business and professional *élite* and foreign owners of Ceylonese property is all that matters. The conception of a 'conflict of interests' between Sinhalese-speaking and Tamil-speaking Ceylonese was possible only if the country's political and material problems were defined in the wrong way. The working people and their families in town and village were persuaded to regard those of the other language group as the enemy while exploitation by the ruling classes and foreign interests went unregarded. Not only were the older, more established communities (which included the 'Moors', 'Burghers' and Malays) unable to act in unity; they were at one in their discrimination against the Ceylon 'Indians', nearly all of whom were descended from nineteenth-century immigrants brought in by the British as indentured labourers to create the plantations. These were the hardest worked, most productive and most oppressed and exploited section of the Ceylonese population. But British and United States Imperialist interests in Ceylon which were obstacles to development benefited by the disunity.*

In west and east Africa, in south-east Asia and elsewhere a great deal of trouble has been taken by foreigners hostile to indigenous initiatives in development to make use of ancient and reactionary racial and tribal suspicions and hostilities. Extensive research has been going on in American universities and in 'the field' to discover how to ruin indigenous development by strengthening the obstacle to development which is being discussed at present. For the tendency among revolutionary left-wing nationalists to end discrimination against minorities and to unite all the poor against the ruling class and imperialist forces is countered by exacerbating internecine hatreds in subtle ways. Work of this kind done in Vietnam and Laos has been widely reported. The interest of the US Department of Defense, through its 'Advanced Research Projects Agency', in using minorities for subversion and counter-insurgency is shown in 'research' discussed in books like *Southeast Asian Tribes, Minorities and Nations.*†

THE CULTURE OF POVERTY

The term 'the culture of poverty' has received a good deal of attention since it was used by the anthropologist Oscar Lewis.

* Fuller discussion of contemporary Ceylon on these lines is to be found in *Organizing for Development: Progress and Reaction in Ceylon 1948–1963* (Colombo, 1964).

† Edited by Peter Kustadter and published in two volumes (Princeton, 1967). 'Only the Communist-dominated parties of East and Southwest Asia,' writes the editor, 'have made reasonably clear statements concerning the rights of the minorities to organize themselves and to preserve or change their cultures' (p. 59). To ruin this nation-building effort, vital for development, is no doubt a laudable policy for the rich who are threatened by such 'Communism'.

It is useful, but if used entirely in Lewis's sense can give an incorrect idea of the cultural factors which assist in producing the widespread poverty in the Third World. Anti-development, it has been argued, results from the systematic working of a certain type of political, economic and social order. That order has its own hierarchy of values and its peculiar ethic. The ideals it invokes lure people towards greater underdevelopment. The prevailing conceptions of normality, justice and rightness make it appear as if those who seek to create a free social order are immoral and culpable. Law, literature and art, philosophy, theology, economic theory, sociology and historical scholarship reinforce and sanctify those conceptions.

The culture of poverty is at work wherever the reversing of the anti-development process so as to bring about the mutual enrichment of all men, the earth and all living creatures is made to appear absurd and impractical. Ethically, it would condemn as theft the attempt by the well-to-do and politically conscious to restore to the poor what is properly theirs. The drama, literature and music of the anti-development order, its television, radio and journalism, draw the community into valuing highly the agonies and hopes, aspirations and joys, fears and ambitions, of the rich, the mighty, the affluent – in the local cities and mansions and in North America and Europe. They thus tend to build up a sympathy for the way of life of the rich and super-rich. Those who weep or laugh over the pains and pleasures of lords and ladies, millionaires and playboys, generals, governors and commissars; or inhabit in imagination the palaces and drawing-rooms of the successful, or feel privileged to share the counsels of the great, become remote from the experiences, problems and aspirations of the poor.

The ways in which people are motivated, and their attitudes formed, by the prevailing culture in an anti-development order, lead them to work for their own impoverishment. Further, the long-established and subtle racialism implicit in the prevailing order acts with great effectiveness as an inhibiting force in a world in which the poor peoples are mainly those of

non-European origin. The prevailing doctrines teach dependence on and inferiority to the 'white man'. Science is irrationally
spoken of as *Western* science. Poor people, the non-whites, are
prevailed upon by the culture of poverty to renounce self-
reliant effort, initiative, originality and discovery as a way to
end poverty. Their own ideas and solutions are by definition
wrong in so far as they contradict or judge those of the dominant classes. For Westerners are *the* authorities on development
and modernization; they are the only model; they disapprove
of peoples of the Third World coming together to exchange
their own ideas and discoveries, to learn from one another and
jointly to discover how the poverty and oppression on which
they are experts can be eradicated. The struggle to reverse the
anti-development process must include an attempt to examine
the credentials of the super-rich.

THE CLOSING OF THE GAP

In digging down to the foundations of the *system* whose working
impoverishes, oppresses and destroys the overwhelming mass
of the people *while* it enriches, exalts and provides security for
the rich we have come to identify the cause of the great poverty
and chronic hunger of which we took note in Chapter 1. The
misappropriation, in every land – every country, every town,
every village – of the community's material resources and
powers, in order to create a monopoly of authority and power
for a numerically tiny, self-perpetuating class, creates the
fundamental condition of world poverty. Not only do the
poverty-creating rich advance their interests through their
monopoly of law-making and police powers, weapons of
destruction, their exclusive property in the means of production, their control of education, and so on, but they also
claim 'legitimacy' in the international system and secure it in
exchange for what they are able to pay the super-rulers in
Washington, London, Moscow, Tokyo and Paris.

The development process was described earlier as a struggle
against all the forces, institutions, practices and structures which

actively promote anti-development. It is only when the masses of the poor in every local situation begin to be successful in this struggle that the process of development – the reconstruction on the lines suggested in Chapter 3 of polity and economy – is practicable. They must take over all that has been forced, beaten, drained out of them, all that has been extorted. They must confront the terrorism of rulers not with fear and submission but with courage, and induce a fear and respect in their oppressors. It is only as they do this systematically and in an organized way that they will close the gap. The classes who have been robbed and cheated by the cumulative effects of traditional, capitalist and imperialist 'development' are the men and women who laboured to produce all the material, social and cultural wealth there is, and their authentic heirs. They alone can create and develop a world which belongs to its people; and they have to advance politically to an understanding of their real powers and their historical mission to liberate all the oppressed. By intensifying world poverty the forces of anti-development are hastening its, and their own, end. That will arrive when the proletarian struggle to eradicate oppression in all its forms becomes worldwide, is led by genuine experts and reverses the history made by the oppressing rich.

In this justifiable and necessary war on poverty will the poor in each land get the support of the poor elsewhere? Will they get foreign aid from the affluent peoples for their struggle for development? Do the leaders and peoples of the high-income countries have the will, the experience and the capacity to assist them? How real is the prospect of aid for the war to eradicate poverty?

CHAPTER 7

The Aid Relationship:
The Benefactors, Models and Teachers

FOREIGN AID IN THE STRATEGY OF DEVELOPMENT

THE working together of certain social, economic and political factors in the way described in Chapter 3 constitutes the beginning of the 'development process'. In taking note of these mention was made of how any community could accelerate the development of the material base of production, exchange and consumption by importing from another 'national' economy vitally needed resources which were unavailable or in short supply locally. In this chapter we consider how realistic it is to expect this form of aid in the struggle against anti-development.

The exchange of manufactures, ideas, skills, technology and useful materials has, of course, been going on since the beginnings of civilized life. Different communities at different times have shown a marked ability to make discoveries or inventions in particular fields of activity; in that way they take a share in the pioneering which is necessary for the continual 'modernization' of human society and its modes of production and its social organization, and its enrichment through scientific and moral discoveries. What was possible for some men, e.g. the Chinese technique of iron-casting or manufacture of gunpowder, demonstrates what is possible for others. What gives point to a discussion of the 'aid' that is offered today from the more industrialized and affluent communities to the less developed is, firstly, the existence of the gap in technology and economic organization that opened up between two large groups of peoples from the seventeenth century onwards. One group transformed the material conditions of their existence by the application of ever-improving methods of machine-production, scientific knowledge and organization to manufactures, military technology and the mobilization of new sources of energies (human and non-human) and skills. The others continued mainly with hand industries until historical changes around them made these of no practical use.

The generations who have to solve the problems inherited by the 1970s are no doubt aware that not very long ago, at the beginning of the Second World War, mankind was still separated into two general groupings enjoying markedly different standards of living. The peoples whose modernization had for one reason or another been retarded in the previous centuries and decades lived mostly in Asia, Africa and Latin America. It is to the other group that those actively interested in 'aid' belong – to that group of peoples who had been free to transform and develop their economies and societies by keeping pace with and assisting the accelerating pace of new development. Once the poor and technologically backward peoples awoke to their situation, they realized that they would have to progress in one massive bound if they were going to reach a stage of development compatible with the most advanced contemporary standards in science, agricultural and industrial technology, equipment and organization. How could they do this most economically? In the circumstances, this was a question which the earlier developers had never had to answer, except perhaps in Russia. Part of the answer was that the poor would not be relying on themselves any the less if *they* decided to make use of needed ideas, skills and equipment which had been tested in the already highly industrialized areas. As long as these helped to speed them on their chosen way to rapid self-development by the whole people, rather than hindered or diverted them, the time, resources and effort spent in trying to develop these ideas, skills and equipment independently would be largely wasted. The time, resources and effort would be more valuably spent in improving on what others had done.

Any arrangement, therefore, which makes it economically and politically feasible to bring about a flow of economically strategic resources in the direction of the already developing, less affluent peoples, and for their own use, will, from the 'civilized' as well as the 'development' point of view, be valuable. The enthusiasts who believe that more goodwill, and bigger and better schemes of 'aid' are urgent and necessary, are in fact arguing that the 'gap' which opened up with the Industrial Revolution and the creation of world empires can be closed if individuals and organizations who benefit from the more developed economies – that is, those in the countries with the superior technical experience and greater productive capacity that an earlier start in modern development has brought – increase their efforts to interest their governments as well as fellow-citizens in intensifying the war against world poverty. That is one way, they believe, in which the impoverishment of the Third World, caused partly by the apathy and weakness of its own peoples, can be ended. If these enthusiasts, to whom we have already referred in Chapter 1, are correct in what they assume about the benevolent and altruistic attitudes and motivations of the affluent, and about the value of 'aid', 'More and more aid' will be a good slogan. Are these assumptions correct, however? Is an increase in what now flows, or is offered, as 'aid' from the rich to the poor desirable? These questions lead to an inspection of the specific character of the relationship which *already* exists among peoples and races. We cannot grasp what is involved in the struggle for development without exploring that relationship and how it grew, and without being clear about what 'international' actually means.

The rich nations and the poor are not groups of the same kind who have had a separate existence. (Russia, the United States and Japan are not nations in the identical sense in which China, Vietnam and Tanzania are.) They have been in contact over a period of centuries, and the contact has not been casual and insignificant. They were, they have been, closely inter-related. They have been living partially integrated in the same 'world'. That is, they have increasingly formed different parts of a single economic and political order. The strength and accelerating enrichment of one and the debility and impoverishment of the other helped to create in the nineteenth and early twentieth centuries an economic unit which bound together what had been geographically and culturally distant peoples. It was a unit, perhaps we should say an economic order, which encompassed and interrelated all the ways in which, in the new capitalist system, people lived and got their livelihood. By the new process of financing and organizing production, trade, distribution and consumption it penetrated almost every community, whether highly civilized or primitive, and determined its role and status. It transformed the geography, history, politics and culture of the whole world.

The existence of this world order was implied in the pictures drawn earlier in this essay of the practices of the international corporations of the industrialized countries which move across the boundaries of states, and of the international flow of money and resources. In so far as international 'aid' for development expresses a solidarity among peoples, action by the peoples of the now affluent countries will be effective if, for example, it can end the oppression of the poor in the Third World by the big corporations and their military–police forces. We cannot discuss how this can come about without first taking a close look at what goes on within the 'rich' countries, what they live for, who makes the important national decisions, what they are after, what their conception of the moral order is, and to what extent the eradication of the conditions that breed poverty is for them a value and an achievement. Only then can foreign aid be discussed in a realistic manner.

AIDERS AND AIDED: A PRELIMINARY SURVEY

Before we begin a discussion of 'aid' and of aid projects it will be useful also to be clear that we are talking about relationships and situations occurring in a number of overlapping historical contexts. A preliminary survey will indicate the ground which we must cover in this chapter. At the end of the Second World War nearly all the civilized peoples were brought to the point of finding practical answers to fundamental questions about their future and the shape of the international order which they would have to build in place of the one that had apparently been shattered by the war. What the poor nations had to say was heard much more loudly than ever before. The subject peoples had recognized that during the period when the European and Japanese financiers and industrialists had monopolized progress they, the subject peoples, had lost out both by being denied independent modernization and by the deformation of their material order and culture. Their resolve, as economically retarded peoples, to make up for what they had lost had been formed gradually, and over a long period of time, in India, China, Egypt, Indochina, Mexico and elsewhere. Given the fact that they had been kept apart, and that some among them had been encouraged to think of themselves in tribal, communal or national terms or only in relation to the rulers of the metropolitan country, and not as the poor classes in the world economy, there was no concerted decision to begin closing the gap which unequal development and exploitation had opened up – between rulers and ruled.* Nevertheless, we can take the year 1945 as the beginning of a new period for the peoples who had experienced the consequences of living in a broken-down traditional society which had been compelled to play a colonial or semi-colonial role in the 'international division of labour'. It effectively marks the end of an age which, as we remarked before, is distinguished by the phenomenal increase, among Europeans and Japanese, of the power of production and of scientific knowledge, and the power to subjugate other peoples. In fact, by 1941–2, when the war became world-wide, it was evident that the seeds of self-destruction sown by the capitalist system had borne fruit.

Both the rich and the poor groups of nations would regard the last twenty-five years as a period when the most talked-about and written-about concern seemed to be the rapid development of peoples – political development, economic development, educational development, scientific development

* International solidarity among the subject, non-European peoples had begun to develop quite early – see Chapter 9 below.

and so on. In the colonial sector of the world, those who lived through the war years had seen popular armed liberation movements in many countries of south-east Asia – the Philippines, Malaya, Laos, Thailand, Burma and Vietnam – and that in China grow tremendously in strength and authority. Through the August Revolution of the Vietnamese, the workers and peasants by their armed struggle against the French and Japanese rulers brought into being in 1945 an independent Democratic Republic of Vietnam. A people who many centuries previously had been an independent and civilized force had recovered the power to play their independent role in the second half of the twentieth century. Actually and symbolically the situation of the poor and oppressed as well as their possibilities had changed. The new government of Vietnam, in its Declaration of Independence of 2 September that year, appealed for the understanding and support of the peoples in the rest of the world, backing its claims with references to the American and French revolutionary declarations.* Then came an even more stupendous achievement of the poor: the revolutionary struggle of the working people, predominantly peasant, of China against their international as well as national oppressors freed all of China except Taiwan. There had (as a climax to nearly half a century of resistance against what Sun Yat-sen had called a 'triple oppression') been eight years of bitter war and direct foreign rule before Japan's surrender; then the civil war had been resumed. In 1949, as the majority of the world's peoples saw it, a century of invasion, annexation, exploitation and humiliation was ended in China by those who had suffered the consequences. They could look forward to a period of peaceful reconstruction, and the fulfilment of the task they had set themselves of creating a world in which poverty is not produced and exploitation not practised. The Chinese, the most populous nation in the world, had become free to conduct their war against poverty.

In several countries where there had been less revolutionary independence movements the leaders, like those of the Vietnam-

---

* See my *From Gandhi to Guevara: The Polemics of Revolt* (London, 1970), pp. 356–9, also pp. 92–8.

ese, expected help, particularly from the people of the United States and the Soviet Union, in their struggle to end their colonial status. The US government had, together with those of other powers, charted the course of decolonization at the end of the war in a number of declarations and actions: the Atlantic Charter of 14 August 1941; the United Nations Declaration of 1 January 1942; the international meeting of 15 May 1943 at Hot Springs, Virginia; the loud proclamation of doom for all those who enjoyed the fruits of aggression and of conquest of foreign territories manifest both in the world-wide anti-Fascist Alliance and in the Summit Conferences at Casablanca (26 January 1943), Cairo (26 November 1943), Teheran (1 December 1943) and Yalta (4–11 February 1945); and the San Francisco meeting to form the United Nations Organization (25 April–26 June 1945). There was the well-known determination of President Roosevelt that the old colonial powers should relinquish their colonial possessions. Many left-wing nationalists in Asia also believed that US–Soviet leadership after the war would ensure that, with the liberation of the peoples in the German, Italian and Japanese empires, all forms of foreign domination would be liquidated, and a new era of cooperation among free and equal peoples inaugurated.*

* In the communiqué of the Cairo Conference, for example, the US, British and Chinese leaders declared jointly that they were 'fighting this war to *restrain and punish the aggression* of Japan. They *covet* no gain for themselves and have no thought of *territorial expansion*. It is their purpose that Japan shall be *stripped* of all the islands in the Pacific which she has *seized or occupied* since the beginning of the First World War in 1914, and that all the territories Japan has *stolen* from the Chinese, such as Manchuria, Formosa, and the Pescadores, shall be *restored* to the Republic of China. Japan will also be *expelled* from all other territories which she has *taken by violence and greed*. The aforesaid three great powers, mindful of the *enslavement* of the people of Korea, are determined that in due course Korea shall become *free and independent*' (italic added). This is a declaration based on *principles*. That Winston Churchill, referring to a former ally of Britain, could be so forthrightly anti-imperialist as to join in issuing this declaration, gave it added significance. The attitude of the United States and Britain to the original Japanese 'aggression, territorial expansion', etc. in Korea and China is highly interesting.

So did some American liberals. A highly sensitive and idealistic American, Harold R. Isaacs, who tried to describe the peculiar character of the historical moment that followed the world war, saw it as a 'turning point'. He wrote:

If the American dream had any reality, now was the time for it to manifest itself. If American professions and good intentions are valid, now was the time to make them good. If the American system of capitalist democracy had within it the promise of fruitful growth for the world, here, perhaps, was the first opportunity to prove it . . .

This war . . . had placed before us once more the whole issue of conquest and power and profit as the basis for existence on the planet. The American victory in the Pacific war was nothing less than the American opportunity to face up to that issue . . .!*

Ever since that time it has been taken for granted in liberal circles that the old relationship of imperial powers and subject peoples (regardless of whether or not it was ever a good thing) was a thing of the past. It was assumed that in place of it there would be a more altruistic relationship, within which part of the costs of the development of independent modern economies and states in the non-European world of Asia, Africa and Latin America would be met by the industrialized and former imperial powers. There would be no need for the subject peoples to *fight* in order to recover their freedom and their own economic resources and to establish their claim to equality of status with those who had for the previous century or two dominated them. The power, privileges and profit of empire would be renounced by its beneficiaries, whether they were Japanese or British, Italian or American.

It is out of a belief in this new, post-colonial goodwill and spirit of international cooperation that there appears to have developed the concern with and aid for the war on world poverty which the organizations noted at the beginning of this essay believe they are conducting. It is part of this belief that the non-industrialized peoples of Latin America, Asia and Africa have, since 1945 and perhaps much earlier, been viewed by North America, Europe, Japan and Australia with friend-

* Harold R. Isaacs, *No Peace for Asia* (New York, 1947), p. 213.

ship and respect; that they are seen as less fortunate communities who need to be helped to modernize, and to 'develop' economically and politically. The 'developing' countries are believed, on their part, to appreciate and be grateful for the way in which the authorities in the West regard them; and to seek after the guidance, patronage and support of the major powers. Hence the creation of such organizations as the United States-sponsored South-East Asia Treaty Organization, the Alliance for Progress (in Latin America) and the Asian Development Bank. Hence also the Russian proposals for military and economic alliances. The French role in west Africa, and the British role in Africa and Asia since the war are also fitted into this new pattern, in which the former conquerors, exploiters and rulers are seen reversing their role.

Thus there already appears to exist a post-colonial relationship of aid-givers and aid-recipients, superseding what was purported to be the old relationship of invader and exploiter on the one side and subject and exploited on the other. If there is still a relationship of dependence it is believed to be a voluntary one, to be explained by the fact that the leaders of the poor countries, while they want to end poverty, recognize their inability to think things out for themselves or help themselves, and seek the superior wisdom, knowledge and skills of their former masters. Among the peoples whose economies have technically been modernized so as to produce a surfeit of material benefits, there are many who would argue that there is nothing humiliating or sinister in this voluntary dependence. They would regard it not as generosity, but as a duty, for them to aid the development process by increasing the supply of goods, technical and organizational expertise and money which are in short supply in developing countries. And they know they are clearly correct if they act in the belief that assistance from the highly developed economies to the economies investing their efforts heavily in expanding and modernizing the productive and distributive apparatus can relieve the tremendous strain on the latter and speed up the process of development. In so far as the peoples of Latin America, Asia and Africa

who are struggling intelligently to overcome the impoverishing
and dehumanizing effects of anti-development can draw as they
need on the economic resources of Europe, North America and
Japan the end of poverty is undoubtedly being brought nearer.

Generosity of this kind is not just a vague emotion of
'goodwill'. Its concrete economic manifestations must show
that activity in the world economy is determined by altruistic
relationships, objectives and values. The devoting of a share of
the productive effort in the industrial countries to the construction of viable, modern and democratically controlled
economies in as yet unindustrialized countries makes sense only
in an international order in which community and cooperation
among peoples prevails over exploitation by and competition
among industrialists and businessmen seeking to enrich
themselves at the expense of the poor. For the generosity of the
rich, unaware of what they owe to the poor, can reveal itself as
as a form of self-aggrandizement. It is therefore not a naive
and vague idealism, but analysis of established and institution-
alized relations between nations and groups of nations which
can tell us what in fact is happening – happening, in this case,
between the already wealthy or highly developed peoples and
the poor peoples who are struggling self-reliantly to overcome
anti-development.

The human concern shown across national and racial boundaries may be something very real. Only utter cynics would
deny that there is a mutual desire to help one another among
working people of different lands. But is there not some confusion in the picture of the post-war world that has been
drawn? Can we go on as if all that there is to the relationships
among peoples is what we have so far talked about in this
chapter? 'Aid'-giving is a concrete phenomenon. Are the rich
identifying their interests with those of the poor to such an
extent that they are using their considerably more advantageous
economic position to start a net flow of basic producing-power
into the economies which are short of certain strategically important economic resources? Are they devoting one day's production out of every hundred or two hundred days', say, to

aid peoples who are actively fighting anti-development? Are they halting the anti-development activities that industrialists and businessmen from their own communities have been carrying on in Latin America, Asia and Africa?

The conventional impressions which we have of the nature of the post-1945 world, impressions which are continually reinforced by the mass media and by scholarly statements, leave a number of substantial questions like these unanswered. They do not explain why there is increasing poverty in the Third World; they do not convince us that the relationship of Britain or the US or the Soviet Union or France to particular 'developing' economies is exclusively or primarily that of aid-giver and aid-receiver, or benefactor and protégé. They do not explain away the evidence that there is a state of cold war between the poor in the Third World and the ruling classes in the First and Second.

THE ESTABLISHED RELATIONSHIP

This preliminary account of the role of 'aid' gives us a shallow and unduly circumscribed view of historical events which originate far back in time, and which stir people very deeply. Even the words used within these narrow limits of abstract idealism are treated as though they were flat and insignificant. The passing of money as 'aid' from one country to another is an act which calls for an effort of historical understanding. What does it signify beyond and beneath the geographical transfer of credits and materials (in so far as that takes place)? What is 'given' and what is 'received' is, of course, a complex reality of economic assets which can be described only with difficulty. But it is more than that. It is part of a sequence of interactions between the powerful and the impoverished, at whose expense the former grow or remain rich. These large groupings of peoples exist in each other's memory, experience and expectations, as a consequence of a pattern of interactions established over a period of time. What is remembered is what happened, what was done or not done, what was undone or destroyed.

The experience has been and is lived. In drama those who play a part are supposed to act in character. It would not be fanciful to see 'aid' in the context of a drama. Observing what is going on between 'developed' and 'newly developing' countries – the rich and the poor – today is rather like watching the third or fourth act of a play which is still not concluded. Who the characters are, what the plot is, the relationships between the characters, and the intensity of the action are lost on someone who has no idea of what has gone on before, and is rather hazy about the meaning of the words in use. We need therefore to recall the earlier acts.

When we speak of Europe in the present context we are referring also to those parts of the world outside the continent which Europeans have taken exclusive possession of. That would include Soviet Asia and North America by the early nineteenth century, and what has come to be Australia. At one time, we must remember, there was the 'shock of discovery' on both sides, and the attraction, for Europeans, of what the non-Europeans produced. There followed the invasions, the conquest, colonial rule, the struggle for freedom, the attempts at reconquest. Having been, and to some extent still being, a reluctant part of the world in which the ruling classes of the European powers of the day dominate, the Third World is not to be viewed 'neutrally', or as a strange and distant society. The areas and resources its peoples claim as their own have existed for Euramerica in very specific ways for more or less long periods of time. They were precious enough to have been sought after, fought over and possessed. The revolutions in the technology of production, in trade and in warfare did not make them less precious. In the next few pages we must make clear what the different parts of the Third World mean for the West (including Japan and the Soviet Union). What do they offer or deny? We must go on to clarify what moral claim the Third World peoples have made and make on the European races. Only then can we discuss what aid the 'developed' countries are actually giving to the war on poverty. Only then can we identify what aims and objectives are being promoted by the 'aid' which is being given and received, and the increase of which is sought by philanthropic organizations.

How far back in time we begin and what course of events we retrace in order to get our discussion into proper context are decided for us by the historical currents, or undercurrents, which still have some force today. What we are going to examine is indicated partly by the fact that the profession of altruistic concern for the non-European peoples is not a new-fangled device to cover up or make up for the guilt of 'imperialist oppression'. The *expression* of concern for the non-European peoples and the profession of responsibility for aiding them are part of a very old tradition: a way of thinking which portrayed the practices of Spanish, Portuguese, French, Dutch and English in America as a mission of goodness. It presented British actions in India as civilizing and redemptive; it interpreted the Open Door policy in China and other Western policies in regard to China as for China's good; it presented the suppression of Filipino independence as a mission of liberation; and Western policies in south-east Asia, including Vietnam, as altruistic. But as it is necessary to pay attention not to what people said or claimed in public but to what they did and tried to do, we look at the actual conduct of those who have acquired a reputation as givers of civilization, givers of knowledge, givers and teachers of the modern way of life, builders of modern society, protectors of the afflicted, relievers of the poor.*

Will the assumptions made stand the test of historical and political analysis? What have the champions of the poor and oppressed themselves had to say about harm and injury done to the poor? We cannot restrict ourselves to a general discussion of the whole modern period. We need to look closely at some aspects of the models of 'aid'-giving. Since the United States is reputed above all others to be the model of altruistic international behaviour, as giver, builder, protector, reliever, and so on, three of the assumed national qualities or qualifications for this role will have, however sketchily, to be examined:

* What is outlined in this paragraph will be discussed in the next chapter.

firstly, its own mastery of the art of development and of eliminating poverty; secondly, the model it offers for the right relationship between a white European ruling class and non-whites; and thirdly, its role in the world of nations, and especially the kind of unselfish interest it has in the world outside. Having done all that, we shall be in a position to discuss 'aid' policies and their reliance and effectiveness in getting rid of poverty.*

EUROPEANS AMONG NON-EUROPEAN PEOPLES

In Chapter 2 we referred to the great historical changes in the world which followed the expansionist nationalism of the Europeans in the post-medieval period. The new energies which carried Europeans to every part of the world, to penetrate the barriers of their ignorance, of distance, of physical danger, of cultural strangeness and armed frontiers, decisively ended the isolation of great civilizations and empires. Peoples were subjugated, their territories occupied, their treasure seized, and their resources put to the use of the expanding capitalist system of production and trade which transcended national boundaries. The Spaniards, the Portuguese, the Dutch, the English, the French, the Russians, the Austrians, the European-Americans, the Germans, the Italians, the Japanese and others undoubtedly forced the survivors of decaying societies they had conquered to seek recovery and to accelerate their own modernization if they were to get free again and survive. The consequences of the creation of colonies and empires by the rising capitalist powers were not simple, and have only recently begun to be described in correct historical

---

* The American millionaire, Henry Luce, expressed a widely held view in 1941 when he spoke of the twentieth century as 'The American Century', and of his country as the 'sanctuary' of 'the ideals of civilization'. 'It is the *manifest duty* of this country to undertake to feed all the people of the world who as a result of the world-wide collapse of civilization [*sic*] are hungry and destitute – all of them, that is, whom we can from time to time reach consistently with a very tough attitude toward all hostile governments' (italic added).

(and ethical) perspective.* It is no surprise that the consequences do not reflect the motives, that defeats and disasters have had beneficial outcomes, while victories and the exercise of dominance have had tragic results.

In every age and in every society there are men and women who are adventurous, or generous – men and women who seek personal fulfilment or the betterment of mankind in work which earns them little material reward or personal glory. Whatever opportunities of service are offered to them are made use of. Administrative, medical and educational work in the colonies attracted some of the best people in the imperialist countries. The social, political and economic meanings of the acts of individual persons are, however, not determined by private motivations or emotions.

In no part of the world was the national economy industrialized while it was a colony or semi-colony. But, as we noted in Chapter 2, there was new economic development of a kind which integrated the territory into the capitalist world economy. At the beginning of the period of what came to be called 'independence' the peoples of Latin America, Asia and Africa were closely related with those of the former metropolitan ruling classes in ways which had no parallel at the beginning of the modern period of world history. Any equality of status they claimed, nationally and racially, and any freedom to determine their own path to modernization and economic and political development, was largely rhetorical. They did not enjoy the respect, nor could they command the fear, of peoples who had ruled over them and still exercised power over their destiny. In the white-dominated world into which they were admitted as 'independent' nations, the rules and definitions had been made by others. There was nothing sinister in this fact. It was an inevitable consequence of what had happened

* e.g. V. G. Kiernan, *The Lords of Human Kind* (London, 1969). There is a considerable body of earlier scholarly literature which is critical of imperialist policies and practices, but they have been limited to certain areas or empires. J. S. Furnivall's *Colonial Policy and Practice* (Cambridge, 1948) deserves study.

H

much earlier, and could not cease to be a fact until equality of status and mutual respect arose out of new conditions which were created or achieved by hard work. The attributing of inferior capacity and abilities, moral and intellectual back-wardness, helplessness and so on to Latin Americans, Asians and Africans was *normal* in and characteristic of the kind of world society which existed.*

The Third World which has emerged from the revolt against imperialist rule has some member nations whose performance is most impressive and the ability of whose peoples to defend themselves is formidable. But by definition it is a 'world' which is regarded as inherently subordinate, dependent and inferior, even by many of its own Europeanized *élites*. Why did the encounter between these groups of peoples produce this kind of relationship, while that between British and Japanese, or Indians and Chinese, did not? Were the non-European peoples in fact inferior? The relation between English and Irish was more like the colonial one of later years. Were the Europeans then just as aggressive and rapacious as any people who discovered that they were superior in armaments? If they were, what could one say about their civilizing mission?

Jonathan Swift's *A Modest Proposal* is a devastating exposure of the cannibalistic nature of the English exploitation of Ireland. There was no tenderness of consideration, no allowing for the inevitability of the suffering that English economic policies entailed, in Swift's treatment of his own fellow-countrymen in this essay. At the time he lived there could hardly be said to exist a modern political consciousness. It is remarkable, there-fore, that the political and economic implications of the relations between different peoples at the time were seen so sharply by a man who was a Tory. Swift lived at a time when

* When the Chinese leaders at the end of their revolutionary war called for a new relationship with the former imperialist powers on the basis of respect and mutual benefit they were accorded scant respect by the scandalized lords of the earth in London and Washington. Today, twenty-five years after her defeat, a newly resurgent Japan even denies the legitimacy of the government set up by the Chinese people in her former imperial possession.

more people were travelling across the sea to distant parts of the world than ever before in history. The sensitiveness he could show as a creative writer to what was going on is instructive. There is a reference, perhaps less widely noticed than *A Modest Proposal*, to the European annexations and colonization by Britons of lands and territory belonging to other peoples, in *Gulliver's Travels*, which was published in 1726. It comes at the end of the book. Gulliver is not inclined to encourage the practice by which 'whatever lands are discovered by a subject belong to the Crown'. He doubts if conquests in the countries he visited 'would be as easy as those of Ferdinando Cortez over the naked Americans'. Even though the Houyhnhnms are not well prepared for war, their 'prudence, unanimity, unacquaintedness with fear, and their love of their country, would amply supply all defects in the military art'. He believes that it is the Houyhnhnms who should send a mission to civilize Europe. And he goes on:

But I had another reason which made me less forward to enlarge His Majesty's dominions by my discoveries. To say the truth, I had conceived a few scruples with relation to the distributive justice of princes upon those occasions. For instance, a crew of pirates are driven by a storm they know not whither, at length a boy discovers land from the topmast, they go on shore to rob and plunder, they see an harmless people, are entertained with kindness, they give the country a new name, they take formal possession of it for their King, they set up a rotten plank or a stone for a memorial, they murder two or three dozen of the natives, bring away a couple more by force for a sample, return home, and get their pardon. Here commences a new dominion, acquired by a title with *divine right*. Ships are sent with the first opportunity, the natives driven out or destroyed, their princes tortured to discover their gold, a free licence given to all acts of inhumanity and lust, the earth reeking with the blood of its inhabitants: and this execrable crew of butchers employed in so pious an expedition, is a *modern colony* sent to convert and civilize an idolatrous and barbarous people.

Some people may argue that Gulliver was wrong in claiming that the countries he visited did not 'have any desire of being

conquered, and enslaved, murdered or driven out by colonies';
and argue also that they did not abound 'in gold, silver, sugar
or tobacco'. The facts support Gulliver. Some of his comments
were a reminder of what, much earlier, Spanish critics, like
Bartolomeo Las Casas, had been writing and saying.* Gulliver's
account of the colonization process also echoed descriptions of
the annexation of territories in the Amazon and the seizure of
Malacca, Mexico, Peru and the Philippines, and anticipated
what was yet to happen in India and parts of the African
continent.†

The remarkable spurt in economic and technological
development that the creators of the capitalist system in Europe
pioneered might not have taken place in the way it did if the
moral standards implicit in Swift's satire and the appeals of
men like Las Casas had been treated with respect.‡ The
mercantile and manufacturing innovators who broke out of the
age-old isolation of peoples to accumulate in the new centres
of scientific and technological advance the hoarded wealth of
different peoples and civilizations were as a race no more
intelligent or ingenious than those of other civilizations and
continents; nor were they more vicious or unprincipled. But
they were more adventurous, energetic and ready to make the
most economically of the opportunities offered by the military
weakness of the non-European peoples. The conquest and

---

* At Valladolid, in 1550, Las Casas engaged in a great disputation with
the jurist Sepulveda over the latter's theological justification of the subjection and enslavement of the American peoples. He vigorously and forthrightly denounced those views as heresy, and prophetically declared that
they would be a licence for greed, brutality and oppression. Las Casas
was less sensitive about the traffic in and treatment of slaves from
Africa. There had been an abortive slave revolt in Mexico as early as
1537.

† See D. F. Lach and C. Flaumenhaft (eds.), *Asia on the Eve of Europe's
Expansion* (London, 1965), for a description of how Malacca was seized.

‡ Humanists, theologians and others who, very occasionally, spoke out
against the bestial and cruel practices of those who owned 'Indian' or
Negro slaves were rebuked or disregarded. The economic necessity of
slaves was accepted by nearly all whites in America.

annexation of foreign territory, and the new 'rights' and 'freedoms' established thereby, ensured to the Western and more progressive nations free access to hitherto unexploited resources of the earth just at the time that the accelerating technological and industrial progress of the capitalist countries enlarged the need for new metals, crops, energies, territories and so on, and the possibilities of their use for profit.

Just as the man who can put others to work for him gains advantages over working alone for himself, so it is with the accumulation of the labour and substance of whole peoples. What is produced by the energies, skills, intelligence and inherited resources of slowly developing communities, separated from one another, can be exchanged by trade between peoples, especially when there is some specialization. But the possibilities of pre-industrial manufacture, trade and social organization were severely limited, and pretty well exhausted by the sixteenth century. Within the existing system, the produce of different peoples like the Indians, Chinese, (indigenous) Americans, Europeans and others, did not, in the absence of a more complex system of international cooperation, provide for the construction of a much more extensive economic base than any which had previously existed. The powers of innovation and of taxation needed for that task did not belong to the old order. Nor did the power of creative self-destruction. By accomplishing the systematic, intensive, rapid and progressive accumulation of the world's produce, Europe, where new technological possibilities were first realized, was the first of the world's major areas to be launched into new forms of development. The ownership of and authority over labour and land was centralized as never before in both Europe and its outlying settlements. Instead of the old patterns of trade, a new economy of plantations, mines and factories came into being. Vertical divisions gave way in time to horizontal divisions.

The mutuality of respect and cooperation among peoples and the other moral and political standards implicit in Swift's satire was out-of-date in the new order. A world ruled from a few centres – Madrid, Lisbon, London and Amsterdam, and eventually Paris, New York, Berlin, Tokyo and Brussels – was inevitably one in which all peoples were part of an all-encompassing hierarchy.

This structural transformation of the world order was inevitable, given the capitalist and commercial initiatives taken in the technological and economic developments of Europe. The hunger for productive resources increased continually, to become virtually insatiable. The more nearly it was satisfied, the more the old order, with all the moral, intellectual, emotional, legal and political underpinning, was broken loose from its foundations.

Speaking in abstractly 'economic' terms, the expenditure of so much that was by traditional standards precious or valuable was 'worth it'.* That in which it was invested grew enormously, and the economic growth gave rise to a wealth of new ideas, new forms of communication, and new human possibilities. Whether the expense, morally and in human terms, was too great was, however, another question, and one which there was much greater difficulty in answering. Human society, as we all know, cannot develop to become more richly human if it dispenses with all moral values and standards. The transformation of the world outside Europe into one of European-owned plantations, mines and colonies involved the transformation also of what civilized people had conceived as normal and proper human goals and obligations – those that men like Las Casas and Swift were sensitive to. In the new world, those who were militarily weak, those who failed to hold their own by strength and cunning, those who became subjects, could hardly be honoured. We could consider, for example, the American peoples, and how the new ways of thinking affected their fate. Their enrichment and development could hardly be seen to be of much relevance for the creation of the new Europe or the enlargement of Papal power. To the men of action there could

---

* The slave trade itself gave an enormous boost to the economic development of the new capitalist nations and to the colonies, Spanish, British, Portuguese and French.

be no point in trying to construct a new world without extracting all that the Mexican, Peruvian and other Indians lived on and would need to live on. This was generally valid as a principle. The new forms of production on the overseas plantations required the *encomienda* system, the slaves and, later, the coolies. It needed in Asia the traffic in opium and the destruction of the indigenous industries.

The notions of inferior and superior races followed the economic and political changes which took place. They were a requirement – a means of morally validating the social relationships emerging with the new forms of economic development. At this moment in the long history of civilized societies the European peoples rapidly went ahead of all others, just as in earlier times the Chinese or the Arabs had. There was on their part the superiority of achievement; correspondingly, there was on the part of civilized peoples who did not innovate and reorganize quickly enough a growing inferiority of performance. They found at one time or another that they could not defend themselves, and they were incorporated into an alien economic system, in which they were expendable. The accelerating anti-development process increased their inferiority in power, prosperity and status.

The essential nature of the development of commercial capitalism was manifested most dramatically in Africa. In the course of supplying the labour for use at less than subsistence cost for the new type of economic development in the newly colonized America, the African continent, with a population of around 100 million in the sixteenth century, lost fifteen to fifty million of its healthiest men and women. They were shipped to America, or they died resisting capture, awaiting shipment or on the journey.* The destruction of civilized life in the afflicted areas was inevitable. Part of the price for the 'development' of European traders, plantation-owners and investors was the potential development of the African societies, where the production of raw material for the slave trade became the main source of profit of the feudal chieftains. The slave-producing

* See Basil Davidson, *Black Mother* (London, 1961).

chiefs sometimes accepted or even sought 'aid' from the slave trading nations. The trickle of slaves became a flood. Destruction on this scale of the basis of economic activity was paralleled in history only by what was done to the peoples of America. It had to become part of the doctrine of the age that non-Europeans held their own lives cheap. Thus the peoples of Africa and America, and the twenty to thirty million Chinese who had to be killed to bring the Taiping Kingdom (1851–64) to an end suffered as people whose claims to territory, freedom and life were of a lower order.*

THE INTERNATIONAL SYSTEM

Whether or not there were alternative paths which capitalist development could have taken is a matter for speculation. But historically it was necessary for the growth of the system which replaced feudalism and other narrowly based pre-industrial economies that both the fruits of previous economic development and the lives of people should be freely available to those who were building the new economic order. Without this freedom, the phenomenal spurt in the development of man's command over nature and over his fellow-man might not have taken place. One can imagine how inadequate the small population of the Netherlands, France or Britain would have been at the time Swift wrote to provide labour for development in America and the Caribbean Islands.† Instead they drew great benefit by monopolizing, during the seventeenth and

* The theologians, too, were prepared to be pretty flexible and accommodated their missionary endeavours to the spirit of their patrons and supporters. West Africa and pre-European America were not the only sources of slave labour. According to Eric R. Wolf, 'Small numbers of Indians, Burmese, Siamese, Indonesians and Filipinos were also brought in to serve in a similar capacity' to Negro slaves in Middle America after the Spanish conquest: *Sons of the Shaking Earth* (Chicago, 1959), p. 30. The great migrations of the masters were accompanied by the great migrations of the servants.

† The population of the United Kingdom in 1750 was only around ten million.

eighteenth centuries, the resources and trade of more developed countries – Indonesia and coastal Ceylon, in one case, and India and America in the case of French and British interests. The freedom to seize, rather than to buy, products, to command and compel, rather than to negotiate with foreign peoples, led to the freedom to take more – land, human beings, and all. Such freedom could not exist among human beings of equal status, where in foreign lands one was a guest enjoying what hospitality one's hosts could want or afford to give.* It could only be the attribute of a race by divine appointment superior in its abilities and calling, divinely endowed with the power of life and death over lesser beings. The habit of thinking about militarily vulnerable peoples and their homelands as being at the disposal of Europeans, and about non-Europeans as inferiors whose treatment need not respect moral norms, was justified by an anthropology in accord with the new economics – that is, a cultural product of the system. In the face of resistance the practice had, as time went on, to be justified philosophically and theologically in more elaborate ways than the contemporaries of Las Casas found possible. Generations of Englishmen, Dutchmen, Frenchmen and white North Americans grew up seeing the 'lesser breeds' as 'without the law', and their territories and persons as fair game. The notions of a 'mission' to help, educate and civilize backward and savage peoples were given currency. Swift's successors, such as Mark Twain, were, however, devastating in their treatment of the justifications for colonial policies given by the imperialists. The 'natives', according to those justifications, had been utterly backward and poor when the Europeans first encountered them. Such horrible practices as human sacrifice (among the Aztecs) and *suttee* (the burning alive of widows) in India were portrayed as features characteristic of non-European societies as a whole. The Indians had not learnt to govern themselves, and had to be taught to govern. They had to be

* This bourgeois-imperialist *freedom* was threatened when the Chinese imperial government's firmness in prohibiting the traffic in opium threatened British trading interests in the 1830s.

taught to read and write. They had to be taught morality. After they were 'granted independence', there had to be a period of tutelage, under those who knew what modernization involved. They had to be kept from being misled by the enemies of freedom. The 'Chinaman' was brutal and barbarous. There was no rational logic in all this, but as one group of nations prospered at the expense of others, its economic and military superiority gave rise to notions of moral, cultural and intellectual grandeur.*

This general and panoramic view of modern world history should indicate how in the era of its overseas expansion Europe has had its thinking about foreign peoples and their ways, its ideology and its folklore, permeated by certain views of peoples whose lands have been coveted and whose human status has been abrogated. It has helped to explain why the fraternity of peoples, which the aid relationship presupposes, was not part of the world order which was created by the world-wide expansion of capitalist Europe. There were men and women of great humanity and high ideals who were not blind to the evil and corrupt practices of the native *élites*, but who objected strongly to the kind of relationship which developed between the European peoples on the one hand and all other peoples on the other. The knowledge of the geography and history of peoples in non-capitalist societies, of their potentialities and worth, has been gained in the course of struggles and activities which had a strong class character. The language, thinking, morality and philosophy of the world we were born into are still permeated by the assumptions about people which we have been discussing. There were many benefits that the subject peoples got from their foreign conquerors and rulers. But the

* 'Upon the whole then, we cannot help recognizing in the people of Hindustan, a race of men lamentably degenerate and base; retaining but a feeble sense of moral obligation; yet obstinate in their disregard of what they know to be right, governed by malevolent and licentious passions, strongly exemplifying the effects produced in society by a great and general corruption of manners, and sunk in misery by their vices . . .' (Charles Grant, *Observations,* quoted by E. Stokes, *The English Utilitarians and India* (London, 1959), p. 31). See also below, p. 242.

'civilizing mission', and benevolence and altruism of the soldiers, traders, governors and preachers from the imperialist powers was mainly rhetorical; there was no love towards or respect for the natives of the colonies; rather, there was hatred and contempt, as talk of the 'yellow peril', 'niggers' and 'chinks' suggested.

It would be a mistake to suppose that international relations in our day are voluntary transactions or interactions among separate nations and states of identical status. The rich and the poor have been intimately involved with one another; and the nations and states which have come into being are not governed by equal obedience for the same laws and by mutual respect for one another's independence, territorial integrity and welfare. The international system itself makes nations and states unequal in the respect that is accorded to them; its continued working depends on the maintenance of double standards. There is a relationship of what we may call subordination and super-ordination, derived from the caste-like distinctions of races and peoples which paved the way, politically and morally, for the appropriation and economic exploitation of the people and resources of America, Asia and Africa. Only a break with – perhaps a breaking up of – the old system could make the giving and receiving of 'aid' for development authentic. This break with the past *may* already have occurred. The practices and values of the era which began with the African slave trade and the wiping out of some of the American peoples may have been brought to an end by the revolutionary destruction of the imperialist system. If this has actually happened, the conditions exist for the kind of economic transaction which we have described as the giving of 'aid' by the beneficiaries of the well-developed economies to those who are building to eliminate the causes of poverty and hunger. On the other hand, if the practices and traditions of exploitation still persist, and find expression in the 'aid' relationship, our conclusions must be different. For if the expectations and ambitions of the rulers of the United States, Japan, Britain, Russia and the other European nations are still the same in regard to the southern continents, as they used to be, the rhetoric of altruism and benevolence must be evaluated differently.

MODEL FOR A MULTI-RACIAL WORLD?

However cynically the currency of international brotherhood and human decency had been devalued by the hypocrisies of the imperialist era, it could still be redeemed for meaningful use if the economic order was so reconstituted as to provide a material base for rapid decolonization and thus for the creation of a political order in which the affluent classes made part of the economic capacity in their control freely and unconditionally available to the poor who were engaged in the reconstruction of their societies. A number of people conceived of the post-war era in these optimistic terms. A conception of this kind would, of course, make economic sense only if it could bring about an increase in the world's capacity for production – that is, if it led to the investment of unused, wasted and inadequately used productive resources in areas where a world economy superior to the old one was being built.

Britain and the continental European countries had played a pioneering role in creating the first modern world order by the empires they built up and the economic development which these empires were made to serve. But was the backing of the United States going to be decisive in decolonization and in pioneering the economic transformation of mankind? The United States had enormous productive capacity, which it was believed to have acquired without resorting to conquest and annexation of the territory and resources of other peoples. Its people were believed to be free of the offensive racialist attitudes to foreign peoples which characterized the British, Dutch and French. Their leaders emerged during and after the war as supporters of anti-imperialist struggles. Particularly in the desperate struggle against the Fascist alliance there grew up a faith in the United States as a powerful force working for the liberation of the poor and subject peoples from the cruel systems and institutions which oppressed and impoverished

them. US collaboration with revolutionary liberation movements in Asia was taken as something more than a military
tactic; it was seen as a political alliance. It seemed as if little of
the old order could survive if victory over both Anglo–
French–Dutch and German–Japanese–Italian imperialism and
racialism was to be achieved. The 'image' of the United States
as the aid-giver and champion of the poor peoples which since
1945 has been in many people's minds was described not long
ago by President Johnson:

In all of recorded history, none have surpassed the American
people in willingness to share their abundance with others. We have
given unstintingly of our material wealth and our precious human
resources to benefit the less fortunate of the earth. We have sought
to restore those whom war has shattered. We have sought to provide
assistance to the newly independent members of the family of
nations who are making the effort to break the shackles of tradition
and achieve a better life for their peoples . . .

The statistics of United States 'aid' to the developing countries
and other manifestations of benevolent and altruistic concern
for the poor have often been reported. The figures are indeed
impressive.

The United States had some of its overseas possessions
attacked and occupied during the war, but its own territory did
not experience a single attack. It was the only anti-Fascist
power to emerge from the war much more prosperous and
more powerful than it was when the war began. The material
resources at the disposal of its people, had they been minded to
take their share in the cost of building an international order
which was free of the characteristics of the old, were enormous.
The kind of claim for the United States made by Mr Johnson
suggested that the American people had indeed identified
themselves and their interests after the war with the forces of
liberation and become a powerful revolutionary force.
Especially as, in the areas of European settlement, the United
States alone had a large proportion of non-white peoples, the
implications of the claim were tremendous. In so far as the
claims made for the United States were valid, and in so far as

exploitation and poverty had been eliminated within that country, the role of 'aid'-giver played by the United States is an important one. It is in fact so important that we are obliged to examine in some detail, though briefly, both the assumptions made about North American wealth and the political and economic system which is functioning in the post-1945 relationship between the United States and the countries of the Third World. If the people of the United States are indeed the inheritors of a tradition which has abolished all forms of oppression and exploitation, they are in a unique position to attend to the needs of others. If they are not, has the liberation of the poor and oppressed been accomplished in recent times within the United States?

The answers to the question with which we must begin are not very encouraging for those who see the United States as an anti-colonialist force in the world. The American Revolution does not put the people of the United States in the same camp as those struggling for national liberation in the late nineteenth and the twentieth centuries. The United States of America came into existence after the rebels in the thirteen North American colonies had declared their independence from British rule and successfully resorted to armed struggle against British forces and their collaborators. But the historical record does not speak of a nation conceived in liberty and in the outlawing of servitude and oppression. The settlers of the seventeenth century and their descendants were among the earliest of those who treated non-white peoples whose territory they took cruelly and barbarously. They were no less cruel and inhuman than the Spanish, Portuguese and French. The connection between the colonists on the mainland and those who ran the plantations in the Caribbean with African slave labour was close; some of them had been, and remained throughout the period before the prohibition of the slave trade, active slave-traders themselves. Not only were large numbers of Negroes held in slavery. The native American tribes who resisted the new settlers were themselves either killed off or, sometimes, more profitably, enslaved. The indigenous

Americans were also at times captured and sold as slaves in the West Indies.*

It will be apt to recall that when the American Declaration of Independence was being drawn up Thomas Jefferson, in deference to the slave-importing states, produced a draft which was a compromise on the issue of slavery. Referring to the British king, it said:

He has waged cruel war against human nature itself, violating its most sacred rights of life and liberty in the persons of a distant people who never offended him, captivating them and carrying them into slavery in another hemisphere, or to incur miserable death in their transportation thither. This warfare, the opprobrium of *infidel* powers, is the warfare of the *Christian* king of Great Britain. Determined to keep open a market where *men* should be bought and sold, he has prostituted his negative for suppressing every legislative attempt to prohibit or restrain this execrable commerce.

Prevailing economic interests in the plantation states of the south and in New England and New York were, however, not identical. But there was enough in common not merely to keep out the condemnation of slavery, but to incorporate acceptance of it into the Constitution of the new republic. Of the four million in the newly formed United States of America, 700,000 were of African descent. Some of them had fought alongside whites for independence. But in all thirteen states they were denied the status of 'free persons'. Some of the founders of the republic were in favour of gradual abolition of slavery, and some were opposed to the slave trade. But all the white leaders could not contemplate living alongside and mixing with black fellow-Americans.

From 1776 onwards the fear of slave insurrections was great, and there was much talk among the authorities of suppressing

* The enslavement of the native Americans was, significantly, the first consequence of the 'discovery' of America by Europe. Columbus took back with him a cargo of slaves – the first to make the transatlantic voyage. On the enslavement and brutal treatment of Indians in North America see David Brion Davis, *The Problem of Slavery in Western Culture* (Ithaca, 1966), p. 176.

black revolt. Subversive influences from outside were also feared, especially when slaves rebelled in the Caribbean islands. The legislation in the years following the establishment of the new republic deprived blacks of almost every political and cultural right which might have been claimed by them. The blacks had never accepted docilely the sufferings and humiliations inflicted on them. It was a matter of deliberate policy to prevent any development of a potential among them for independent thought or activity, any independent movement or association.

The black non-citizens were completely at the disposal of their masters. Theodore Weld (one of a long line of white American 'protesters') in the report *American Slavery As It Is*, which he compiled and introduced in 1839 for the American Anti-Slavery Society, undertook, successfully, to prove:

That the slaves in the United States are treated with barbarous inhumanity; that they are overworked, underfed, wretchedly clad and lodged, and have insufficient sleep; that they are often made to wear round their necks iron collars armed with prongs, to drag heavy chains and weights at their feet while working in the field, and to wear yokes, and bells and iron horns; that they are often kept confined in the stocks day and night for weeks together, made to wear gags in their mouths for hours or days, have some of their front teeth torn out or broken off, that they may be easily detected when they run away; that they are frequently flogged with terrible severity, have red pepper rubbed into their lacerated flesh, and hot brine, spirits of turpentine, &c., poured over the gashes to increase the torture; that they are often stripped naked, their backs and limbs cut with knives, bruised and mangled with scores and hundreds of blows with the paddle, and terribly torn by the claws of cats, drawn over them by their tormentors; that they are often hunted with bloodhounds and shot down like beasts, or torn to pieces by dogs; that they are often suspended by the arms and whipped and beaten till they faint, and when revived by restoratives, beaten again till they faint, and sometimes till they die; that their ears are often cut off, their eyes knocked out, their bones broken, their flesh branded with red hot irons; that they are maimed, mutilated and burned to death over slow fires . . . not merely that such deeds are committed, but that they are frequent; not done in corners, but before the sun: not in one of the slave states, but in all of them: not perpetrated by brutal overseers and drivers merely, but by magistrates, by legislators, by professors of religion, by preachers of the gospel, by governors of states, by 'gentlemen of property and standing', and by delicate females moving in the 'highest circles of society'.*

Economically speaking, a society founded on such practices, and organized on such a basis, cannot be engaged in a struggle against anti-development forces, unless very radical changes have since been made. Some Americans with noble ideals have indeed fought hard to liberate the blacks. The position of the blacks has not, however, changed radically in the last two centuries, though the slaves were emancipated in the Civil War. President Abraham Lincoln never intended to make the United States a land in which men and women of white and black races lived together as equals, nor did he achieve equality for all.†

Today, as reliable reports and even official reports testify, blacks are far from living in security, dignity and community with whites. There was a long period when black Americans submitted to the treatment they received. But in recent years they have made it clear that they find their situation intolerable.

---

* This and the previous quotation are from Joanne Grant (ed.), *Black Protest: History, Documents, and Analyses, 1619 to the Present* (Greenwich, Conn., 1968). The attempt systematically to degrade the Negro slave and destroy his humanity is a function of the depraving effects of a prosperity based on the slave-trade and slavery.

† Lincoln's aims and policies cannot be explained in simple terms. But the saving of the Union was his main aim, and military necessities were sometimes predominant. Over 180,000 Negroes were fighting for the Union at the end of the War. The slaves were not vital to the economy of the northern states, and Lincoln could seriously think of getting rid of the blacks by settling them in colonies outside the United States. The actual liberation was very much the consequence of what the Negroes did on their own initiative, in conditions of civil war.

The very character of 'modernization' in their country had condemned them to an increasing inferiority. The political, social and economic subordination attributed to blacks appeared to be part of the American way of life, and essential for the maintenance of the system. In an economically stratified society, where the ascription of inferiority to particular groups of Americans had to be justified by pseudo-scientific ideologies, the universal application of constitutional rights required revolutionary action. For decades Negroes had no protection against lynching. By the 1960s the average wage of a non-white American was half that of whites, while the unemployment rate was double. Forty-eight per cent of non-white families lived in serious poverty. Non-whites, according to one report, had nearly double the infant mortality rate of whites, and had twenty-seven physicians serving every 100,000 of them while the corresponding figure for whites was 157. Fifty-six per cent of non-whites lacked housing facilities, and only twenty per cent of whites.* The non-whites are compelled to bear the greater part of the costs and a smaller share of the benefits. In the actual fighting in Vietnam the percentage of blacks fighting (and of black casualties) is much higher than that of blacks in the population.

It was not because people have not been aware of the misery of blacks in the United States that these conditions persist. There have been liberal and humanitarian white Americans wanting to ease the lot of the blacks, which they regard as scandalous. But the practical determination of the blacks (and other non-white groups) to emancipate themselves has grown; it has become too much for the stability of the existing economic and political system. The overturning of the existing order (which, of course, extends far outside the present boundaries of the United States) during the 1950s and 1960s could be prevented only if the black militants were met with an increasingly elaborate and terrifying machinery of established law and order. For even the mildest of the acts of black emancipation, such as the research into, and the teaching about, the distinguished

* See Grant, *op. cit.*, pp. 477–8.

role of the Negroes in American history, is felt to do violence to the existing order and its claims to be what President Johnson said it is.* The liberation of non-whites has come to be regarded as subversive. The race problem has grown progressively worse, as even official reports like that of the Kerner Commission on Civil Disorders have made clear: the United States has tended to become 'two societies – one black, one white, separate and unequal', with conditions bordering on an unequal civil war. Black political leaders have been met with harassment, beaten up, and, as the evidence makes indisputably clear, summarily executed in the streets by the forces of white 'law and order' – the guardians of the existing system, mainly police and 'security forces'. Their telephones have been tapped; they and their white associates are treated as national enemies. Attempts have been made – in full view of the whole world – by the government, newspapers, university academics and others to vilify and smash organizations working for the liberation of black Americans. The number of black leaders, local and national, shot without trial and seriously injured or killed in 1968 alone is instructive.†

The ability of the established power within the United States to make free with the lives and liberties of the poorest group of American citizens may be connected with a report from the capital, Washington, which appeared not long ago:

* See 'The Unknown Negro in US History' by Tom Wicks, *NYHTI*, 27 February 1968.

† The vigorous protest against this by small sections of the American people of all colours must, of course, be noted, even if it has been futile. The very sober liberal writer, Ronald Steel, was one of many who reported after an investigation on the situation of the Black Panthers, the main target of police attack. 'Anyone who is a Panther today, or who contemplates joining the party, knows that there is a good chance that he will be jailed or die a violent death. Panthers have already been murdered by the Police, many have been beaten and wounded, and others are almost certain to be killed in the months and years ahead . . .' (*New York Review of Books*, August 1969, p. 23). Prophetic words they turned out to be, as the purge of the black militants continued.

POLICE ORDER ON 'WOPS' AND 'KIKES'
CAUSES OFFENCE

Washington policemen have been ordered not to address citizens as:
'Wop, kike, chink, dago, polack, bohunk, limey, frog, and kraut.'

The order has been issued by Mr John Layton, the police chief,
who also required the men to refrain from *harsh, violent, coarse,
profane, sarcastic, insolent, and obscene language.*

This move towards civility has presumably been welcomed by
hyphenated Americans of Italian, Jewish, Chinese, Polish, Bohemian,
English, French, and German extraction, but the order caused a
furore in the local press.

Mr Layton did not enjoin his men to refrain from *calling Negroes
'niggers, boy, smoke, spook or coon'*, and the inference apparently is that
the police of this southern town are still segregationists.

The omission certainly reduces the force of the order because
rather more than six of every 10 Washingtonians are Negro. The
proportion of Afro-American families, to use the term the community prefers, is much higher, and partly explains why nine of every
10 children attending district schools are Negro.

UMBRELLAS BANNED

It is a double pity, because Mr Layton clearly meant well. He told
his men not to smoke in public, swing truncheons, carry umbrellas,
or play cards on Sunday.

They must also not publicly *comment on the demerits of laws and
ordinances*, but uphold them without *bias* or *prejudice*, and without
regard to race, creed, national origin or economic status. *Suspects*
should not be *humiliated, ridiculed or beaten*, and *interrogations* must not
be *conducted in a manner to compel confessions.*

Judging from public complaints, all this is a considerable advance
on past police behavior.*

The fate of other non-white peoples in the United States
also suggests that the United States is one of the countries least
qualified to aid the struggle of the non-European peoples
against the forces working for poverty and hunger. There is no
reason for singling out the dominant groups in that country
for a special concern for the oppressed races. The position of

* *NYTI*, 1 December 1965 (italic added).

those who come to be incorporated into white-dominated America – American Indians, Chicanos, Asians and other similar groups – has been described by well-known authorities. It is similar to that of the more oppressed of the colonial peoples in the other continents. The plight of the American Indian in 1969, the unadorned facts of health conditions, infant mortality rates, life expectancy, malnutrition, educational opportunities, employment and treatment at the hands of government agencies, almost surpasses belief. White America's claim 'we have given unstintingly of our material wealth and our precious human resources to benefit the less fortunate of the earth' may be sincere. But this much-advertised compassion and altruism is manifestly irrelevant to the war on poverty and the development process.

If the American system is a direct cause of the extremist form of anti-development among some twenty-nine million non-whites in the United States itself – a process which the forces of goodwill and altruism among the people are unable to reverse – it seems unlikely that these forces can do much to aid the struggle against anti-development overseas. However, it is still possible that the special claims made for the United States may be justified if the working people of white America have actually succeeded in overcoming anti-development and creating a model of economic development.

THE MOST DEVELOPED COUNTRY?

The conspicuous failure of United States society on the racial score is explained partly by a social structure which gives enormous economic and political power to a small minority. The achievement of the United States in overcoming poverty and hunger is often commended as a model for poorer peoples. But inquiry into this achievement leads one to doubt its qualification as a model of economic development, and to believe that its experience has value for the poor peoples only in a negative sense. For the American economic system works so that not only are there a few very rich and a great many poor, but that the rich get richer and the poor poorer. The fact that personal income averages are continually reported to be rising does not mean that poverty is being eliminated.

In *The Rich and the Super-Rich*, Ferdinand Lundberg quotes two government statisticians who conclude from a review of Robert Lampman's 1962 study that 'top wealth-holders owned 27·4 per cent of gross and 28·3 per cent of net prime wealth in 1953, but increased their share to 30·2 and 32·0 per cent respectively by 1958. These data support Lampman's conclusion that the share of top wealth-holders has been increasing since 1949.'* Lundberg argues persuasively, providing ample statistical evidence, that in terms of the economic structure of the US, the top 200,000 families, and certainly the top 700,000, almost totally controlled the economy of the country. That is, the decisions about the nature of the economy, production, employment and investment were confined to about one per cent of the population. For the twenty-two per cent of the country's wealth controlled by 200,000 households was mostly in the form of strategic stock-holdings in the major corporations. Lundberg draws attention to other calculations: that forty-four per cent of spending units in the country lived below the maintenance level set by the US Bureau of Labor, while 27·5 per cent lived below the emergency level. Or, as Michael Harrington (who is one of the country's leading authorities on the subject) put it,

two-thirds of the families in America have less than the $9,191 a year required to maintain a 'moderate standard of living'. . . . That means that the have-nots and the have-littles, the impoverished and the struggling, comprise the overwhelming majority of the population.†

* *The Rich and the Super-Rich: A Study in the Power of Wealth Today* (London, 1969), p. 25. British studies have shown that in Britain, too, the rich have, contrary to public belief, been getting richer, and income and property have been concentrated in the hands of a small minority: one per cent of the British population hold forty-two per cent of the total personal wealth; the top five per cent hold seventy-five per cent of it.

† Michael Harrington, 'The Road to 1972' in *Dissent*, 1969. The income figure appears to be high. The cost of living at even the most

Rural poverty has become a hard-core phenomenon. Poverty begets poverty in a vicious circle. To date, policies and programs designed to cope with this social cancer have been too little, too late. They assist a family here and there, provide a few new jobs here and there, but they have not come to grips with the hard-core poverty problem – with the millions of men and women who grow up, marry, raise more children, and die in poverty. These millions live out an existence contributing little or nothing to the daily operation of society and the economy and exert a positive drag on the development of society and the expansion of the economy.

This is not a quotation about Brazil or India. It is taken from the findings of the Citizens' Board of Inquiry into Hunger and Malnutrition in the United States. Their report, *Hunger USA*, which was published in April 1968, described conditions of appalling poverty and malnutrition in American communities. The fact that this group, sponsored by the Citizens' Crusade Against Poverty, issued this report did not mean that there was great sensitiveness among national leaders to the problem of poverty and hunger. This and other reports – including one which showed that free and subsidized school lunches were benefiting middle-class children rather than the poor, and a CBS television documentary on 21 May 1968, *Hunger in America* – failed to move administrators and legislators. A Congressional committee, supposedly dealing with poverty, was reliably reported to have instigated the FBI to discredit the work which was being done. And FBI agents 'investigated' (but failed to frighten) groups and organizations which had reported widespread hunger and malnutrition.*

* *NYHTI*, 8 December 1968. The same newspaper carried a news item on 18 April 1969 on a survey of 'hidden hunger' being conducted by officials of the US Department of Health, Education and Welfare. The survey was already showing a remarkably high incidence of vitamin deficiency, anaemia, retarded growth, etc. In one school '92 per cent of Project Headstart children . . . were found to have vitamin A deficiencies on a level lower than that in children already blind from that disease'. The director of the National Nutrition Survey, Dr Arnold E. Schaefer,

frugal levels must take into account rents, medical care, winter clothing, heating and travel.

The *Washington Post*, which in an editorial quoted from *Hunger USA*, went on, however, to disagree with its criticism of the big subsidies being paid by the government to rich farmers.* Yet, as two writers in the *New York Herald Tribune* reported, in 1969 about $390 million of Federal funds were allocated

to maintain 10,000 affluent American farmers and farm corporations in the style to which they have grown accustomed.

This tells us something about the order of priorities in this country and it says something about our system of politics.

This system which, they argue, has fixed very low ceilings for relief payments to the poor,

has decreed that ceilings of that sort are inappropriate for the welfare handouts to wealthy commercial farmers. Accordingly, one large farm corporation received more than $4 million in subsidies from the federal government in 1967 and more than $3 million in 1968. The *average* payment to the 10,000 most favoured commercial farmers in the country last year was $38,610.

* *NYHTI*, 25 April 1968.

giving his preliminary report in January to the Senate Select Committee on Nutrition and Human Needs, said 'It is . . . perhaps shocking to realize that the problems in the poverty groups in the United States seem to be very similar to those we have encountered in the developing countries.' Cases of marasmus and kwashiokor were also to be found (*US News and World Report,* 28 April 1969). This was not surprising, as a group of leading medical men had, after a survey in 1967, seen 'evidence of vitamin and mineral deficiencies; serious untreated skin infestations and ulcerations; eye and ear diseases, also unattended bone diseases secondary to poor food intake; the prevalence of bacterial and parasitic disease, as well as severe anaemia . . . in boys and girls in every county we visited, obvious evidence of severe malnutrition, with injury to the body's tissues – its muscles, bones, and skin as well as an associated psychological state of fatigue, listlessness and exhaustion. . . . In some, we saw children who are hungry and who are sick – children for whom hunger is a daily fact of life and sickness, in many forms, an inevitability. We do not want to quibble over words, but 'malnutrition' is not what we found. . . . They are suffering from hunger and disease and directly or indirectly they are dying from them – which is exactly what "starvation" means.' Quoted by Elizabeth Drew, 'Going Hungry In America', *Atlantic Monthly,* December 1968.

They refer also to the fact that the influential Senator James O. Eastland, as a plantation-owner in Mississippi (where as everyone knows the condition of the poor is worst of all) received $116,978.*

The ways in which subsidies, economic legislation, federal projects, tax 'reform' and the like benefit the rich rather than the poor are frequently reported and sometimes discussed in the United States. Anti-corruption crusades by people like Ralph Nader force into the open the corrupt practices of particular corporations, legislators or government departments. One such exposure, recently, compelled the government to begin an investigation into the involvement of nine major oil companies in what one government lawyer was reported to have described as 'one of the most remarkable cases of naked corruption ever exposed'. Corruption on a large scale allows the rich to enrich themselves at public expense on a massive scale. Tax regulations allow avoidance of income tax. For example, in 1964 there were thirty-five millionaires who paid no taxes at all on big incomes.†

Regular and systematic corruption in awarding contracts, maintaining standards, accounting, etc., involving millions and even billions of dollars must be mentioned not for their moral implications, but as indications of economic inefficiency. Such ways of diverting wealth and economic power to the rich and unscrupulous as is customary is wasteful, and a mark of incompetence. It is anti-development in its consequences. While the most eloquent pleas for the elimination of poverty in the United States are heeded only perfunctorily or not at all (as the figures show), projects for the corporations, often with inflated budgets which sometimes singly exceed the GNP of

* Richard Harwood and Laurence Stern, 'Welfare for Rich Farmers', *NYHTI*, 4 July 1969. Elizabeth Drew, in the article cited earlier, mentions the fact that the Eastland Mississippi plantation was allocated $211,364 from public funds in 1967.

† *NYHTI*, 27 May 1967. Complaints about the poor quality of the services rendered by the richest corporation, American Telephone and Telegraph, have been mentioned earlier; and also the devastating consequences of the frantic search for profit. See Chapter 2 above.

sizeable Third World countries, are allocated billions of dollars.*
Thus, while the total wealth in the possession of the 'top'
industrial corporations, leading financial companies and richest
families was, as we noted in Chapter 2, quite fantastic, total
indebtedness in the United States was staggering in its dimensions.† It was a measure of economic incompetence.

'Subsidized affluence', as we have noted, is possible in other
ways in a system which used revenue from general taxation to
award lucrative manufacturing and other contracts to some of
the richest industrial corporations. On the other hand, the
forces which 'combined to produce a militant and powerful
opposition to the government's war on poverty programme'
have been successful in getting large allocations out of public
revenue for police and para-military action against the discontented poor and their champions among the more affluent.‡
The 'law and order' forces thus trained, organized, armed and
maintained have been used with the utmost vigour against
any attempt to eradicate the causes of impoverishment and
oppression. It is not the high incidence of murders, armed
robberies, rapes, of which we spoke earlier, or of large-scale
corruption in high places and misappropriation of funds, but
radical action against poverty and oppression that is now
accounted the most serious crime. While, as we noted in
Chapter 2, the actual crime rate was rising alarmingly, it was
political dissent which was worrying the FBI and the government.§ A political and moral order which is manifestly callous

* The way in which US government agencies devise projects and other
expensive contracts for the major corporations is a complex subject. The
work of Senator Proxmire has exposed some of the activity that goes on.

† The figure given by Dick Roberts, in his article 'The Financial
Empires of America's Ruling Class', *International Socialist Review*, May–
June 1969, p. 26, would, if written out, be $1,747,000,000,000.

‡ The words quoted are those of the *Guardian's* Richard Scott, 8
November 1967. Chicago today, Daley, Hoffman and all, is the exact
antithesis of the moral and social order the poor seek to develop.

§ 'Crime among American youth, particularly in the case of such
organizations as the Black Panthers, has become a self-conscious act of
political rebellion, the executive director of the American Bar Foundation

about human suffering, subservient to the rich and powerful, and repressive of the poor and compassionate, is a model more useful to the oppressors of the poor than for the war to eradicate the forces which impoverish and destroy men.

The way in which the dominant values and patterns of authority affect people's sensitivity to true development is suggested by the results of experiments based on their reactions to the American Declaration of Independence. Some Americans have refused to endorse it on the ground that it is a subversive document. Support for even the eighteenth-century liberalism of the founding fathers has, in the prevailing climate of values, come to be seen as 'Communism' and 'alien subversion'. Experiments by University of Maryland researchers with US troops were revealing. Asked to sign if they agreed with the statement, 'We hold these truths to be self-evident, that all men are created equal, that they are endowed by their Creator with certain inalienable rights, that among these are life, liberty, and the pursuit of happiness', seventy-three per cent refused. One must assume that most of them have been indoctrinated so that they would fight people who defended the US Constitution.

In order to back and, when necessary, compel acceptance of the prevailing conception of what the United States stands for, there are not only executive, legislative and police forces, but also a vast military organization. The military bureaucracy in the United States now takes $80 billion annually out of public revenue which might otherwise presumably be available for

---

said today. . . . Mr Hazard said the "politicalization of youth crime" is posing the most serious threat to the already uncertain stability of our nation. . . . Mr Hazard, a law professor at the University of Chicago, said there were signs in Chicago, San Francisco and New York that "some youth gangs appear gradually to be reshaping themselves into something like an underground political movement with more or less definite political objectives relating to income, jobs and, more generally, to life opportunities"' (*NYHTI*, 31 July 1969). *A History of Violence in America* (New York, 1969) by H. D. Graham and T. D. Gurr shows that the American people have always been subjected to violence.

the domestic war on poverty and has, in 1969, a military force of 3,400,000 trained American men and women at its disposal, not to speak of non-American military forces at its command.* The Pentagon has been a fascinating subject of study. Its central administrative building is the largest in the United States. It tops the list of owners of property. Apart from the armed forces at its disposal, its enormous budget, obtained through political influence, enables it to award contracts (totalling tens of thousands) which industrial and other business concerns, at home and abroad, find lucrative. In this way, the employment of millions of civilians is controlled by its spending. Military expenditure remunerates workers in over 5,000 American towns or cities, and scientists, social scientists and administrators in most of the leading universities. The demands made by the military machine appear to have outraged a few scientists, theologians, scholars and housewives, and the moral sensibilities and personal liberties of large numbers of young people. The number of young Americans who are refugees on this account is remarkably high, and desertions from the armed forces have also been very high.

The military role in the United States is also played by the para-military character of the local police forces, the activities of 300,000 National Guardsmen, and the large number of reservists trained for what is called 'riot duty' within the country. Military action, including the use of armed helicopters and chemical weapons, has been taken in US cities. Reports from usually reliable sources also indicate that concentration camps for dissenters have been kept prepared by the government. The rulers of the United States – that is, government officials, leaders of industry and business, legislators, military and police chiefs – apparently see in the country widespread discontent on a scale amounting to actual revolt.

The gross national income of the United States is enormously high. So is the proportion of the world's resources used up by

---

* The amount that on average every working American contributes to the military budget annually (over $1,000) is worth comparing with the average annual income per head of poor class families.

the world-wide American economy. But neither the wealth, nor the power to dispose of it, appears to belong to the American people. The values and complex processes of the democracy indicated in Chapter 3 – the active democracy of working people who have the power to serve their own and mankind's interests – is hardly imaginable to Americans. To work for it would be treason. According to one of the most distinguished American historians, Professor Henry Steele Commager, the United States started as 'the most democratic of political systems' and has become 'one of the least democratic'. It was, according to a report of his views, 'a nation unable to stop a war that the majority found misguided, and immoral, and unable to solve its most pressing domestic problems because minorities would not let the majority have its way'.* Professor Commager's view of the way in which the US political system is regarded abroad differed from that of President Johnson. It is the correct one. The poverty and oppression of millions of Americans is evident in the repression of dissent, in the violent denial of the human right to change society and to create institutions and organizations.

The reason for this discussion of the United States is our interest in the special role which it is believed to be marked and equipped for in leading the struggle against the forces of anti-development. (Other industrialized countries, some independent of, some subordinate to, the United States, are also believed to play a similar role.)† A country which is itself a

---

* *NYHTI*, 6 November 1968.

† A more thorough and extensive discussion of the qualifications of the highly reputed 'aid'-donors and the models of development should have included an inquiry into the experience and competence of the Soviet Union and perhaps Britain, France, Japan and Israel. Needless to say, the Soviet Union will not emerge any more credibly than the United States as a nation which is fitted by its experience, record of achievements and values to help in the development process. The change in Tsarist Russia, politically backward and greedy for foreign territory, as a result of the Bolshevik Revolution, was tremendous, and stirred the imaginations of the Chinese people. But Lenin had a premonition before his death of the relapse of Russia into its pre-revolutionary backwardness – the subsequent

model of what we have described as 'development' must by
that very fact have an important role to play, because of its
experience, interests and values. But nothing that we have so
far noticed about American society, American politics or the
American economy suggests a special fitness for overcoming
poverty or a desire on the part of those in authority to do so.
Since the United States is *par excellence* the dispenser of 'aid',
the 'aid'-giving role becomes somewhat incredible. Will the
relationship that the US has had with neighbouring and distant
peoples make it more credible and instructive? We must now
turn to an examination of US activities abroad to find out.

---

barbarities, purges, tortures, mass killings of leaders of the working class,
economic 'development' by massive exploitation, including forced labour.
The worst features of Tsarist society which Stalinism brought back, the
repression of socialist democracy and bureaucratic-military dominance
could hardly make Russia a source of enrichment for the oppressed and
poor in other lands. The Russians, like the Americans, have a task setting
their own house in order, fighting poverty there, learning how to deal
effectively with the power of oppressive rulers whose ambitions are
world-wide in scope. The foreign relations of the Soviet Union tell as
dismal a story of insensitiveness to and lack of concern for the fundamental revolutionary tasks.

CHAPTER 8

The Aid Relationship:
The Rhetoric and the Reality

IF every generation made a clean break with the past and began 'from scratch' historical analysis might be a simple matter. But the understanding of the present depends on some knowledge of the past. People are either performing duties which were customary in the past, or they are deliberately struggling to put an end to archaic practices. Even the trauma of a harrowing collective experience such as subjection to a savage conqueror, or migration to strange and distant lands, does not result in total amnesia. Until they are worked on and transformed, old ways will persist into 'new' periods of history.

It *may* be that the highly industrialized rich countries do now show respect for the revolutionary aspirations and rights of the impoverished peoples on the other side of the wide gap in power and standards of living. If this altruistic relationship has been realized through 'aid' programmes, it is for us to ascertain in what ways the present international relationships actually help the development process.

Only a revolutionary change in the society and politics of any of the former imperial countries could turn it into an ally of the former colonial subjects who through the decolonization process are trying to make their leap into the twenty-first century. Britain's transfer of power in her colonies (to native rulers of whose 'fitness' to continue in the colonial traditions she was sure) did not mean the restoration to the natives of their wealth and resources held by Britons. The first and essential step in the development process could therefore not be taken in a country like India. The post-independence arrangement there was understandable; it would have been surprising if the British government had helped the Indian people to decolonize. The claims made on India's limited resources by British industrial interests were legitimate, by the standards and usages of the period of the subjection of Asian peoples. Britain was considered by many scholars and even working-class people to have done a good job of work in India – even though the poverty and misery of the mass of the Indian people, the lack of educational, industrial and political development in 1947 were appalling.

An 'aid'-relationship which is of genuine assistance to the Indian people must presuppose on the part of Britain a far-reaching transformation of the economic relationships between the economies of the two countries. It must also presuppose that the mass of the Indian people, under leaders of their own making, are prepared to take complete possession of the material base of their economy through revolutionary action, and by intelligence and hard work to institute, in place of the anti-development process, the process of development which will progressively enrich their own powers and productive capacity.

An 'aid'-relationship does exist between Britain and India. Is it conducive to anti-development or to development? Similar questions can be asked about Britain's 'aid'-relationship with other countries of the former British empire, and about France's relationship with the peoples she is, to judge by her statistics of 'aid for development', generously helping. The answers will become easier, perhaps, when we have further explored the relationships between the United States and the peoples of the Third World.

THE EVER-OPEN DOOR

The thirteen colonies which came together to form the new republic had territory eight or nine times that of the United Kingdom. Their population was only four million. Over the next century-and-a-quarter different social forces and ideologies and economic motivations were at work in the new nation, and it is not easy to summarize what happened. It is true however, that the United States was an expansionist power. The story of the United States was one of continual growth at the expense of the territory and resources of neighbouring peoples. American historians have shown how varied the pressures for expansion were at different times, and how hotly various expansionist proposals and actions were opposed or debated. The outcome of these was that by the end of the nineteenth century the United States, which had been a nation on the Atlantic coast of North America, had become a major power bordering the Pacific Ocean, and with about four times its original territory. If the long-standing hope of annexing Canada had been realized there would have been another doubling of territory.*

The first victims of United States expansion were the indigenous tribal communities whose land was coveted – the American 'Indians'. The process has been described by scholars, among them Albert K. Weinberg, who in his excellent study *Manifest Destiny* quotes a US Secretary of the Interior's description of it as 'in great part a record of broken treaties, of unjust wars, and of cruel spoliation'. Weinberg points to the way in which the expansionist doctrines justifying the treatment of the Indians had a 'natural growth'. 'Its first stage . . . was its extension to territorial issues other than those involving Indians.' It was not merely the pretence that in their unprincipled and brutal treatment of the Indians they were following 'God's' ordinances which was extended to justify further expansion. Racialist doctrines played an important part in this. In the arguments that went on for and against the seizure of all of Mexico, the racial inferiority of the Mexican

* See Julius W. Pratt, *The Expansionists of 1912* (New York, 1925); Albert K. Weinberg, *Manifest Destiny: A Study of Nationalist Expansionism in American History* (Baltimore, 1935); Foster Rhea Dulles, *China and America: The Story of Their Relations Since 1874* (Princeton, 1946); Frederick Merk, *Manifest Destiny and Mission in American History* (New York, 1963); Basil Rauch, *American Interest in Cuba 1848-1855* (New York, 1948); Richard van Alstyne, *The Rising American Empire* (New York, 1960); Walter LeFeber, *The New Empire: An Interpretation of American Expansion 1860-1898* (Ithaca, 1963).

I

people was an argument used on both sides, the opponents of annexation being concerned not for the rights of the Mexicans but for the sectional or regional interests within the United States which would be adversely affected by the victory of the expansionists. 'The Mexicans are *Indians* – Aboriginal Indians,' Merk quotes one journal as arguing:

Such Indians as Cortes conquered three thousand [*sic*] years ago, only rendered a little more mischievous by a bastard civilization. The infusion of European blood, whatever it is, and that, too, infused in a highly *illegitimate* way, is not enough, as we see, to affect the character of the people. They do not possess the elements of an *independent* national existence. The Aborigines of this country have not attempted, and cannot attempt to exist *independently* along-side of us. Providence has so ordained it, and it is folly not to recognize the fact. The Mexicans are *Aboriginal Indians,* and they must share the destiny of their race . . .

How are we to maintain our control over the Country – on what terms, under what contingencies – is a matter of detail, and subject to future events; but we do not believe there lives the American, with a true understanding of this country's interests and duties, who, *if he had the power,* would deliberately surrender Mexico to the uncontrolled dominion of the mongrel barbarians, who, for a quarter of a century, have degraded and oppressed her . . .*

The designs of some expansionists on Mexican territory, and the war – an act of aggression, as several political leaders and historians recognized – against Mexico into which President Polk manoeuvred the United States in 1846, bring into clear view the handicaps of the young republic in learning to conduct itself internationally. Firstly, the fairly easy disposal of the territories and lives of the American Indians, and of treaties

---

* *New York Evening Post,* 24 December 1847, quoted by Frederick Merk, *op. cit.* 'Broken treaties, unkept promises, and the slaughter of defenceless women and children all along with the un-European atrocity of taking scalps, continued to characterize the white Americans' mode of dealing with the Indians. The effect on our national character has not been a healthy one; it has done much to shape our proclivity to violence' (Richard Maxwell Brown, 'Historical Patterns of Violence in America' in H. D. Graham and T. D. Gurr, *A History of Violence in America* (New York, 1969), p. 67).

made with them, established a precedent for dealing with other non-European peoples whose ancient and traditional rights seemed to be in the way of Manifest Destiny. There were people in the United States who pressed for alternative standards by which to evaluate the treatment of the native Americans, but they were powerless to restrain the dominant economic interests. Except in dealings with the major powers of the European continent (and later imperialist Japan) international relations with other peoples tended to be conducted on a unilateral basis, as between a superior and an inferior. Secondly, transatlantic developments were not the centre of attention in Europe. As long as the imperial privileges and economic stake of the major world powers in the Americas were not challenged by United States expansionism (and they sometimes were), the United States had a free hand in her dealings with the republics in Central and South America. The pattern of 'international relations' to which she grew accustomed was compatible only with an international 'order' of a very peculiar kind – an order not formed and maintained by all the members of the international community, but one imposed and determined by a nation claiming more than ordinarily human status. No Latin American republic could match the United States in military power, and the mystical, quasi-theological rhetoric of those who dreamed of a vast empire gave each use of force against a neighbouring country an aura of divine sanction. Dissenters were always eloquent, but impotent.

Speaking in Buenos Aires at the end of the century, the Argentinian Roque Saenz Pena (who was later to become his country's President) expressed the Latin American view of US conduct. He was looking back at the doctrines and actions of three Presidents – Monroe, Polk and McKinley. '[They] are not three doctrines, they are three acts sanctifying a single usurpation: the intervention of the United States in the destinies and life of the peoples of the Americas.' Pena pointed out that Monroe's declaration of 1823 was an 'arbitrary act', whose claims to authority were 'fictitious'. In the course of an argument which exposed the pretentiousness of the US claims, he wrote that 'we will have to conclude finally and emphatically that force creates doctrine, that the army establishes rights'. He proposed a principle enunciated by Simon Bolivar on behalf of the Latin American nations, but rejected by the United States – one that would subject the United States, as much as other American states, to the rule of law.*

The Latin American republics did not have the same kind of problem as the United States in finding their identity as nations in a world of nations. It was perhaps the difficulty in finding the sense of completeness and identity as a people – with a given territory, traditions, a common experience, shared cultural forms, and the discipline of interaction with neighbouring powers and nations – which may account partly for the fervid expansionism, the rhetorical bombast and disregard for law and morality which could justify the fantastic territorial ambitions of the imperialists. It was not with men that Americans abroad were dealing, but with 'God'. It was not enough to force the Mexicans to give up Texas and California. Canada, all of Mexico, Cuba, all of South America, the Pacific Islands and, indeed, the already heavily populated lands of the Asian mainland seemed to be open. An awareness of historical conditioning and limitations of the existence and claims of other peoples and of the importance of being careful about long-term consequences – all of which go to constitute maturity – was in the circumstances slow to come.

It might be pointed out that American foreign policy has a vocabulary all its own, consciously – even ostentatiously – side-stepping the use of terms that even hint at aggression or imperial domination, and taking refuge in abstract formulae, stereotyped phrases, and idealistic clichés that explain nothing. Phrases like 'Monroe Doctrine', 'no entangling alliances', 'freedom of the seas', 'open door', 'good neighbour policy', 'Truman Doctrine', 'Eisenhower Doctrine', strew the pages of American history but throw little light on the dynamics of American foreign policy. . . . There is

* See David Marquand Dozer (ed.), *The Monroe Doctrine* (New York, 1965), pp. 40 ff.

a strong pharasaical flavour about American diplomacy, easily detected abroad, but generally unrecognized at home . . .*

When a spokesman for the imperialists, Senator William Beveridge, explained their aims, in 1900, he therefore spoke in language like this:

The Philippines are ours forever . . . and beyond the Philippines are *China's illimitable markets.* We will not retreat from either. We will not repudiate our duty in the archipegalo. We will not abandon our duty in the Orient. We will not renounce our part in *the mission of our race, trustee, under God, of the civilization of the world.* . . . We will move forward to our work . . . with gratitude . . . and thanksgiving to Almighty God that he has marked us as his *chosen people,* henceforth to lead in the regeneration of the world. . . . *Our largest trade* henceforth must be with Asia. *The Pacific is our ocean* . . . and the Pacific is the ocean of the commerce of the future. Most future wars will be *conflicts for commerce. The power that rules the Pacific, therefore, is the power that rules the world.* And with the Philippines, *that power is and will forever be the American Republic.*†

At the time that words like these were being uttered, much to the dismay of people like former President Grover Cleveland, an anti-imperialist, the bitter and savage campaign against the independent Filipino Republic was being carried on by troops who had learnt their fighting against the American Indians. By the end of the nineteenth century, having conquered all the North American territory apart from British Canada, up to the Pacific coast, US expeditionary forces were fighting their first war of conquest in Asia, against the youngest of the independent Asian republics. After the troops of the Filipino Republic were defeated, the resistance of the people continued, and exemplary campaigns of terror had to be conducted to persuade the peasants that continued resistance to US

* Van Alstyne, *op. cit.,* p. 7.

† *ibid.,* p. 187, italic added. These were crude but prophetic words. The relation between the rhetoric and the ambition has remained constant. The Pacific has come to be regarded as an American 'lake', and the boundary of US 'security' is beyond its western shores. See also Beveridge's words quoted in my *From Gandhi to Guevara: The Polemics of Revolt* (London, 1970), p. 48.

occupation and rule would be very costly. 'Pacification' was finally successful. But the outcry in the United States over the atrocities committed by US troops forced the government to hold a Senate investigation, and some of the details of the allegations by soldiers of torture, destruction of towns, killing of prisoners, women and children were established as fact. The attitudes and moral standards which had justified the treatment of the Indians, and later the Mexicans, characterized the first military encounter with technologically less developed Asian peoples. (The tortures and massacres were justified by the military and their civilian supporters, who did not exclude missionaries.) The Filipino Revolutionary Committee had in 1898 sent a representative, Mariano Ponce, to Japan for help, and there he had made contact with the Chinese revolutionary leader, Sun Yat-sen. The US campaign in the Philippines not only showed what wars of imperial conquest or reconquest were going to be like in Asia in the twentieth century. It also helped accelerate international cooperation among colonial peoples. 'Up to now,' the Filipino President Aguinaldo is reported to have said, 'I have trusted the white men but I have been deceived by the Spaniards and now by the Americans; nothing remains but to draw the sword. . . . To oppose the white man and gain freedom and independence, the colonial races must join together.'*

But it was China that was the El Dorado. It was necessary to get control in Hawaii and the Philippines in order to get a foot in the door into China. For the Open Door into China was vital to US business and industrial interests. 1898, the year of US intervention in both Cuba and the Philippines in the course of liberation wars against Spanish rule, was the date of the founding of a journal, *Asia*, and of the Committee on American Interests in China and the American Asiatic Association. During the greater part of the nineteenth century those who

---

* William Elsbree, *Japan's Role in Southeast Asian Nationalism* (London, 1953). It is interesting that a photograph of a heap of bodies of women and children massacred by US troops in 1906 at Bud Dajo was published in the United States, and stirred up protest.

sought to add to the territory and resources of the United States had had what one of them called 'the subjugation of a continent' to keep themselves and the American people busy. The Asian mainland was half-way across the world from the original western boundary of the United States, and there was much land to be conquered and a fleet to be built before the expansionists could travel far westwards 'looking for fresh worlds to conquer'.* As early as 1784, an American ship, the *Empress of China*, had sailed from Boston and reached Canton; and there was some trade between the two countries. The U S merchants in Canton were not capable of the sophisticated appreciation of Chinese thought and civilization which was to be found among well-educated Europeans. They subsequently played a part in the illegal opium trade. It was after the First Opium War, when the defeated Chinese empire was forced to yield to British demands, that the first official contacts between China and the United States were made. In 1844 Caleb Cushing led the mission which negotiated the Treaty of Wanghia. By this treaty Americans got all the priveliges that the British had secured after their aggression in 1838; they also got, through what came to be called the 'most-favoured nation clause', all the privileges which at any time the Chinese government allowed to other foreigners. The rights of 'extra-territoriality' and other encroachments on Chinese sovereignty which the United States had gained after the First Opium War were added to when, immediately after China's defeat in the Second Opium War, the American envoys got the Sino-American Treaty of Tientsin signed even before the British and French got their treaties. In regard to China, the foreign policy principle of 'active intervention to secure for our merchandise and our capitalists opportunity for profitable investment', as Senator Taft described it, was established quite early. Like the American Indians and Latin Americans, the Chinese were held to be acting aggressively, in resisting attack or refusing 'free' trade and movement. Wells Williams, the missionary, was a member of the delegation that pressed the

* Foster Rhea Dulles, *The United States Since 1865* (East Lansing, n.d.).

Chinese for concessions in the Treaty of Tientsin which would be ruinous to China; he wrote during the negotiations: 'I am afraid that nothing short of the Society for the Diffusion of Cannon Balls will give them the useful knowledge they now require to realize their own helplessness.' It was also his opinion that 'We shall get nothing important out of the Chinese unless we stand in a menacing attitude before them . . . for [the Chinese] are the most craven of people, cruel and selfish as heathenism can make men, so we must be backed by force if we wish them to listen to reason.' The Chinese were, indeed, far too unaggressive and unmilitant a people to resist, and the Americans, as well as the other European peoples, were accorded a 'legal' basis for future interventions in China's internal affairs.

The United States acquired no colonies in Africa; in Asia all the areas of major economic significance other than the Chinese empire were by the end of the nineteenth century possessions of the European powers (particularly Britain, Russia, France and Holland) and Japan. As Walter LeFeber and other scholars have shown, the 1890s were a period when United States manufacturers had cause for anxiety about future prospects, and the need for assured markets abroad was great.* That was the time when the 'most-favoured nation' status which had been won by treaty, and which gave the manufacturers and businessmen all the access to the China market that any other foreign power had, seemed to be threatened. The break-up of China among the other imperial powers, somewhat on the African pattern, seemed imminent. In 1895 Japan, after defeating China in war, had wrung from her by the Treaty of Shimonoseki concessions and indemnities which China could clearly not afford. She had also, in seizing Korea, threatened free United States access to Korean markets. Unless there was, first, consensus among the powers exploiting China's weakness and her resources and, secondly, the preservation of China's 'territorial integrity', America's Open Door into China would be lost. The exchange of notes between Britain and the United States on the policy of the Open Door helped to prevent the

* LeFeber, *op. cit.*

partition of China. Japan's seizure of Korea, and brutally imperialistic policies in China, were consented to on the assumption that the Open Door and 'most-favoured nation' principles would be respected.

In the US State Department's famous White Paper of 1949, after the failure of US China policy, Secretary of State Dean Acheson in his Preface still expressed hope of the Open Door into China. He also claimed that 'our friendship for that country . . . have [*sic*] been attested by many acts of goodwill over a period of many years'. The widespread belief that US relations with the Chinese people had and have been characterized by friendship and goodwill can only be due to the personal feelings of several individual Americans. They have shown generosity and even love for the Chinese people. Individual persons have gone to China to work for a country which would belong to the Chinese people. But in the century following the Treaty of Wanghia the relationship between the United States and China most certainly lacked the respect for China's development, independence, dignity, progress and revolution which friendship and goodwill must mean. The only Asian people with whom Americans had (before 1898) a close relationship experienced contempt, exploitation, patronage and, later, enmity. American 'aid' to China was fairly substantial during the half-century that ended in 1949; it was unfortunately disastrous in its consequences.

China had from the latter part of the eighteenth century begun experiencing the systematic impoverishment and political collapse produced by a combination of circumstances – rapid increase in population, itself partly a consequence of earlier progress in agriculture; neglect of the villages and their irrigation and other common facilities; increasingly exploitative taxation by an increasingly idle and socially irresponsible ruling class; the illegal opium trade; peasant revolts which failed to ease the misery of the masses. The material base and the economic system which had sustained a much more populous society through agriculture, internal trade and social organization than ever before in history had stopped growing. The disruptive and destructive effects of the invasion of China by international capitalist forces caused tremendous suffering and poverty. The most important part of the problem of gross poverty which was inherited by Asians, Latin Americans and Africans in the twentieth century was created in China; it could be solved only by the overthrow both of the ruling classes and of the new type of colonialism being practised by the foreign capitalist powers in China.

In 1895 Sun Yat-sen began his attempts to organize the forces of revolution, to overthrow the existing oppression and to create a new political and economic order, of which he had at the beginning only a vague conception. From that time onwards there were Chinese organizing their own people to fight the causes of the increasing poverty, misery and backwardness of the vast population. At crucial moments – such as the attempts to create a Chinese republic, the movement to end extra-territoriality and other humiliating consequences of the 'unequal treaties', the May Fourth movement, Sun Yat-sen's setting up of the government in Canton in 1924, the counter-revolutionary *coup* by Chiang Kai-shek in collaboration with imperialist and gangster interests, the struggle against Fascist Japan – the practical opportunities for foreign 'friendship', 'goodwill' and 'benevolence' were tremendous. If these had been taken, how different economic conditions in China might have been! A close study of the record of United States intervention in China suggests that American interests were much closer to those of China's enemies than to those of the Chinese people. The obsession with the Open Door was so great that the economic well-being of the United States seemed to depend on it. In fact, those who wanted a China which was 'freely' at the disposal of United States manufacturing and financial interests determined, as episode after episode proved, the country's policy towards China.

It was Woodrow Wilson who said in 1913:

The masters of the government of the United States are the combined capitalists and manufacturers of the United States. It is written over every intimate page of the record of Congress, it is written all through the history of conferences at the White House, that the suggestions of economic policy in this country have come from one source, not from many sources. The benevolent guardians, the kind-hearted trustees who have taken the troubles of government off our hands have become so conspicuous that almost anybody can write out a list of them ...

Suppose you go to Washington and try to get at your government. You will always find that while you are politely listened to, the men really consulted are the men who have the biggest stake – the big bankers, the big manufacturers, the big masters of commerce, the heads of railroad corporations and of steamship corporations.... The government of the United States at present is a foster child of the special interests.*

But Wilson himself had approvingly summed up the nature of the United States relationship with weaker peoples, when, in 1907, he had written:

Since trade ignores national boundaries and the manufacturer insists on having the world as a market, the flag of his nation must follow him, and the doors of the nations which are closed against him must be battered down. Concessions obtained by financiers must be safeguarded by ministers of state, even if the sovereignty of unwilling nations be outraged in the process. Colonies must be obtained or planted, in order that no useful corner of the world may be overlooked or left unused. Peace itself becomes a matter of conferences and international combinations ...†

THE NEW DIPLOMACY

Because of its irrational nature, it is almost impossible to discuss the world order as it has been conceived by the dominant forces in the United States. There is too much of fantasy

* Quoted in F. Lundberg, *The Rich and the Super-Rich: A Study in the Power of Wealth Today* (London, 1969), p. 430.

† Quoted by van Alstyne, *op. cit.*, p. 141, from William E. Diamond's *The Economic Thought of Woodrow Wilson* (Baltimore, 1934). Van Alstyne adds: 'Wilson is the quintessence of American imperialism and of its tragedy. His imperfections are far from personal. They reflect historical national patterns of thought and the immaturity of a nation that materially had been highly privileged but intellectually had made little progress since the days of its founders ...'

and make-believe about it. If the entire world is to be at the free disposal of the business, financial and manufacturing interests of the United States, with their insatiable demand for cheap and docile human 'labour', raw materials and consumers willing to pay the prices demanded for US commodities, it would be a monstrosity. The notion that Third World peoples must be obedient to the commands of the United States government derives from delusions of self-importance among some Americans, but from nothing which is observable except the power of guns and of money. Until the world has been conquered or bribed, the world order which compels that obedience cannot be said to be in existence.

When the comparatively new nation, the United States, made its appearance in south-east Asia, nothing in the long history of international relations in that area had prepared people for the notion that their role in future was to help realize the destiny of the ruling class of the United States. Though the United States had conquered the Philippines at the turn of the century, it was not until the defeat of Japan in the Second World War that the American encounter with the peoples of south-east Asia became a direct one. If opportunities for helping the Asian peoples to overcome the impoverishing consequences of colonialism and war were desired, they were not lacking. The Vietnamese, who had regained their independence without foreign help, and were entitled to United Nations membership, and the security which that was supposed to provide, could have been shown 'friendship'. The Indonesians could have been given similar help. President Ho Chi Minh is reported to have said to a US government representative: '... my people look to the United States as the one nation most likely to be sympathetic to our cause'.

The cause of freedom for the much-exploited and impoverished people of the smaller nations of Asia – the freedom, that is, to create for themselves genuinely developing societies, secure against foreign interference, exploitation or conquest, and, in cooperation with other nations, a more decently human and democratic international order – was indisputably one of the noblest in all human history. These peoples had learnt a great deal about the nature of oppression, and in Vietnam (as to some extent in Indonesia and the Philippines) it was the common people – the peasants and the proletariat – who formed the backbone of the popular movement to free their country from French capitalist interests and local landlords and mandarins. The kind of democracy which could be realized in the new phase of human history was a most exciting prospect.

How the United States first allowed and later actively helped and encouraged the French to try to reconquer Vietnam is a story too well known to need recounting here. *Nothing could show more unambiguously and forcefully the utter contempt of the European peoples for the Asians, for their rights, aspirations and welfare, and for the development and progress of the peoples who had to bear the burdens of technological and scientific backwardness and distorted economies as they tried to modernize, than the Western measures taken in August 1945, itself, to usher in a new era of colonial rule and exploitation.* The trust of the Asian leaders in the war-time declarations was treated as a laughable matter. Not even a show was made of honouring agreements solemnly entered into, as the Vietnamese, for example, discovered again and again.*

* The Cairo Declaration, with its high-sounding and pious condemnation of imperialism which we have quoted in Chapter 7, was apparently a dead letter by the end of the war. Since the British and the Americans had the power of the gun, no one was in a position to challenge the casuistry which could justify the bizarre military operations undertaken in southeast Asia immediately *after* the end of the war. In Vietnam the Japanese, from whom earlier the people of Vietnam had retaken their country, were ordered into action against the Vietnamese by the British commander. One instance of the cynical breaking of agreements was the attempt of Admiral d'Argenlieu in June 1946, in violation of the terms of the armistice, to split independent Vietnam by proclaiming an 'independent' Cochin China, with Saigon as the capital. The puppet ruler installed by the French did away with his own life. But here was a ruse which was to be tried again and again, and which was occasionally to work – the breaking of agreements and the attempt to get new footholds in Asia by setting up puppet regimes with puppet rulers whom the imperialists could 'recognize'.

The Japanese, in order to get their Greater Co-Prosperity Sphere (however short-lived it proved to be), had to fight against the old imperial possessors of Indonesia, Indochina, Burma and other colonial territories. The 'development' they planned and got carried out was not any the less colonial and anti-development in character than the old colonialism. The 'free world' co-prosperity sphere is not any the less anti-development, either. The United States has made it clear beyond all doubt, and has tried hard to make it clear to all Third World peoples, that any attempt by them to get control over their resources and to develop the base for their material existence as a people by struggling against anti-development and imperialism is a declaration of war on the omnipresent and ubiquitous claims of US business interests. Our present inquiry is concerned only with the feasibility of the United States' actually providing 'aid' for the war on world poverty. We can say that neither evident inclination nor practice suggests that the US has abandoned the racist and oppressive policies traditionally associated with 'manifest destiny', 'dollar diplomacy', 'the big stick' and 'world policeman'. The liberation of the poor is the last thing the rulers of the United States have sought, as they have visited on the peasant peoples of south-east Asia violence which for its intensity, cruelty and destructive effect surpasses *all* previous instances of savagery.

In the summer of 1954 the French government abandoned its ill-conceived attempt to reconquer its former subject peoples in south-east Asia. The contempt with which the British, French and Americans had regarded the peasants of Vietnam in 1945 had proved to be mistaken. '*Les jaunes*' had found that the very people whose Declaration of Independence had influenced their own, and to whom they had looked for help in 1945, were paying eighty per cent of the cost of a Franco-American attempt at reconquest. But they had gone on fighting to defend their independence. The French disaster at Dien Bien Phu showed that the immense economic and military resources of the imperial powers were never again going to be decisive in the affairs of the Third World – altogether a day for celebration, from the point of view of those who favoured the liberation and development of the poor peoples, and the closing of the 'gap' between rich and poor. However, on 22 April 1954 Walter Robertson, US Assistant Secretary of State for Far Eastern Affairs, expressed the US viewpoint to C. L. Sulzberger, who wrote about it much later in the *New York Times*. 'This has been one of the worst days in *United States history*. We must recognize that it is *impossible for us to lose south-east Asia* – which would follow the loss of Indochina. ... *Our whole civilization* would be affected. We must intervene. . . .'* Earlier that month the US government had allocated, for 1955, a sum of $1·33 billion as 'aid' to the French puppet regime which had been set up in Saigon as an alternative to the independent government. This allocation was one third of the total foreign aid budget.† As *US News and World Report*, in its issue of 16 April 1954, put it: 'One of the world's richest areas is open to the winner in Indo-China. That's behind the growing US concern. . . . Tin, rubber, rice, key strategic raw materials are what the war is really about. The US sees it as a place to hold – at any cost.'

At the Geneva conference in 1954 the French agreed to give up their military and political campaign against Vietnam and Laos, and they were given the facilities for withdrawing gracefully. Their Indochinese opponents made important concessions for the sake of peace. John Foster Dulles and some of the US military chiefs had wanted to use nuclear weapons against the Vietnamese (a good indication of what concern they showed for Asian peoples who had never attacked even a single American) but General Ridgeway helped to prevent this happening. For some of the things that happened after the Geneva accords one cannot do better than quote General James M. Gavin, who was then Chief of Plans in the Army, directly under Ridgeway:

* *NYTI*, 11 January 1967, 'The Day it All Began', italic added. The notion that the US possessed south-east Asia is significant.

† G. McT. Kahin and J. W. Lewis, *The United States in Vietnam*, p. 32.

With the folding of the French the Pentagon staff assumed that the burden of fighting Communism in Asia had now fallen upon the United States. Secretary of State Dulles and the CIA agreed with the Pentagon. At that time Secretary Dulles was building a paper wall of treaties to contain Communism. The Joint Chiefs [of Staff] began a high priority study of a proposal to send combat troops into the Red River Delta of North Vietnam.

Gavin then reports that it was assumed that the attack would mean war with China. As during the Dien Bien Phu crisis, Admiral Radford, together with the Air and Naval Chiefs, wanted to take the risks involved. 'Just south east of Haiphong harbour is the island of Hainan, which is actually part of Red China [*sic*]. The Navy was unwilling to risk ships in the Haiphong area without first taking the island.' Ridgeway went over the head of his superior direct to President Eisenhower, and succeeded in getting him to put a stop to the invasion and aggression which were being planned.

However, there was a compromise. We decided to support what we hoped would be a stable, representative, independent government in South Vietnam. The fact that this was contrary to the Geneva accords seemed irrelevant. We thought then that our most serious problem was the selection of a premier for South Vietnam, to serve under the technical head of state, Emperor Bao Dai. The job fell to Ngo Dinh Diem. I visited Saigon early in 1955 to discuss political and military-aid matters. I met Diem, who struck me as very non-political, self-centred and quite unresponsive to the needs of his own people.*

The United States installed a puppet regime in Saigon before the French could fulfil the terms of the Geneva agreements.

---

* 'We *Can* Get Out of Vietnam' in *Saturday Evening Post,* 24 February 1968. To set up a 'government' *representative* of US interests, *independent* of the Vietnamese people, on part of the territory of the Democratic Republic of Vietnam, and under a puppet 'quite unresponsive to the needs of his own people' (whom he was trying to betray) was undoubtedly the act of a nation which had a very low rating, politically and morally. No doubt any attempt by the Chinese to oppose the seizure of Hainan would have been denounced as 'Communist aggression', and accepted as that by the UN, the American public and the British public.

Its officials and experts trained military and police forces which could, through torture, terror, imprisonment and execution, systematically destroy the basis in the villages in the southern zone of the proud nationalism which the French had found invincible. The illegal Saigon regime became the beneficiary of enormous amounts of AID funds, PL480 funds and military aid. Even if all this is regarded as a good thing, in so far as it was aimed at destroying the 'Communists', it was the opposite of development aid. For the US regime in Saigon from the beginning brought great suffering and impoverishment to the men and women who had successfully defended independent Vietnam against the French, and devastation to their villages. This side of the anti-Communist heaven, it is impossible for any society to make economic progress by dispensing with the men and women who cultivate the fields, fish in the rivers and seas and produce in the factories; it is impossible to help a nation 'modernize' by obliterating towns and villages, mining rivers, wiping out factories, fields, water-conservation schemes, hospitals, schools, places of meditation and worship – by trying to bomb them back to the Stone Age! Economically speaking, pimps and prostitutes, mercenary soldiers and black-marketeers and other hangers-on of invading armies do not *produce* anything except venereal disease, idleness, dead bodies and wilderness. Even the cleverest of Eugene Staleys and Walt Rostows cannot make 'development' theory of such practices.

In fact, the Vietnamese people are irrelevant to the 'development' of 'the Republic of [South] Vietnam' which the United States created.

Geographically [said Henry Cabot Lodge to an audience in Cambridge, Massachusetts], Vietnam stands at the hub of a vast area of the world – Southeast Asia – an area with a population of 249 million persons .... He who holds or has influence in Vietnam can affect the future of the Philippines and Formosa to the east, Thailand and Burma with their huge rice surpluses to the west, and Malaysia and Indonesia with their rubber, ore and tin to the south.... Vietnam thus does not exist in a geographical vacuum – from it large storehouses of wealth and population can be influenced and undermined.*

This is a most unfortunate way of thinking about the modern world, and especially about an area of the Third World which could, if left to its own people, not only have solved many of its own problems, but helped to solve those of other peoples who have by their own initiative, hard work and creative abilities tried to find a dignified, secure and viable way into the twenty-first century.

In 1963 there appeared a collection of papers by various 'scholars' whose names will be familiar to students of international politics as able promoters of United States interests in the Third World. The editor, William Henderson, reflected on the 'historic tasks' which he assigned his country.

They are, in short, nothing less than to assist purposefully and constructively in the process of *modern nation building* in Southeast Asia, *to deflect the course of a fundamental revolution into channels compatible with the long-range interests of the United States*; they place upon our foreign policy demands of a wholly new dimension, of a kind that we have not had to cope with hitherto. They demand a degree of involvement in Southeast Asia that few could possibly have imagined even a decade ago. They call for a *new diplomacy*.

There is no space here to discuss what would be required of the United States in order to practice successfully *the new diplomacy of nation building* in Southeast Asia. At a minimum, it would require a greater commitment of material resources. But this has not been the principal shortfall to date . . .

Much more critical is the inadequacy of our human resources with which to pursue a manipulative, constructive diplomacy among the modernizing countries of Southeast Asia (and, indeed, in the other underdeveloped regions of the world) . . .†

* Reported in *Boston Sunday Globe,* 28 February 1965. 'That empire in Southeast Asia,' said Senator McGee ten days earlier, 'is the last major resource area outside the control of any one of the major powers of the globe. . . . I believe that the condition of the Vietnamese people, and the direction in which their future may be going, are at this stage secondary, not primary.'

† Italic added.

The conception of US agents playing the role of 'nation building' in other countries posed the question 'Which nation?' It is the *American* nation whose expansion the southeast Asian peoples are being made to serve. Henderson quotes from another writer, John H. Ohly: 'The test is not the test of whether military or economic objectives are served, but the test of whether, in the aggregate, various forms of aid and combinations thereof, best serve the total pattern of US objectives, regardless of whether one labels them as "military", "economic", or "political".'* Or, as Professor Hans Morgenthau put it in his 'A Political Theory of Foreign Aid': 'We have interests abroad which cannot be secured by military means and for the support of which the traditional methods of diplomacy are only in part appropriate. If foreign aid is not available, they will not be supported at all.' The 'aid' which Congress must vote and the people must pay must, one assumes, bear some relation in volume to the interests and objectives of the industrial and business corporations and the military. What relation does 'aid' bear, we must wonder, to the subversive thoughts of the villagers who have yet to exercise their rights to produce their livelihood in their fields, factories and mines?

MORE OF THE SAME 'AID'?

The magnificent rhetoric which clothes the transactions between rich and poor peoples in sentiments of friendship, goodwill and altruistic love depicts our age as the noblest in all of human history.

Nearly everyone who has had an interest in 'aid to developing countries' has heard of United States Public Law 480, under

* Quotations from William Henderson (ed.), *Southeast Asia: Problems of United States Policy* (Cambridge, Mass., 1963). Henderson was Adviser on International Affairs, Socony Mobil Oil Company, Inc., and had been Executive Director of the Council on Foreign Relations. For fuller discussion of US objectives in relation to independent Third World initiatives see my *From Gandhi to Guevara*, *op. cit.*, pp. 25 ff. How the 'new diplomacy' worked in their country is described by Hamza Alavi and Amir Khusro in 'Pakistan: The Burden of US Aid', *New University Thought*, 1962.

which Food for Freedom or Food for Peace assistance is given by the United States. A very high proportion of the food that is given at all has been given under PL 480 programmes. The giving away of one's own food in order to help the hungry or the victims of famine is a noble act, and the popular titles of the Law suggest both generosity and idealism. The Act as it was passed by Congress in 1954 was in fact entitled the 'Agricultural Trade Development and Assistance Act of 1954', and Section 2 stated:

It is hereby declared to be the policy of Congress to expand international trade among the United States and friendly nations, to facilitate the convertibility of currency, to promote the economic stability of American agriculture and the national welfare, to make maximum efficient use of surplus agricultural commodities in furtherance of the foreign policy of the United States, and to stimulate and facilitate the expansion of foreign trade in agricultural commodities produced in the United States by providing a means whereby surplus agricultural commodities in excess of the usual marketings of such commodities may be sold through private trade channels, and foreign currencies accepted in payment therefore. It is further the policy to use foreign currencies which accrue to the United States under this Act to expand international trade, to encourage economic development, to purchase strategic materials, to pay United States obligations abroad, to promote collective strength, and to foster in other ways the foreign policy of the United States.

Considering that the duty of the US government is to safeguard and promote the interests of the ruling class, the aims of the bill are unexceptionable. It would be tedious to quote the Act in full, but there is *nothing* in it which suggests either an understanding of the development process as it has been described in this book, or an altruistic concern for other peoples who want to develop independent and viable economies which will secure them against pressures, threats or invasions from the major powers. In 1966 the Act was amended; or, rather, a new Food for Freedom Act was substituted for it. The Committee on Agriculture examined the draft bill and reported favourably on it, with minor amendments.

The language of the new Act was, understandably in view of the rhetoric which had become popular under Presidents Kennedy and Johnson, much more moralistic and idealistic. It was also a response to those who pressed for more 'aid'. The new bill went beyond the old one in permitting, as the Committee said, 'deliberate production of food in the United States to feed hungry people in other nations'. Some quotations from the Report of the Committee on Agriculture will be instructive.

The new program will *encourage the development of free enterprise in the recipient developing countries* . . .

While other peoples are underfed, *America's problem* has been overabundance.

We have now 60 million acres of farmland in retirement, bedded down under various farm programs. These programs came into being as a means of *preventing our agriculture from suffocation* under an avalanche of surplus food and fiber.

In an all-out world war on hunger, we may bring these acres out of retirement, to produce enough food, if it could be delivered to the underdeveloped countries, to drive hunger and starvation out of *the free world* while these countries are building up their own agricultural production . . .

An expanding agriculture should *cause rural America to flourish.* This should support on our farms many thousands of people who otherwise would be crowded into our cities. Greater activity in rural America should *give new strength to the economy of the whole Nation* . . .

Opportunities for industry and business, as well as for agriculture, *are virtually limitless* in this new undertaking.

If total farm exports were to rise by 50 per cent, in the war on hunger, this would mean substantial additional inputs of fertilizer, of machinery, of all the materials that go into the production of crops and livestock.

This would *create new markets for industry and business.*

This should be accompanied by *a new surge in foreign trade* as Asia, South America, and Africa, where the great population explosions are occurring, build up their own food-producing capacity and general economies, and develop transformation and distribution systems capable of getting food, and manufactured goods as well, to their people.

The agricultural development of underdeveloped nations affords this country perhaps its *best opportunity in all history to expand the foreign markets for American products*. New billions of dollars' worth of manufactured goods should cross the seas. All the facts and statistics show that the faster another nation improves its agriculture, the stronger its economy becomes, and the greater the volume of our commercial markets in that country . . .

The United States should recover the costs of financing its leadership in the world war on hunger. It should *get back in dollars and cents, in the long run, as much as or more than it invests* . . .

Subsection (*b*) (*1*) continues the provisions of existing law which direct that not less than 5 per cent of the currencies which accrue from title I sales of agricultural commodities be available, subject to appropriation, for use to finance programs to *maintain and to develop new and expanded dollar markets abroad for US agricultural products*. Since the time of its original enactment the development of new markets for US agricultural commodities has been one of the major objectives of the legislation. These currencies generated from the sale of agricultural commodities abroad can be put to no more constructive use than for the financing of activities to build and maintain, wherever opportunities to do so are presented, commercial markets which will be of lasting benefit to American agriculture. These market development programs are managed and carried out by US non-profit trade and agriculture groups pursuant to agreements with the Department of Agriculture and have been remarkably effective in the development and maintenance of foreign markets for US agricultural commodities . . .

The committee noted with approval that in two or three instances market development programs have been combined with food donation programs. Programs of this type should be encouraged. *Free sampling is one of the oldest and most effective types of market development* . . .*

The funds accumulated abroad in any country in local currency can be used instead of dollars by United States embassies and other government agencies for their running expenses; and a proportion of them is made available by this legislation for the use by US corporations to expand their activities in the 'aid'-receiving country. The President, by the terms of the Act, is required to 'take steps to assure a pro-

* Italic added.

gressive transition from sales for foreign currencies to sales for dollars at a rate whereby the transition can be completed by December 31, 1971 . . .' (Section 103 (*b*)).

The questions about the philanthropy of all this are perhaps easily answered. What is more important is the relationship of what is being promoted and achieved through PL 480 and Food for Freedom on the one hand to the self-initiated and self-directed development process in the still-isolated and vulnerable national economies of the Third World, on the other. Countries which experience famine as a result of natural disasters can decide to undergo a period of great hardship in order to retain their power to struggle in their own way against the forces of anti-development – and against defects in methods of production, deficiencies in scientific and technological skill and an exploitative political and economic system; to do this the mass of the people should have power, and the burdens of poverty should be shared by all people and regions. Countries which want to avoid the hard road to development can accept Food for Freedom only by making a commitment to anti-development. For the programme is intended and organized so as to *obstruct* the development process as it has been described in this book.

A publication of the Agency for International Development is quite candid about the fact that 'aid' is a process which helps enrich and 'develop' the business of United States farmers, industrial and financial corporations and government agencies like the military forces. *The Aid Story** has charts and statistics to convince the American public that AID INSURES AMERICAN INVESTMENTS IN LESS DEVELOPED COUNTRIES and that AID BUYS US GOODS and also that MOST AID DOLLARS STAY AT HOME. In 1965, for example, ninety-two per cent of the 'aid' funds spent on commodities benefited US business and industry. Facts of this kind, which are *all* the significant facts about who benefits by the 'aid' funds taken from public revenue, have had to be advertised in recent years because the overseas opposition to the US presence abroad has made it

* (Washington DC, n.d.)

necessary to persuade taxpayers that the United States must
continue to be generous in this manner.

As we have suggested before, it is not extraordinary that the
powerful business and industrial corporations should use the
state apparatus and media of publicity to further their own
interests. They would be incompetent if they did not. The
long-term need for more markets and industrial resources
must be met, if the immense productive capacity concentrated
in their hands is to continue to be profitable, and also if they
are to keep the mass of their fellow-citizens satisfied with their
domination by continuing to increase the opportunities for
remunerative employment. If there were no 'aid' and no
war-related expenditure and investment (in its multifarious
senses), and if individual and civic-institutional demand for
goods and services alone maintained the level of employment,
it would be well below the level of the total labour force. If
the demand overseas for the products and services of US
corporations, banks and other agencies had not expanded after
the Second World War, or if it had remained level or even
fallen, the story would be other than that which we have been
reading regularly in the newspapers: the saga of the tremendous
increases in the profits of the major corporations. The privately
controlled productive apparatus in the United States is producing well below capacity and in a highly wasteful manner.
The cutting down of both investment and production would
have had serious consequences, which would be aggravated if
the production of weapons for use against the Third World,
research by scientists, engineers and social scientists on United
States problems overseas and loans to particularly cooperative
Third World regimes for purchases of US goods and know-
how were to stop. If, on the other hand, India could be
persuaded to cooperate in 'international development' which
would in time produce a privileged economic stratum, twenty
million or more in number, living at something near the
material affluence of the US, with another moderately affluent
group of about fifty million, the future would be brighter
than if India refused to get into debt now and took the

revolutionary socialist path of self-reliance and mass democracy. The control that 'aid' has given US officials and industrialists over India's development will impoverish the Indian masses but benefit the rich.

The US, and even the other ex-colonizing powers like Japan, Britain, Germany and France, are no longer imperialist in the nineteenth-century sense. That is, they do not seek to take possession of territory belonging to peoples in Latin America, Asia or Africa, and to administer it directly from Washington, Tokyo, Bonn or Paris. Indeed, what was necessary from the sixteenth to the nineteenth centuries to create and establish the legal, political and geographical foundations of the international capitalist order, with its variety of practices and spheres of operation, does not need to be repeated. That order was repudiated by those who felt themselves victimized and oppressed by it, but at the end of the war they lacked the military power to liberate their homelands; they also lacked a voice in the so-called 'international' bodies like the United Nations Organization. The superpowers realized that the violent upheavals and social and political transformations which were on the agenda following the anti-Fascist world war (see Chapter 1) could be forestalled only if the colonial areas could be developed and modernized on the appropriate lines.* The more pragmatic and self-confident colonial powers, especially Britain, had shown the way by devising institutions and training native *élites* for an eventual 'peaceful' transfer of governmental functions. In view of the mass upsurge of anti-imperialist activity just before and during the war years it seemed prudent to let Latin America, Asia and Africa be governed internally by native rulers, provided that the

---

* The refusal of the Chinese revolutionaries to tolerate the restrictions placed on the Asian peoples by the post-war deals between the major military powers, and their successful assertion of the complete sovereignty of the Chinese people over their own homeland, was a disaster for the powers. The implications are discussed at length in my 'The Human Implications of the Revolution for the World', in *China: Yellow Peril? Red Hope?* (London, 1968).

international framework of the old order was kept intact. The humiliation and crass racialism of continued direct rule through an expatriate colonial administration was widely recognized as an evil: it was clearly a provocation to the entire native population (who had somehow acquired notions about the dignity and status of non-white peoples) and a cause of international instability. Respect for the goals, hierarchies and values of the already established international order had already been forfeited by fratricidal conflict among the imperial powers; and this conflict had also temporarily lost them the power to enforce the over-riding authority of the governments of the white and quasi-white nations in regard to what the non-European peoples were allowed or not allowed to do. If the normal course of political struggle, among traditional or pre-colonial authorities, colonial *élites*, radical intellectuals, rebellious peasants, trade unions and others, to decide the character of resurgent nationhood had been allowed to develop; if the oppressive rule of native guardians of the international order had given rise to the armed revolt of the people; or if the presence of surviving foreign white governors had alienated potential members of a native colonial *élite* ambitious for office, peace and stability would be endangered. 'Peace' was the non-disturbance of the political and economic activity abroad for which the world order had been framed.* Peace had therefore to be ensured.

In the last two decades colonies and empires in the old sense have *not* been sought by the United States, Britain, Japan, Germany, France, Russia or Australia. It has been realized that between native rulers to whom political authority over formerly subject races and peoples had been transferred, on the one hand, and the dominant forces in the world economy, on the other, co-existence and cooperation could be achieved through a

---

* There are scores of newspaper and magazine items which emphasize this fact. Business must not slacken: 'Private Corp. is Urged as AID Adjunct' (*NYHTI*, 28 December 1968), 'Moguls join the Indonesian oil rush' (*Sunday Times*, 3 November 1968), 'Investors' sights on Far East' (*NYHTI*, 12 February 1969).

modification of the established order. To rule out the kind of modernization and development which would have to take place outside the established order, and therefore would disrupt it, the kind of modernization and development would have to be devised which would ensure continuity with economic and political operations of the imperial powers in the past. For example, economic growth would have to make *some* people in *every* part of the world richer and more powerful. An analysis of the activities associated with a number of international agencies, organizations, institutions and programmes financed by major corporations will show that considerable research and writing by sociologists, political scientists, economists, historians, philosophers and journalists is meant to provide a rationale for measures taken to ensure that modernization and development are 'stable' and 'orderly'. Among the intellectuals who have had the task of providing a systematic theory or ideology for what we may rightly call neo-colonialism the emphasis has shifted a little. In the early days a person like Professor Rupert Emerson of the Massachusetts Institute of Technology (and also of the State Department and the C I A) sought to provide an apologia for the old type of colonialism, which American liberals had tended to regard as vicious. The concern for political stability manifested in recent works, such as Samuel P. Huntington's *Political Order in Changing Societies*, and the counsel they give to policy-making colleagues of the authors', are much more sophisticated.* The new Machiavellianism tries to persuade its patrons that expanding markets, and freedom and legitimacy for international financiers and industrialists and military officers can be secured in the long run

* (New Haven and London, 1968.) Huntington had, before his book appeared, served on a number of organizations and programmes concerned with furthering US business and military interests in Latin America, Asia and Africa: the Institute of War and Peace Studies, at Columbia; the Brookings Institution; the Social Science Research Council; the Council on Vietnamese Studies of the Southeast Asia Development [*sic*] Council; A I D; the Office of the U S Secretary of Defense. The commitment and the practice from which the experience of the 'problems' and knowledge of the world is derived is unmistakable.

only if the power of policy-making in the local capitals is secured for the established powers; certain types of 'reform' and 'change' and 'democracy' can frustrate and defeat the rebellious poor by giving a larger number of the natives than before a vested interest in securing the international order against the disruptive consequences of the genuine development process, which liberates the poor. The masses, too, must be 'mobilized' into an alien system which will prevent them from mobilizing themselves under their own leadership, and from mobilizing also all the resources which rightly belong to them in order to achieve *their* own revolutionary development. As for middle-class intellectuals and others who are not loyal to their class but have 'revolutionary proclivities', the advice of this Harvard expert is unambiguous: they have violently to be got rid of.* What the dissenting teachers and students of Peking in 1919 and their Latin American contemporaries, and succeeding generations of intellectuals and students in the Third World, have achieved by collaborating with the poor is too well remembered. After mentioning the fact that Kerala was the Indian state with the highest literacy rate, Huntington declares: 'Political participation by illiterates, however, may well, as in India, be less dangerous to democratic [*sic*] political institutions than participation by literates. The latter typically have higher aspirations and make more demands on government. ...' The conclusion of Huntington's skilfully argued thesis for pre-emptive modernization under United States auspices is clear: 'Either the established *élites* compete among themselves to organize the masses through the existing

* 'For the governments interested in the maintenance of political stability, the appropriate response to middle class radicalism is repression, not reform. *Measures which reduce the numbers, strength and coherence of the radical elements of this class contribute significantly* to the maintenance of political order. Government actions designed to restrict the development of universities may well reduce the influence of revolutionary groupings' (*ibid.,* p. 373, italic added). Huntington does not say if the 'aid' which makes possible the sophisticated operations of counter-revolutionary practice – the training and activities of torturers, maintenance of special prisons, etc. – 'contributes significantly'.

political system or dissident *élites* organize them to overthrow that system. *In the modernizing world he controls the future who organizes its politics.'*

Who can blame the Huntingtons, Rustows, Rostows and Pyes for not favouring dissidents in societies where the indices of poverty characterize the lot of over ninety per cent of the people? They are not dissidents in their own society. Ever since Rudyard Kipling celebrated, in the 1890s, the acceptance by the rulers of the United States of their Anglo-Saxon duty by assuming (what Kipling called in his poem) 'the white man's burden' the impoverished, conquered, humiliated and pacified natives have remained 'half-devil and half-child' in the eyes of the pious and the dutiful. What began in Cuba, the Philippines and China in the 1890s came in time, in spite of US interventions, to make the Third World. But the kind of 'aid' that the United States and other powers give makes good imperialist sense and sound morality. One rarely finds a statesman or an editor who questions the rightness of 'pacification' and the destruction of 'Communists' in the villages and jungles of Asia and Latin America.† But in this essay on world

* *ibid.*, pp. 49, 461, italic added. It is no wonder that in the affluent countries the very people who have a sensitive understanding of the true nature of the development process and a commitment to assist the world's poor are not only denied access to positions of influence or command in politics, economic life, the universities, the mass media and social life, but even regarded as 'subversives'. The bi-partisan policy, on both sides of the Atlantic, of fighting those who have 'higher aspirations' for this poverty-stricken, cruel and barbaric world has the intention of compelling those who are friends of the Third World poor to 'participate' in injuring them.

† 'A germ of hope for the poor of the world,' loudly proclaims the *Guardian* in 1968, describing the completion of a British military counter-insurgency project, part of British aid to Thailand. The Royal Engineers had built a road in north-east Thailand: 'about as cost-effective a form of aid as you can get . . . one of the most effective forms of defence spending that could be devised for the unstable world of the 1960s and 1970s'. 'Our servicemen could repeat the Thailand story in a score of countries in Africa, Asia and even Latin America.' Another article, identical in ideology, explains candidly how 'urgent . . . is the need to counter the growing danger of civil unrest and insurgency in the north-east provinces. . . . This part of the country is fertile ground for political agitators, for the

poverty, one is obliged to ask questions about what the affluent
and resource-hungry 'aid'-givers seek in the tri-continental
'south'. What is it that they expect of those who collaborate
with them in ruling over the poor peoples? What is actually
demanded in the name of stability and of what is continually
labelled 'peace'? What claims do they make on the meagre
resources which have so far been discovered or developed
within the homelands of the poor peoples? What in terms of
the development process described in Chapter 3 is the cost to
the poor nations of the Third World of satisfying the 'development' and modernization demands of the 'aid'-donors?
What, in specific terms of bodies broken, blood spilt, homes
destroyed, fields devastated, villages burnt out, water resources
poisoned or wasted, factories and schools obliterated and other
similar phenomena, is the cost of independent-minded peasants
and factory workers being incorporated forcibly into the stable
world order? To be able to help capable and intelligent people
who are in the most unfortunate material circumstances, both

land is arid and poor, the peasants are barely able to eke out a living, and
for decades the Bangkok government have taken no interest in the land
or its people. The Government representatives, mainly police, are un-
popular.' British aid includes 'the construction of the Leong Nok Tha
air base', and the education of 'some 1,000 Thai children and students . . .
in Britain. . . . A British education has become a status symbol among the
main Thai families, who retain the leadership in Government, the armed
services, banking, and business. The Crown Prince is in an English
preparatory school and will go on to Rugby.' If those obscure villagers
became too politically agitated about their misery and oppression, the
shock-waves to the system would send dominoes crashing not only in
Bangkok but also in the public school system, the newspaper offices, the
UK Ministry of Defence and, above all, the City. British liberals try to feel
superior to and holier than American liberals, and at the same time
applaud Britain's attempts to compete with other imperialist powers in
slandering and oppressing the poor of the Third World. This is pathetic.
The behaviour of the privileged *élites* among industrial workers, for example the readiness of US trade union bureaucracies to work with the
CIA overseas, unites some 'socialists' with liberals in the fear that the
masses at the bottom of the imperial hierarchy will capture the outposts of
empire.

individually and as a group one must cross the barriers of class, race and nation, and attempt to share an experience that is unlike anything one has ever known. This necessary and qualifying experience of oppression, hunger and destitution can be obtained by appropriate commitment and action. What evidence is there of a *caring* and spirit of self-denial, self-emptying – so necessary for authentic foreign aid – among 'the lords of human kind'? When those who proclaim their good-heartedness and altruism are religiously inclined, their rhetoric includes references to 'justice'. But we cannot help observing that in order to be in a position to render unto other men the things which are theirs one must first pay the debt of bearing true witness. 'Aid' can be of help only to peoples for whose persons, whose right to live, whose unique and distinctive ways, whose right to defend themselves, there is true respect.

We can learn a great deal about the reality of 'aid' by studying the history and techniques of pacification: that of the British in Burma and Egypt, the Americans in the Philippines, Vietnam and Laos, and, by proxy, in Guatemala, of the French in Algeria and Vietnam, the Japanese in China and Korea. But to continue to look behind the rhetoric for any substance would be pedantic. The rhetoric of concern and care issues from the world of Lyndon Johnson, Spiro Agnew, Walt Rostow, General Westmoreland, Robert McNamara, Leonid Brezhnev, Marshal Grechko, Eisaku Sato, Michael Stewart, Edward Heath and their French, German, Canadian and Australian counterparts. To discuss their rhetoric as though they were speaking for the oppressed and the poor (rather than against them) would be to invite ridicule. Their arrogant and bullying tone when they address the poor and their leaders conveys a great deal. What they have done and are planning to do may be, as many worthy people tell us, highly commendable morally; but there is no doubt that it accelerates the processes of anti-development, and makes the war on world poverty more difficult than ever before. And it is unmistakably evident that their presence within the Third World – the diplomatic and cultural missions, undercover agencies, military forces corporations, banks, experts and others – is not based on an experience of abolishing poverty, the capacity to understand what the true process of development is, a commitment to abolish the causes of oppression and impoverishment, or a will to help the poor in their struggles against the forces which oppress them.*

Those who believe that they are 'liberal' are just as irrelevant, or relevant, as the establishment forces which are doing all they can to strengthen the local outposts of the maintainers of world stability and order. So, too, are the dogmatic and sectarian armchair revolutionaries whose ambition to mastermind the world revolution leads them to slander and obstruct the 'backward' and untutored militant poor. They are all, in mind and spirit, in commitment and action – in all excepting rhetorical manifestoes and journalistic exploitation of their humanitarianism – far from the real struggle of the poor. A genuine reverence for life in all its varied historical and material forms, for the earth and all the non-human life to which man owes and must always owe so much that sustains, invigorates and delights him, must manifest itself in a life-affirming self-denial – in humility, continence, frugality and unselfconscious involvement in all one's given and potential communal identities. A people must come to an awareness of their own very limited place in the universe before they can enter into fraternal and civilized relations with other peoples who have their respective place too. The international 'order' which in practice denies the vast majority of people free access to what the earth and scientific knowledge and their own energies and skills offer them for life and work, denies the available production facilities, and denies the right to struggle against oppression and servitude, has its peculiar superstructure of attitudes, assumptions and notions which give it moral validity, theological justification and intellectual plausibility. 'Radicals' who share these assumptions – who think of non-European peoples as 'backward', for example – are hardly in a position to stand

* For some further implications of this see Ronald Segal on the subject on pp. 135 ff. of my *From Gandhi to Guevara, op. cit.*

beside the poor who are vanquishing the enemies of true development.

The rich – those with affluent styles of living, who have had many years of formal education, who have many machines and gadgets – are not more intelligent, inventive, original, creative politically, culturally and materially than the poor – those who live in huts, work with simple implements and have read few books. They are not more courageous, better organizers, more resolute or better internationalists. *Nowhere* in the world are the rich, whatever their rhetoric, a model for the revolutionary poor, who do not necessarily admire the kind of 'development' we described in the early part of Chapter 2. If the peasants, factory workers, fishermen, teachers, transport workers, miners and other working people in a Third World country collectively organize themselves for political study and action, and take over the development and administration of their own land, and take on themselves the task of eliminating poverty and oppression, waste, ignorance and disease, of resisting foreign interference and invasion – and if this demonstration of the development process becomes world-wide, the world system whose preservation has come to mean 'stability' and 'peace' will collapse. Industrial raw materials will be flowing towards new factories, and new trade routes and markets will come into being, as hundreds of millions of newly liberated, alert, self-reliant and creative brains, nimble and skilful hands, restored energies, and new machines in the Third World begin to turn out of socially owned factories and farms high-quality products which can enrich the life, work and thinking of all.

This process of development will lead to the fall of many 'dominoes' – not only local tycoons and dictators, but ultimately the more distant beneficiaries of the 'stability' and 'peace' which will end. The McNamaras, Rockefellers, Brezhnevs and their peers will fall to the level of ordinary working people. For development cannot take place until the poor and oppressed unite to ensure that their fields, factories, homes, villages, dams, power stations, scientific laboratories,

K

schools, theatres and even temples are not bombed, napalmed, or destroyed in any other way. That is a far more difficult task for the poor than seemed the prospect twenty-five years ago. As things stand, their suffering is going to increase. For they threaten the existing world order by their commitment to authentic development. If, instead of forming tastes, wants and habits as potential consumers of what US, Japanese, Soviet or West European industrialists decide to produce and export to them, they themselves become producers, the economic implications would be enormous. With eighty per cent of the world's population by about 2000, the peoples of the Third World with their already revealed capacity for originality, inventiveness and hard work, and having mastered the best in the heritage of science and technology, will hardly be consumers of what the remaining twenty per cent produce. One day they will, if they are not to remain poor, be responsible for about eighty per cent of, say, the current consumption of minerals. They must have their own shipping, have a say in the prices of goods, and have an international currency which will certainly not be either the US dollar or anything devised by the 'Group of Ten'. Anyone who has looked at US calculations of what US corporations want of the world's mineral resources and production will realize what all this means for the long-term future of the existing order.*

The Third World peoples who are on the way to constructing a wholesome and equitable world order are inextricably part of the whole world of peoples. Development and modernization must include the creation of a worldwide moral order in which the abolition of poverty is both conceivable and realizable. The world policemen are incapable of creating the required

---

* It is no wonder that Robert Barnett, a senior State Department official, takes the initiative in creating the 'Asian' Development Bank, or that McNamara moves from conducting the war on the Vietnamese peasants to directing the International Bank for Reconstruction and Development. United States dependence on foreign minerals was explained in the Report of the President's Materials Policy Commission of 1952 (the Paley Report).

moral order – one which governs the way that the fruits of the earth and human labour are allocated, and how men and communities of people relate to one another. Without that, the poor have no option but to see the development process as one which includes the development of the capacity to defend their homelands and their achievements, their right to internal revolution and democracy, against the most sophisticated weapons of those who claim ownership of the whole earth. Advanced electronic devices, chemical and biological weapons, nuclear weapons and other means of terror and destruction are being prepared, at immense cost, for use against them, the 'Communist menace'. The choice of defeat or surrender is not theirs.* The 'advanced' technology of the industrialized countries is not there to aid them in the struggle for development but to crush and terrorize them. The well-remunerated and expert skills of scientists, industrial workers and propagandists are mobilized against them. While the rhetoric in the 'aid'-giving nations speaks of heart-felt concern and altruistic service, the reality is a deadly war against the poor involving invasion, occupation, torture and devastation. For many in Guatemala, Peru, Brazil, Vietnam, Laos, Thailand and elsewhere, it is 'aid' that brings the most terrible personal suffering.

* The US government took action to crush an armed revolt by the grossly oppressed and impoverished Filipino peasantry. The guerrillas surrendered. But the misery of 'peaceful' submission is indicated by the incredibly low calorie consumption figures. The national *per capita* average in 1957–9 was 1,760, in 1960–62 1,810, and in 1962 1,800 (UN, Food and Agriculture Organization, *The State of Food and Agriculture 1964* (Rome), p. 228). That the systematic and thorough destruction of the Vietnamese nation has been planned and carried out by the US there can be no doubt. The evidence is overwhelming. The mentality of the civilian and military leaders who have cold-bloodedly planned and acted is perhaps diseased beyond cure. For the Vietnamese, as for other victims, death and extinction is preferable to submission. They should think of the Jews who submitted to the Nazis.

CHAPTER 9

Joining the Real War on Poverty

IT is part of the argument of this essay on world poverty and
the meaning of modern development that the poor have in fact
been receiving very little assistance from the rich, in their
struggle to eradicate their servitude. Outside help cannot be
given by men and women who do not understand the nature
of the plight of the poor peoples, have no respect for their
dignity, rights and aspirations, and no sense of what has to be
done by Third World peoples. The discovery of 'world
poverty' after the last world war was only superficial. The
'hungry two thirds' remained a set of statistics; those who
hungered and thirsted most deeply and agonizingly were in
caves, jungles and remote villages, spiritually and intellectually and often physically inaccessible to the people who
knew the statistics. It is also part of the argument that
the lavishly advertised 'progress' made by formerly colonial
subjects whose leaders have cooperated with and accepted
the tutelage of affluent countries will not stand up to examination.*

The last five chapters have outlined the plight of the poor
peoples, and the complex social, political, cultural and economic machinery which enriches and exalts a few by draining
from more than half of mankind all that they must possess and
use to make them human. Those chapters have tried to outline
the nature of the poverty of which in the last fifty years the
poor have become increasingly conscious. They do not
provide a systematic theory of world poverty; the time for that
is still to come, and the immediate and urgent need is to break

* See discussion of the 'success stories' in Chapter 1.

the domination in international discussions and strategy of those who have consistently lied about the poor and thereby added to their misery and suffering. Many people, in the industrialized affluent nations as well as in the tri-continental south, have been deceived about the nature of world poverty and the urgency of eradicating it. A genuine recognition that their own humanity might be disgraced as long as most of mankind is oppressed is so dangerous that it is evaded. Instead, they compromise with superficial and haphazard remedies which allow essential poverty to go on unimpeded. World-wide collaboration in exploring and exposing the *systematic* character of increasing poverty is therefore urgent.

The desperate situation of the poor in many lands does not leave room for tender-hearted treatment of the pious and seemingly generous do-gooders who approve of and even promote the economic, political and military actions of their chosen leaders in the distant lands of the Third World peoples. *Every day* more houses are being destroyed, more workshops, schools, hospitals, factories, roads, dams and bridges are being blown up, more animals and people crippled or destroyed, more land made uncultivable. Men, women and children are hunted down in their own land by foreigners, as though they were vermin; stocks of food are seized and destroyed; many of those captured are raped, tortured or press-ganged into military service against their own people. *Every day*, in the lands of the rich, industrial workers are making bombers, helicopters, naval vessels, tanks, military trucks, bombs, pellets, bullets, rifles, bayonets, napalm, chemical and biological weapons, mines, detection devices and other hardware for use against the poor. Politicians are hammering out policies for action against the poor who have organized and have started breaking out of their poverty. Chaplains are hopefully invoking the assistance of divine powers, and assuaging the moral pain of those who have to maltreat, bomb, torture or kill the poor. Able-bodied men acquire the skills necessary to terrorize the poor in tropical non-European lands, and to occupy those lands as soldiers and executioners. Journalists are busy concocting accounts to show how vicious and aggressive the resisting poor are. Scientists are making ever deadlier weapons. Scholars are publishing studies and recommendations on how to break down the newly created organizations of the poor and counter their determination to free themselves. Airmen are flying bombers and transport planes, sailors are crossing oceans with cargoes of bombs, napalm and troops, engineers are building military roads and airports so that the poor in their villages, caves and mountain fastnesses can be more easily reached with the products of the industry and technology devised by the rulers of the affluent nations. There is no sinister conspiracy here: it is only the normal working of an international system in which the revolt of the poor against their subservient status and their oppressors is regarded as a disaster. Millions of people performing their normal roles are therefore daily intensifying the poverty of the world's poor – in Guatemala, Vietnam, Laos, Cambodia, Thailand, Brazil, Mozambique, Rhodesia, South Africa and dozens of other lands. Those who can lead the poor out of their impotence and backwardness are being destroyed one after another: a roll of honour the growing length of which is a measure of increasing impoverishment. The urgency cannot be disputed.

Many people who read the reputable sources of information about the Third World must find the kind of world portrayed in this book incredible. Where is the generosity, the goodwill, the self-sacrifice of altruistic Europeans and North Americans? Is it not true that the activity described – the hostile military, diplomatic and political actions of the powers in the Third World – is really directed not at the poor but at the 'Communists'? Questions like these will certainly form in the minds of some readers. Nevertheless, the daily impoverishment of the poor is so concrete that it can be expressed in statistical terms. And in so far as it is the increasing pace of impoverishment that is one's main concern, it is entirely irrelevant whether the victims of invasions, bombing, napalm, defoliation, rape, torture, starvation in concentration camps, pacification and genocide are Communist babies, Roman Catholic nuns or

Rotarians. One may even grant that someone or some nation labelled by British or American authorities as 'Communists' is worthy of instant death. But the issue in the war on poverty is poverty. Historic *communities* and *countries* have had directed against them in the last twenty-five years more destructive force than they experienced in the previous 2,000 years. Entire *villages,* ancient *cities,* a *countryside* cultivated over many centuries, *factories* providing work and much-needed goods, *rice-fields*: these, not 'Communists', have been and are being destroyed in the lands of the poor at tremendous cost to the common people of the United States, Australia, New Zealand, Britain and other 'aid'-giving countries.

The reason why people talk of fighting poverty while in fact they are fighting the poor explains why the post-war discovery of world poverty did not get very far. The experience of the poor is that the affluent are greedy and cruel. But until they are inside the workings of the rich nations they will not believe how little they can appeal to the understanding, sense of justice, knowledge or compassion of the peoples whose active consent, labour and contributions help to prop up their worst oppressors at home and to sustain the oppression from abroad. Human feelings and respect for the poor do not flourish in the mental and moral climate produced in the West by the cynicism of affluence. The world, as seen in the facts of history and social analysis, standards of right and wrong, what is and is not shameful, is a bizarre one. It is not the inhuman treatment of the poor that angers and outrages many people, but rather the candid portrayal of and protest against this treatment. It is not surprising that it is the confirmed experience of the self-reliant poor everywhere in their dealings with the rich that neither among the people who seek to disarm them by terror and violence nor among those who try to disarm them by pious appeals to non-violence are there many who on considerations of justice, right or compassion will return to them those things that belong to them. In the world order which creates and requires the poverty of the majority of mankind, moral and ethical considerations have ceased to exist: that is a fact revealed by careful observation. We cannot expect that poverty will be eliminated because it is scandalous. The rich, with their ideology of anti-Communism, are incapable of being scandalized by anything but the overthrow of aggression and tyranny. The violence which impoverishes and destroys most of mankind must cease completely if the poor are to be liberated. But it cannot be stopped by rhetorical humbug and fictitious moral appeals; increased 'aid', relief operations, do-gooding sentimentality and such things only add to the difficulty of eradicating the violence.

The micro-sects of the revolutionary left, with their disputes over the exegesis of sacred texts; the voluntary aid agencies; the so-called international agencies: these have done very little for the poor in the last twenty-five years. The great victories in the war on world poverty have been won by the exploited and oppressed themselves. The traditions, institutions and resources which shape the struggle of the poor in different countries vary considerably. Therefore the geography, sociology, economics and politics of the revolutionary war on poverty have varied. But there is also a community of historical purpose, a solidarity in taking the development of mankind into a new stage, which makes it possible to speak meaningfully of a Third World of the revolutionary poor. It is a 'world' in which the spokesmen for the poor in one land – Nelson Mandela, Mao Tse-tung, Che Guevara, Josue de Castro, Mehdi Ben Barka, Soong Ching-ling, Luis de la Puente, Frantz Fanon, Julius Nyerere, Ho Chi Minh or Fidel Castro – become the spokesmen for all. The poor who are seriously aware of what they are up against and of how long a march they have to make to free themselves from the trammels of the oppressive world order and to achieve genuine development know also that they must collaborate when they can, share one another's experiences, support one another and regard the success of one as the benefit of all.*

* Some of the documentation for this has already been given in my *From Gandhi to Guevara: The Polemics of Revolt* (London, 1970).

The sensational predictions of world-wide catastrophe which were noted at the beginning of this book are in fact based on appraisals of the world situation which are inaccurate and out-of-date. Repeated declarations that there is increasing poverty outside the 'developed' countries and their foreign enclaves, and plaintive appeals to the rich to offer better terms of trade or to invest in the lands of the poor to avert revolution, suggest that the situation of the poor now is as bad as it was some years ago. They serve to prevent recognition of the fact that the war waged by the poor against the causes – political, social and economic – of their poverty has already been an important aspect of the last few decades of world history. Indeed, the sensational and almost incredible development actually achieved by the poor in the world's most populous country is of crucial importance in showing us what needs to be done, what the consequent problems are, and what, even in the worst conditions, the self-reliant poor are capable of accomplishing. The poor in China are certainly not the only people whose successes are instructive and of strategic value. But there are reasons why it must be regarded as nonsensical and dishonest to profess an interest in overcoming world poverty while being indifferent or hostile to the magnificent victories of the revolutionary poor in China, who form one third of all those in the tri-continental southern hemisphere.

China by the beginning of the twentieth century had developed into the classic case of a once great and prosperous people brought to a collective material and spiritual destitution by anti-development forces. It had been the greatest, and technologically the most advanced, of the non-European civilizations, and a country of continental proportions; its rapid and continuous decline created a vortex of poverty into which the immense possibilities of all mankind were in danger of being sucked. The process of collapse and disintegration seemed irreversible. In the period before the capitalist powers forced their way in with their opium, their gunboats and marines, their unequal treaties, extra-territoriality, annexations and consortia to begin China's 'international development' there had already been a decline in the material and spiritual conditions of life of the mass of the Chinese people. For at the very moment when the population explosion of the eighteenth century demanded rapid economic development and industrialization, the ruling gentry and bureaucracy were intent on enriching themselves by extremely corrupt and oppressive practices. Concentration of land-ownership in the hands of an influential few went with an increasingly landless peasantry. The great rebellions of the poor and discontented had been abortive. Already with nothing but increasing misery and backwardness to look forward to, the mass of the people had then to bear meekly the burdens of being a colony not of one but, as Sun Yat-sen pointed out, of all the imperialist forces – Britain, France, Russia, the United States, Germany, Japan, Austria, Belgium and others. The Chinese people, like their neighbours, suffered the deeply impoverishing consequences of their country being compelled to play a helpless and subservient international role at the bottom of a hierarchy of greatly unequal classes, races and nations. Those parts of China not annexed or administered 'extra-territorially' were nominally independent; but the imperial regime, and later the warlords and Chiang Kai-shek, were independent only in so far as their oppression of the peasants and urban labourers was advantageous to the foreign powers. The economic process which had drained out the life and resources properly belonging to the millions of Chinese was further developed to drain them out of China – in the form of taxes imposed to pay 'indemnities' to the invading powers, of resources used up cheaply for capitalist industry and trade, of profits earned on trade with merchants and landlords, of interest on loans, of coolie labour abroad and in the concessions, sweated and child labour in the factories, prostitution, conscription and so on. The disparities between rich and poor, educated and uneducated, the interior and the coastal regions, countryside and cities, became wider than ever before. Servilely accepting the false necessity of eating bark and leaves after producing grain, of living in squalor, of selling off their children or themselves for the casual pleasure of others, of toiling with little reward for doubly alien masters, of enduring the withering racial contempt, of the superstitions and the dumb hatred, the dehumanized Chinese peasants and workers appeared to have lost all power to improve their lot. Yet today, fifty or sixty years later (and in most parts of China just twenty years later), they have made that experience a distant memory.

If the achievement of the Chinese people consisted only in the rapid increase in the Gross National Product it would hardly be worth the special consideration which is being given here to China's transformation. Rapid increases in the statistics of production and industrialization have been achieved in other countries by enterprising *élites*, at tremendous cost to the lower classes and to other nations and to their own humanity – costs which never enter into the calculation of how much progress has been made. China's economic growth is faster than that of nearly all other 'developing' countries, but the hard facts of the elimination of poverty in China are more substantial and complex than anything that the old-fashioned tables of statistics used in computing capitalist commodity production can show. China's 750 million now have enough food to eliminate not merely starvation and chronic hunger, but even malnutrition, and the food within reach of all is richer in quality and variety than ever before. This is evidence of a fantastic leap forward both in the volume of food that is produced and purchased collectively, and in the people's power to determine what should be produced and how it should be distributed. All throughout China people are beginning to live in simple but dignified conditions, with clean surroundings, air and water, and almost totally free of infection and vermin. The massive sales of sewing machines alone indicates how adequately clothed people are beginning to be, and the availability of electric lights in remote rural homes is another aspect of the change in the living conditions of a hundred million families who till recently were impoverished. All the communities dispersed throughout China are enjoying the benefits of well-organized health services and medical care, and easy access to local, provincial and national hospital treatment and surgery as good as the best available to the super-rich in the capitalist countries. In the fight to liberate the poor the special poverty of the physically handicapped has not been ignored; it says a great deal for the revolutionary daring and human solidarity of the poor and their regard for the preciousness of human beings that in the exercise of the power they have won in China they have set about trying to make the deaf hear, the dumb speak and the paralysed walk, with some success. The rich land, once taken from them by landlords and foreign and local enterprises, is theirs again, to work, live on and enjoy – an increase of 'wealth' which it is not easy to measure. Increase of agricultural land is only one of the material resources with which the once-starving and technologically backward poor have begun creating what is clearly a modern industrialized economy aiming at the best scientific and organizational standards. All through the country the Chinese people, led by the revolutionary poor, have acquired new irrigation works, power stations, hydro-electric plants (including some of the world's biggest), entirely new industries, factories, tools, scientific equipment, computers, nuclear plants, bridges, roads, railways, shops, schools, machinery, ships and much else, mostly of their own devising and creation. Tasks which used to require backbreaking toil and much time have been considerable eased by the application of inventive abilities and capital investment to the needs of the poor peasants and workers; and the burdens which have to be borne are now shared widely. The people have built up and maintain scientific and technological institutes which are indisputably helping them to create a more humane twenty-first century world order. Education in the widest sense is a right enjoyed by all at no cost, and some of it is directed towards training ordinary people to take intelligent and independent initiatives in their own revolution. The facilities for secondary and higher education have been multiplied many times over in the last twenty years, and practically every child is provided with primary education. Education was highly valued in pre-revolutionary China, but it was the education of an *élite*; as recently as 1949 eighty per cent of Chinese were estimated to be illiterate. With over a hundred million children in school and various programmes of adult education in factories, communes and other places, a considerable proportion of the world's poor are well on their way to the total elimination of illiteracy. Since the educational aim is to produce not mandarins but revolutionaries 'serving the people' of China and the world, this could, if the champions of the poor succeed in producing the literature which is needed, be a step forward in development which, again, it is not easy to compute. The future which belongs to the youth of China is richer than that offered to the youth of any other land. The extent to which the Chinese people have been enriched by their numerous social, political and industrial experiments, their successes as well as their failures – that, too, cannot be measured, for it is immense. But all these, like the rights, powers and status now enjoyed by women whose elder sisters and mothers had bound feet, are tangible, real and highly precious gains by the poor in fifty years of development effort.

The war of the poor against poverty is, certainly, not a matter of slogans and manifestoes, but an ongoing fact. It has been going on in a world in which the rich in their insatiable greed for what belongs to other people have the tentacles of their rapacious technology and politics reaching out to every land and into the ocean depths. The poor have pioneered a totally different road to the true development of the politics, exploration and production of human well-being. And in doing so they have, in accordance with their own aspirations as they are summed up in Mao's Marxist teachings on revolution, placed the lowest value on the bourgeois greed for 'fame, material gain, power, position and limelight'. The transformation of China which the poor have achieved – on a scale and with an originality which are impressive – is the outcome of a profound transformation, begun many years ago, of what has been called in this book the 'culture of poverty'. It was the spirit of revolt among the people, and the rejection of both the old order and of imperialist 'development', which turned young peasants, workers and intellectuals into revolutionaries, and made them search for a revolutionary ideology and a revolutionary party. China's transformation was effected through Sun Yat-sen's efforts to overthrow the old order, the May Fourth Movement of 1919, the tremendous events of 1924–7, life under the Chiang dictatorship, the struggle against Japanese rule, and the revolutionary war which ended in 1949 with the creation of the People's Republic. And Mao Tse-tung, who had in the course of that struggle emerged as the ablest leader of the revolutionary poor, was speaking with an unrivalled know-ledge of what poor peasants and workers could accomplish when he wrote in 1955:

In a few decades, why can't 600 million paupers, by their own efforts, create a socialist country, rich and strong? The wealth of society is created by the workers, the peasants, the working in-tellectuals. If only they take their destiny into their own hands, follow a Marxist-Leninist line, and energetically tackle problems instead of evading them, there is no difficulty in the world that they cannot resolve.*

One can understand, in view of formulations like this, why anti-Communism was used by the Japanese as an excuse for their conquest of China, why the United States aided Chiang Kai-shek, why China has been harassed by the superpowers and, indeed, is now under threat from the three richest powers – the United States, Russia and Japan – and why it has trade embargoes to contend with. The power and ability demon-strated by the poor in governing China – where nearly a quarter of the world's people live – has been a scandal in a rich man's world order; a people's government in Peking, with claims to an effective voice on matters of world peace and international justice, has been too much for the United Nations Organization,

* Quoted in Stuart Schram, *The Political Thought of Mao Tse-tung* (London, 1969), p. 351.

which was formed to be dominated by a rich man's club. The Chinese have consequently had to struggle for their development in the face of virtual expulsion from the UN, the absence of all help from its agencies, and no protection but that provided by their own liberation army, their militia and their government against foreign attempts (which still go on) to overthrow their power and restore the old order. One of their provinces is a US protectorate, and a base for counter-revolutionary political and military action. Yet, in a world of highly sophisticated military technology, the people have achieved enough powers of resistance to deter invasion and attack, and have for twenty years been able to concentrate on the task of development. The path of development so ably pioneered by the revolutionary poor in China is, of course, no short cut to the total elimination of all that creates oppression and poverty. The politics of the ongoing Chinese revolution are very complex and very demanding. The creation of a society in which frugality, hard work, simple tastes, courage, loyalty to the poor and the overcoming of selfishness are highly valued is seen by the revolutionary leadership as a necessary condition for accomplishing the tasks which have yet to be done. The aim is not to enrich a few millions but to set all oppressed people free.* Already the poor in China have made a modern freedom for themselves: they are in fact free to defy the nuclear threats of the rich who hate them, free to shape 'a world belonging to the people', free to go into space, free to have human relations which are not marred by the necessity of mutual exploitation, free to synthesize new materials, free to help the poor in other lands on the basis of equality and mutual benefit – free to make decisions whose implementation, in the absence of the powers they have acquired by their development, would have depended on the permission, goodwill or benevolence of the rich. The concrete, material achievements of the Chinese are therefore of

---

* See my *China: Yellow Peril? Red Hope?* (London, 1968); Han Suyin, *China in the Year 2001* (London, 1967). Relevant Chinese texts are Mao's *Serve the People, Where do Correct Ideas Come From?* and *On the Correct Handling of Contradictions Among the People*, available in many editions.

the greatest importance, even though no system of calculating them in figures has yet been devised. There are pockets of extreme poverty in the United States which do not appear to exist at all in China. The Chinese are beginning to export high-quality products and precision tools to the developed countries. Kurt Mendelsohn, a physicist at Oxford who has travelled widely, reported on the basis of three visits to Chinese industrial and scientific establishments that Chinese-made materials and equipment used in industry and advanced scientific research equalled the best available outside China. Other experts in the field have agreed with this assessment. China is self-sufficient in oil and has surpassed all other countries in some fields of the oil industry because of the inventiveness and skill of the workers. The Chinese are net exporters of food, and among the world's leading exporters of textiles – even though they are all adequately clothed and fed. The poor who have become engineers and technicians are relatively young and inexperienced, but they are undoubtedly among the best in the world. In so much else – land conservation, for example, or rural industrialization – the progress of the working people in technology and productivity is so rapid as almost to baffle an outside observer. And it is almost eccentric of the Chinese people to have a currency so stable that prices tend to fall, and to be completely free of national debt.*

What is remarkable about this proletarian struggle for development is that it does not depend on the exploitation and coercion of the working people by a ruling *élite* or the exploitation of other lands and peoples. There were once some Stalinists in the Chinese leadership, but they have been discredited or corrected. It is evident that those once oppressed, deprived

---

* Information about China has to be culled from widely scattered sources. Books of interest are: Kurt Mendelsohn, *In China Now* (London, 1969); Joshua Horn, *Away with All Pests* (London, 1969); Keith Buchanan, *The Transformation of the Chinese Earth* (London, 1970). At the time of writing all published economic studies are based either on capitalist or Stalinist assumptions.

and dehumanized can humanize, educate and modernize themselves and their community in the act of working as intelligent revolutionaries to create a society free of poverty. The war against poverty can make them rich in the material products, the knowledge and the human relationships which, in their turn, enrich and liberate the human spirit. The immense debts which accompany United States and Soviet development (but which are left out of the calculations) are not, so far as it is possible to observe, to be found in the development process initiated by the poor in China. The poor, in other words, are succeeding without having to oppress and impoverish others. Poverty is under attack in Vietnam, Laos, Guatemala, Portuguese Guinea, Cuba and some other places, too. And it is clear that it is authentically eradicated by what was described earlier as the 'leap forward' of revolutionary daring: by wresting power from their oppressors, and by hard political and economic work, the poor can make the withered life of the feudal, capitalist and imperialist wilderness bloom with new life and hope and, perhaps, love. The great promise of the human city was once turned into slums, sweatshops, bombed-out ruins and mansions of corruption and vice. The long-delayed promise may yet be realized by the political and material transformation of the countryside, as in China, by the labours of the poor, now liberated: not just deserts into gardens, but garden cities where there are imperialist-made deserts and cemeteries.

The war of the poor against the rich may go on for many decades before it can be won. What can those who want to aid the poor do, living as they do in societies whose technology and politics create poverty?

There are three ways of joining the war on world poverty. First, there is the use of existing programmes and activities to put people in the affluent countries in actual touch with the facts of world poverty, and with the poor themselves. This may be resisted by those who manage the voluntary agencies and the government agencies. It is only in situations where the struggle against anti-development is in fact being waged by the poor that foreign aid can help to eradicate poverty. Those who collect money for voluntary agencies or do educational work for them would be honest only if they explained this to the people among whom they work or from whom they collect money. Sweden is a rare example of a nation in which government and voluntary action reflects a genuine respect for the rights of the poor. The fostering of respect for the much-exploited non-European peoples, and for their rights, is far more valuable than persuading people to give money.

Secondly, truly useful aid can be rendered by non-cooperation with the machinery of terror, oppression and exploitation. Poverty in the Third World is the product of indigenous anti-development forces. The very process of development cannot, to use Walt Rostow's term, 'take-off' until the poor bring themselves by their own work to the point of overthrowing the power of their home-grown tyrants.* But what prevents them from doing so in many parts of the world (and almost prevented them in China and Vietnam) is the hard work put in by millions of people in the economically advanced countries to build and service the imperialist economic and military machines. Industrial workers, journalists, politicians, housewives, students, teachers, broadcasters, scientists, pilots, soldiers and traders can singly and in cooperation render concrete aid in the distant struggle for development. They can do so by refusing to play essential roles in the apparatus of oppression. How many lives and injuries among the poor would be saved if they did that, how many dwellings, villages, cities, factories; how much iron, bauxite, copper, petroleum, skilled labour would remain for the use of the proper owners! People who stopped making napalm, bombs, B52s; stopped

---

* For some decades now the tyrannical ruling classes in major nations have been living in fear, for they have seen the writing on the wall. Chiang Kai-shek was not able to save them in China. As for Brazil, see Josue de Castro, *Death in the Northeast* (New York, 1969), pp. 117 ff. Continuing massacres of leaders of the poor have not solved the problems of the oppressors there.

piloting helicopter gunships; stopped spraying defoliants; stopped buying things made from material obtained by corporations which have robbed or cheated the poor or manufactured by sweated labour; stopped spying on, betraying or attacking the poor in their own lands; stopped misrepresenting the truth in the interests of their own ruling class; stopped agreeing to tax increases for the benefit of those who profit by war industries and the exploitation of the resources and wealth of Third World peoples: people who did all these things would make an immense contribution to the war on world poverty. They would be friends of the poor.*

There is a third way of helping the poor, and of bringing about a world free of poverty, misery and backwardness. It is the revolutionary way of turning swords into ploughshares. The brutal, inhuman world order which exists only to exalt and pamper the rich can be replaced with an order in which no oppression or lordship is permitted. Those who are concerned for the victims of the present system, those who want to 'serve the people' of all the world, can work to take over the shaping of the technology and ideology, the productive apparatus, the seats of power, the prostituted organs of education and information, which are theirs by right in their own lands. Instead of merely refusing to serve the corporations and the military bosses who dominate the world they can overthrow their usurped power and dominance. They can thus eliminate the poverty of body and spirit which degrades their own lives, in the United States, Britain, France, Germany, Japan, Russia, Belgium, Canada and Australia. *Then* only will they be in a position to offer the use of their tremendous industrial resources for the development of the material and social conditions of the peoples of Latin America, Asia and Africa. The majority of those invited for training and experience in modern skills will not be policemen and soldiers and spies (as they are now) but men and women who are committed to serving their own people. The poor who want to end their poverty are up against an enemy who is in control of the mightiest war machines in

* Action on the lines indicated has begun in the United States.

history. It is very substantial aid indeed for the mass of the
people in the United States, Russia and Japan to overthrow
that enemy of mankind. But those who want the poor to dare
almost impossible feats – who on occasions insist on the poor's
dealing non-violently with armed invaders – do not often dare
to contemplate revolutionary change in their own countries.
Their respect for the pretensions of the rich is greater than their
pious concern for the liberation of the oppressed and poor;
proletarian democracy appears more intolerable than the
unchallengeable power over their lives of those who monopo-
lize the productive resources as well as the right to dictate
what they may or may not do. All this is understandable. But
it also makes it clear that for those who have been integrated
into the relatively affluent strata of the world society it requires
a tremendous moral and political transformation before they
can stand beside the poor in sympathy and solidarity. The kind
of revolutionary change described here is, however, the only
way in which the anti-development systems can finally be
transformed into the opposite.

One factor common to all three modes of foreign aid for the
poor is the immediate cessation of certain forms of what has
passed for 'aid' – what the Pearson Report calls 'international
development', for example. *All* forms of 'partnership' in the
Third World between the super-corporations and international
financiers on the one hand and the poor, *all* support for and
praise of and attribution of legitimacy to regimes which
have not been set up by the power of the people, *all* forms
of provision for military and police action, pacification,
torture, and other similar activity, *all* interference in internal
concerns of other peoples must be brought to an end. In
the case of the United States in particular, complete isolation
from the affairs of the Third World, which are properly the
business of its peoples, would give a great boost to development.

To reach the stage of being able to make the man-made
wilderness bloom and the solitary places glad with human joy –
or, to be more prosaic, to end poverty and all that produces

poverty – mankind would have to progress well beyond its present stage of development. The destiny of the whole earth is involved in the abolition of anti-development. Whether or not the achievement will match the hope depends not on the poor alone but on the poor working with genuine allies among the rich, the blacks with the whites. There is a big gap between that and the present reality.

Index

Africa, 14, 15, 17, 30, 68, 70, 80, 84, 110, 152, 153, 159, 163, 183, 185, 209, 283

agriculture, 3, 8, 57, 73, 74, 77, 78, 79, 81, 278 *see also* land

AID (Agency for International Development), 23, 25, 26, 251, 257

aid, anti-development effects of, 247–53, 259, 263, 269
  arguments for, 18 ff., 30, 191
  foreign aggression as, 270–73
  military component of, 33, 34, 39, 40, 249, 251
  statistics of, 22, 25, 26, 34, 37, 249
  true value of, 83, 180–92, 213, 283–6

aid programmes, 18, 20, 23–8, 263–4 *see also* AID, 'Food for Freedom/Peace'

American Indians, 235–6, 241

anti-Communism, 115, 146, 148, 263, 274

anti-development, 82–5, 86–188, 271–2, 275, 276
  attitudes of rich to, 1 ff., 265, 273
  beneficiaries of, 90, 124, 132–4, 224, 226, 227 *see also* rich
  bureaucracy in, 153–7
  capitalist production and commerce in, 104 ff., 122, 165, 180 *see also* capitalism
  class relations, 10, 56, 74, 84, 85, 91, 107, 111, 123 ff., 128, 131 ff., 135, 143 ff., 147, 187–8, 224, 243, 273–4, 276
  the colonial heritage in, 11 ff., 95, 154, 209, 244
  education and, 129, 156–7
  diplomacy for, 245 ff.
  exploitation of women in, 75, 148–9, 276, 277
  genocide as, 172–3, 223, 269
  housing conditions and, 96 ff.
  human wastage in, 92–3, 103, 143, 165, 251
  imperialism as, 92, 94, 95, 148, 149, 164, 180, 208–9, 244, 245, 251, 276 *see also* corporations, imperialism
  indebtedness as, 34, 35, 37, 120, 159–61, 228
  inflation as, 66
  international co-operation for, 139, 150–80, 259–61, 275–6
  the military in, 34, 124, 142–3, 144
  'mobilization' for, 85, 260, 262
  pollution and, 49 ff., 96, 101
  role of scholarship in, 173, 185, 224, 225, 252, 261

anti-development – *cont.*
social disintegration as, 51, 53, 98, 99, 118, 121–2, 123
taxation in, 89, 119, 144, 166, 243
see also disinvestment, land, starvation

Brazil, 31, 102, 115, 122
imperialist exploitation of, 168–74, 178
poverty in, 16, 64, 66, 91–2, 96, 97–8, 103, 104, 105, 128, 129–30, 132, 133–6
repression and torture in, 92, 124, 140–42, 145, 172–3, 269
revolt of poor in, 75–7, 140–42, 158
Britain, 15, 20, 36, 47, 49
rich and poor in, 9, 33, 42

capitalism, 11, 17, 46–9, 51, 52, 94, 107, 165 ff., 244–5
Ceylon, 37, 66, 95–6, 104, 115, 154–7, 158, 184–5
children, 78, 93, 96, 100, 101–4, 150, 279
Chile, 65, 67, 98, 100, 103, 126, 128, 131, 132, 135
China, 4, 31, 65, 67, 183, 195
foreign aggression against, 34, 115, 147, 149, 201, 204, 240–44
foreign intervention in, 23, 33–4, 244, 250
oppression and poverty in, 9–10, 16, 88–91, 97, 107, 113–14, 130, 242–4, 276
pioneer, as a, 194, 263, 267, 274, 279, 281, 283

pre-modern achievements of, 59–60, 106
revolution in, 10, 75–6, 188, 193, 194, 244, 262, 280
the transformation of, 37, 80, 111–12, 275–83
city, the, 58, 73, 77, 96 ff., 283
colonialism, 9, 12, 32, 62, 204, 205
heritage of, 14–17, 115
impact on traditional society of, 115–22, 203–13
corporations, business, 26, 46 ff., 141, 164, 171–3, 174–9, 192, 255
corruption, 145 ff., 227–8
crime, 51, 114, 227–8
Cuba, 5, 67, 128, 129, 263, 283
culture of poverty *see* poverty

de Castro, Josue, 76, 104, 105
decolonization, 12, 195
development, academic study of, 18, 28
collective character of, 80, 81, 91, 277 ff.
conditions for, 53 ff., 76, 80–81, 84, 91, 96, 187–8, 268
see power
discovery and invention in, 58, 59
in historical perspective, 16, 17, 40, 41, 52–62, 73, 74, 189–99, 203–12, 277 ff.
political character of, 79 ff., 140, 179
the process of, 62, 72, 73–85, 181, 187–8, 190–92, 266–9, 274, 277
rapid, 51, 52

self-reliance in, 11, 74, 84
socialist, 77–82, 277–83
the way taken by the poor to, 72, 84, 247, 274 ff., 279, 281, 283
the working class in, 188, 247, 282
disease, 51, 75, 93 ff., 150
conquest of, 278
disinvestment, 150–61

education, 66 ff., 74, 77, 79, 81, 82, 278, 279
pre-school, 102 ff.
Egypt, 100, 134

famines, 10, 94, 105 ff., 109
fear of, 2, 4, 83
'Food for Freedom/Peace', 24, 34, 251, 254–7
food supply, 3, 4, 13–15, 94, 105–8, 110–14, 277

'gap' between rich and poor, 19, 32, 35, 66, 68, 71, 123, 189–90
growth rates, 35, 36, 82, 277

health, 82, 277, 278
housing, 35, 79, 96–101, 277

imperialism, 17, 30, 202–14, 239 ff. *see also* anti-development
British, 11, 115 ff., 196, 259
French, 244
Japanese, 11, 33, 95, 96, 195, 242, 248
the new, 162–87, 244, 246 ff., 259 ff.

Russian, 112, 200, 242
Spanish, 202 ff.
income, 46, 47, 48, 61
distribution of, 36, 124–7, 224
national, 15, 16, 63 ff.
sources of, 127, 132 ff.
India, 10, 47, 61, 62, 67, 77, 91, 92, 97, 104, 152, 193, 204, 233–4, 258–9
poverty in, 15, 16, 37, 66, 98, 99, 107–10, 114, 118, 121, 129, 143, 153–4, 157–8, 159–60, 165, 183–4
colonialism in, 107, 115–21
industrialization, 74, 77, 79, 155, 203, 282
industry, 79, 81, 278
inequality, *see* income, land, power
international development, 18, 26, 28 ff., 32, 33, 62, 162–88
international order, the, 11, 190–92, 204, 210–14, 272
investment, foreign, 26, 162 ff., 168, 174, 175–9
in development, 82, 83, 84, 277–80

Jamaica, 65, 66
Japan, 11, 12, 30, 52
Johnson, Lyndon B., 5, 24, 31, 215, 255

Korea, 11, 31, 34, 35, 37, 65, 67, 115, 144, 145, 166–7, 184, 195, 242

land, ownership of, 132 ff., 235, 276
reform, 12, 138

landless labourers, 120, 132, 276
Laos, 11, 130, 147, 185, 249, 265, 269, 271–2, 283
Las Casas, Bartolomeo, 206, 208
Latin America, 17, 23, 24, 30, 37, 68, 84, 97 ff., 103, 111, 124, 158–9, 163, 164, 182 ff., 194, 238
liberation movements, 11 ff., 194–5
literacy, 128, 143, 262, 279

malnutrition, 13, 14, 89, 92–4, 121, 137, 225
Mao Tse-tung, 10, 75, 274, 279, 280
Mexico, 31, 35, 102, 103, 115, 127, 128, 209, 235–6, 238
migrations, 99, 157–9, 202, 210
military, the, 144 ff., 228–30
  expenditure on, 142, 143, 144, 147, 271, 284
mobilization *see* anti-development
models, 63 ff., 68–73, 214–23 *see also* China, United States
modernization, 68, 69, 70, 71, 81, 122, 136, 261, 277 ff.

national liberation, struggle for *see* liberation movements

Open Door, 201, 240 ff., 244
oppression, 10, 56, 92, 114, 134, 135, 154, 194, 218, 223, 229–31, 264, 268–72

Pakistan, 31, 36, 37, 104, 142, 158

partition and disunity, 149, 174, 181–5
Pearson Commission, 29, 32, 39, 286
peasants, 10, 11, 64, 76, 89, 111–12, 119–21, 131–2, 135–7, 139, 141–2, 154, 247, 248, 260, 264, 267
Peru, 98, 103, 111, 125, 126, 128, 132, 136–8, 163, 164, 177, 209, 269
Philippines, 11, 37, 66, 104, 115, 130, 131, 194, 239–40, 251, 269
planning, 79–81
population, 2, 3, 6, 60, 124, 243
poverty, 42, 45, 49, 51, 53, 72, 74, 75, 110 ff. *see also* anti-development
  collective character of, 86–92, 179–80, 181, 191–2, 194, 273
  culture of, 77, 87, 185–8, 229, 263, 271–2, 273, 280
  discovery of, 9 ff., 90–91
  dynamic character of, 123–50, 160, 166
  in pre-modern times, 43, 44
  revolt against, 43, 76, 274 *see also* China, revolution
power, political, 48, 76, 77, 80–82, 84–5, 124, 130–43, 154–6, 187–8, 194, 253, 267, 269, 277
productivity, 14, 56, 61, 82–3, 277
prostitution, 75, 148, 149, 251

racism, 12, 62, 66, 68–72, 112, 156, 186, 206–14, 217–23,

242, 246, 247, 248, 251–2, 263, 265, 266
revolt of the oppressed, 9–12, 89, 113, 114, 272, 276
revolution, 12, 274, 277 ff.
    in development, 54 ff., 76–85, 268
    fear of, 6, 7, 262, 263
    world-wide, 62, 81, 187–8, 190–92, 266–9, 274, 281–3
rich, the, 14–15, 45–52, 63–4, 90, 124–8, 130–35, 151–9, 160, 224–8
    interests and outlook of, 1–8, 18, 24, 43–4, 79, 87–8, 115, 130, 136, 138–50, 153, 154, 158, 164–5, 169, 170, 174–9, 186, 197, 225, 228–9, 239, 245–53, 258–68
    qualifications for ending poverty of, 38–41, 61–2, 69–72, 107, 136–7, 144–5, 149, 170–72, 177–8, 180, 201–2, 215, 223, 231–2, 254, 271, 273–4
    as ruling class, 12, 122, 123, 124, 128, 131–3, 135, 139, 142, 143, 144, 147, 151, 153, 163, 165, 176, 178, 184, 186

school attendance, 103, 104, 128
science and technology, 18, 19, 57–8, 74, 77, 79, 83, 190, 268, 278–82
slavery, 206 ff., 210, 216–19
socialism, 11, 12, 77 ff., 277 ff.
South Africa, 65, 115, 124, 165–6
starvation, 4, 5, 8, 88 ff., 92–4, 225–6

Thailand, 11, 37, 67, 104, 124, 130, 131, 145–50, 194, 263–4, 269
Third World, 4, 5, 31, 61, 64 ff., 86, 100, 163, 175, 181 ff., 200, 204, 246, 252, 263, 268, 274

United Nations, 4, 7, 8, 12, 13, 14, 27, 28, 97, 195, 246, 259
United States, 15, 22 ff.
    attitude to non-white peoples of, 209–14, 216–23, 235–69
    expansionism of, 235 ff.
    military and police in, 220–22, 228–30
    as model, 66–75, 201
    rich and poor in, 9, 46–51, 130, 223–9, 282

Venezuela, 64, 67, 98, 103, 126, 127, 128, 130
Vietnam, 31, 220
    impoverishment and oppression in, 91, 92, 94, 115, 119, 122, 130, 144–5, 146, 147, 148, 149, 181, 185, 201, 246–52, 265, 269, 271–2, 273, 284
    revolutionary struggle in, 11, 194, 246, 248, 274, 283, 284
violence, 7, 89, 90, 92–6, 139–40, 180, 265, 269, 271–4

Wilson, Woodrow, 244–5
world development *see* international development